IMAGES
of America

SALINAS VALLEY

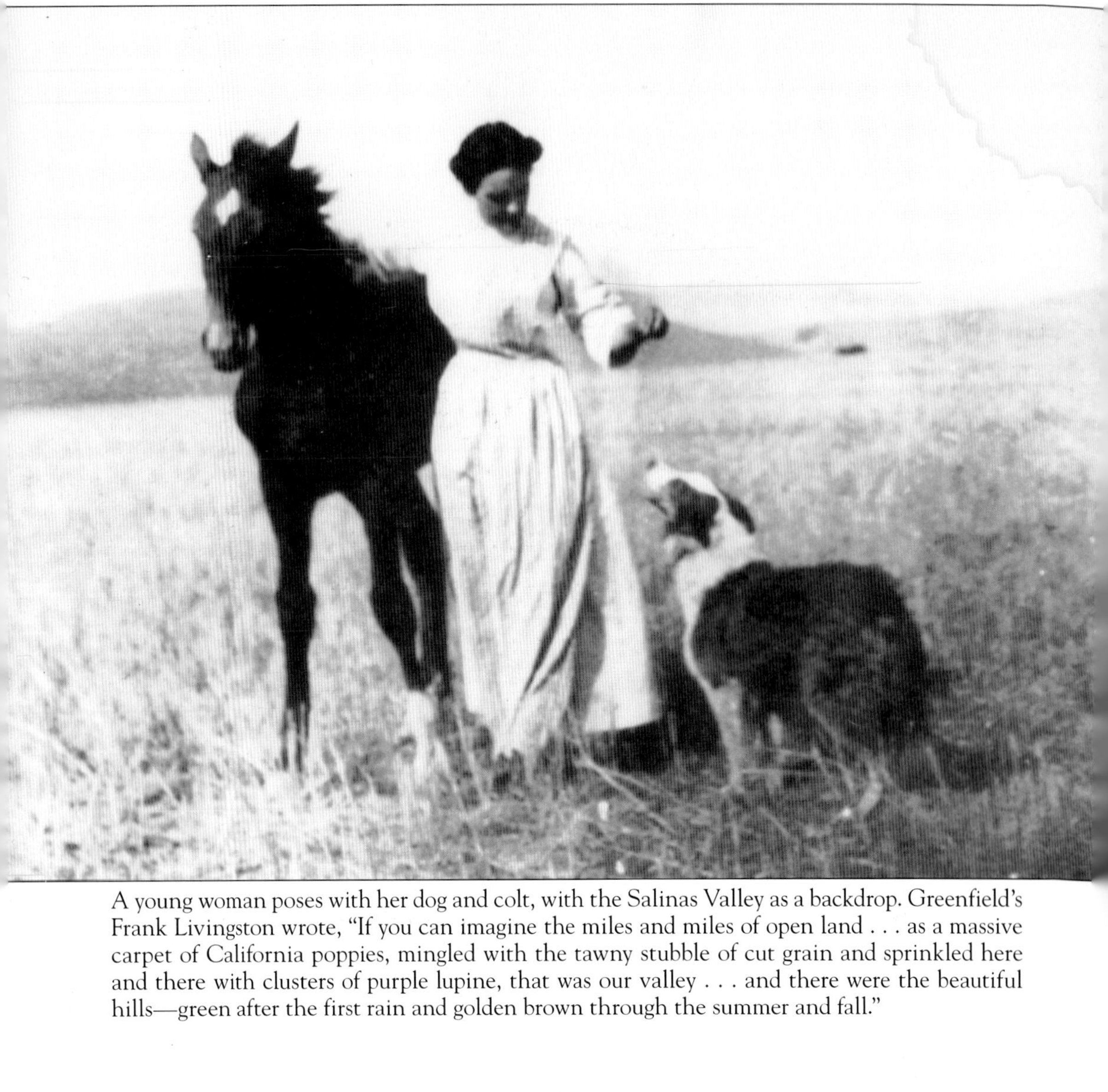

A young woman poses with her dog and colt, with the Salinas Valley as a backdrop. Greenfield's Frank Livingston wrote, "If you can imagine the miles and miles of open land . . . as a massive carpet of California poppies, mingled with the tawny stubble of cut grain and sprinkled here and there with clusters of purple lupine, that was our valley . . . and there were the beautiful hills—green after the first rain and golden brown through the summer and fall."

ON THE COVER: This 1894 photograph offers a sweeping vista of the town Gonzales, fertile farmland, and the snowcapped peaks of the Santa Lucia mountain range.

IMAGES
of America

SALINAS VALLEY

Margaret E. Clovis
Monterey County Agricultural and Rural Life Museum

ARCADIA
PUBLISHING

ISBN 978-0-7385-3048-2

Published by Arcadia Publishing
Charleston SC, Chicago IL, Portsmouth NH, San Francisco CA

Printed in the United States of America

Library of Congress Catalog Card Number: 2005928795

For all general information contact Arcadia Publishing at:
Telephone 843-853-2070
Fax 843-853-0044
E-mail sales@arcadiapublishing.com
For customer service and orders:
Toll-Free 1-888-313-2665

Visit us on the Internet at www.arcadiapublishing.com

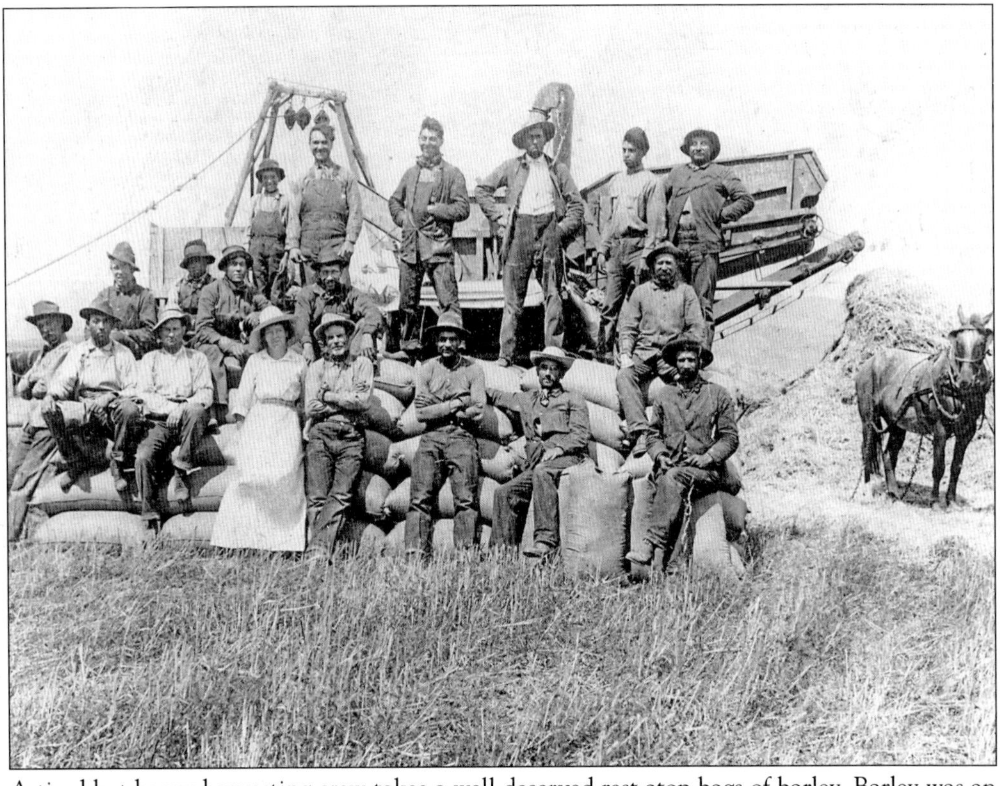

A tired but happy harvesting crew takes a well-deserved rest atop bags of barley. Barley was an important crop in Monterey County during the second half of the 19th century. Oxen, horses, and mules furnished most of the traction power during this time. Barley, used as feed for the draft animals, was in great demand.

CONTENTS

ACKNOWLEDGMENTS

The majority of the photographs featured in this book are from the collection of the Monterey County Agricultural and Rural Life Museum at San Lorenzo Park in King City. Photographs from several other Monterey County repositories were used in the book as well. I wish to thank Pat Hathaway from the California Views Collection; Dennis Copeland from the California History Room, Monterey Public Library; Ray Melendez from the Monterey County Library; Joyce Lombardi from the Monterey County Library, San Ardo Branch; Mona Gudgel from the Monterey County Historical Society; and Raquel Arroyo from the Soledad Historical Society.

In addition, I wish to thank individuals who shared their private collections, remembrances, and historical information, including Edward Whalen from the Monterey County Historical Advisory Commission; Frances Rogers Johansen from King City; Helen McDonald from Greenfield; Bob Oates from King City; and Pat Terry, who provided the rare photographs of Fort Romie.

Ernie Binsacca and Linda Sayler, members of the Monterey County Agricultural and Rural Life Museum Board of Directors, assisted with the identification of photographs and contacted private collectors. I am indebted to Lee Gularte, chair of the Monterey County Historical Advisory Commission, for her help and support in contacting private collectors.

Special thanks to John Castagna for his expertise in scanning the photos and making them look their very best. Finally I wish to thank Lynn Learch and Christine Raarup for typing and proofreading the manuscript and keeping me organized.

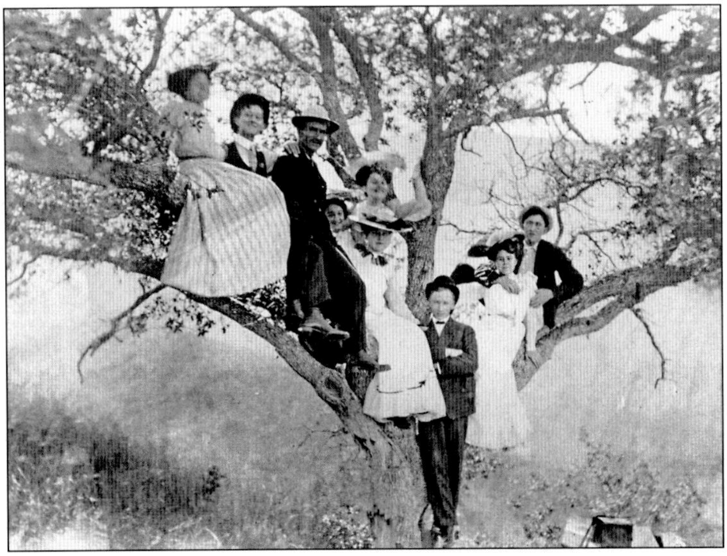

Camping trips and picnics were a favorite Salinas Valley pastime at the turn of the 19th century. Velma Dayton wrote that, "A bunch of us young folks would go for picnics on horseback, tie our lunches behind our saddles. What fun we had." Here ladies in spring dresses and gentlemen in hats have clambered up an old oak tree while a friend snaps their photograph with a trusty brownie camera.

INTRODUCTION

The long, narrow Salinas Valley is flanked by the Santa Lucia and Sierra de Salinas mountain ranges on the west and by the Gabilan Range and Cholame Hills on the east. Through its center, the Salinas River meanders its way to Monterey Bay, ducking underground during dry summer months. It is considered the longest underground river in the United States. This is the valley memorialized by John Steinbeck and known as the "salad bowl" of the nation.

For 7,000 years, three Native American tribes populated the valley. The Ohlone tribe occupied the northern portion of the valley, encompassing the area south of Salinas to Gonzales. The Esselen territory took in Soledad, Greenfield, and Paraiso Springs. The Salinan tribe lived south of King City.

The Salinas Valley attracted settlers for many different reasons. First to arrive were the Spanish missionaries who founded Mission Soledad. They brought local Native Americans to the mission, but they failed to thrive. European diseases, poor living conditions, and cruel treatment led to more deaths than births.

After the missions were secularized, great tracts of land were divided into Mexican ranchos. Native Americans slipped back into the mountains or found employment at the nearby ranchos of San Vicente or Los Coches. Vast herds of cattle waded through the valley's deep grasslands, providing the foundation for rancho life and economy. A devastating drought in the mid-1860s killed much of the livestock, and the industry never recovered.

Although thousands of settlers poured into California during the gold rush, few found their way to the Salinas Valley until the 1860s. Disappointed gold seekers turned toward the land and there was plenty of land in the Salinas Valley. Spurred on by the Homestead Act, settlers began to stake out small farms. Towns soon followed, situated at well-traveled crossroads. Grain became the county's principal product. Between 1857 and 1865, grain acreage increased from 2,450 to 27,358 acres. Farmers had difficulty getting their crop to market with far away Monterey and Moss Landing the only shipping points. In stepped the Southern Pacific Railroad, which extended its line to Salinas in 1872 and then continued south. As soon as tracks were laid, towns were established, including Chualar, Gonzales, and Soledad. In 1886, the railroad reached Charles King's ranch, and King City was founded, followed shortly thereafter by San Lucas, San Ardo, and Bradley.

Chinese laborers leaving the gold fields found employment in Salinas Valley grain fields. Farmers negotiated reclamation leases with them to drain land crisscrossed by sloughs. By 1880, Chinese farmers were leasing 1,000 acres of Salinas Valley land. They were followed by the Japanese, Filipinos, and many other people from around the world looking for a better life.

New industries were introduced when more immigrants moved to the area. The Swiss, Portuguese, and Danes started dairies. By the 1920s, 300 Salinas Valley dairies milked over 25,000 cows, making Monterey County the largest milk-producing county in the state.

Life was not all work. People gathered for parades, picnics, and pageants. One popular destination was the Paraiso Springs resort in the valley's foothills outside of Soledad. Guests stayed in quaint Victorian cottages, soaked in mineral-charged waters, and enjoyed grand vistas of the valley.

At the end of the 19th century, the introduction of large-scale sugar beet farming by sugar king Claus Spreckels led to Salinas Valley colonization schemes, such as Fort Romie in the Mission District near Soledad. Here the Salvation Army built a community where the poor could get a foothold in life. Clark Colony (now known as Greenfield) soon followed, distinguished by a maze of irrigation canals that are still in use today.

During both world wars, the Salinas Valley played its part, producing beans, evaporated milk, and guayule rubber for the home front and overseas. A 1942 treaty with Mexico allowed Mexican nationals called *braceros* to come to the United States as laborers. By 1951, growers' demand for laborers led to a permanent *bracero* program.

Many people have contributed to the growth and development of the Salinas Valley—Mexican rancheros, hardy pioneers, optimistic town boosters, and versatile farmers. Their hometowns—Chualar, Gonzales, Soledad, Greenfield, King City, San Lucas, San Ardo, and Bradley—have supported, and still support, a mighty agricultural industry now valued at over $3 billion. Fragments of daily life, captured by the camera for over a century, tell a familiar but potent tale of struggle, triumph, and simple pleasures.

These images, gathered from libraries, archives, and individuals, highlight the contributions of the many people throughout history who have made the Salinas Valley what it is today.

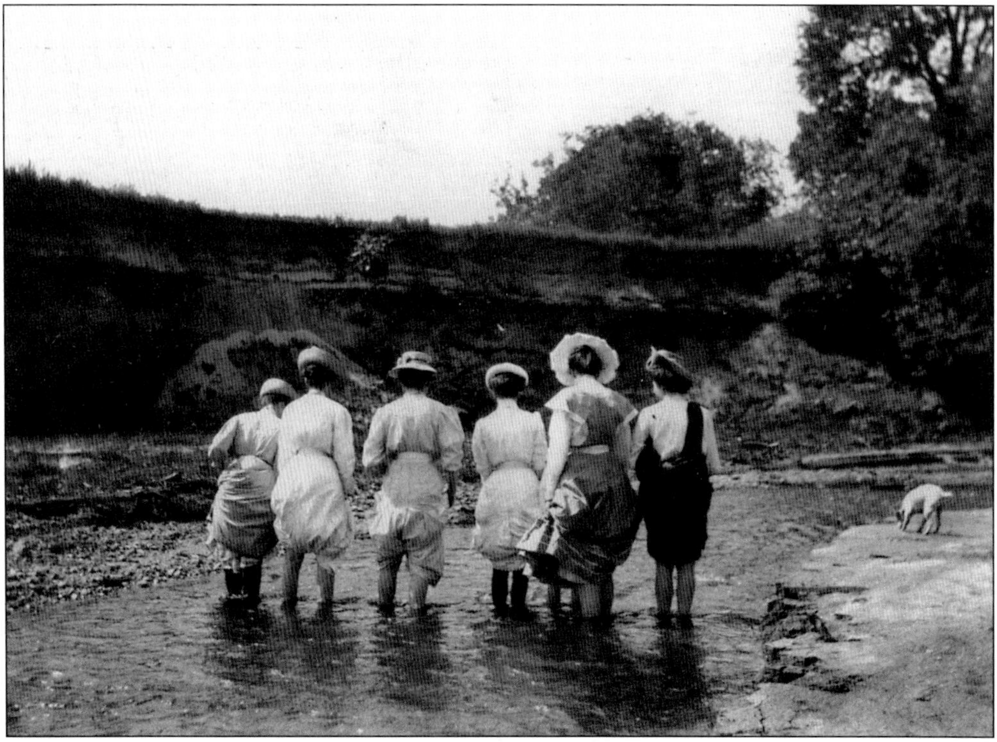

Six Gibson girls tucked up their skirts and waded in the cool Salinas River during a Salinas Ladies Club picnic. Picnics were a popular pastime in the valley, especially in groves along the Salinas River.

One

The Early Years

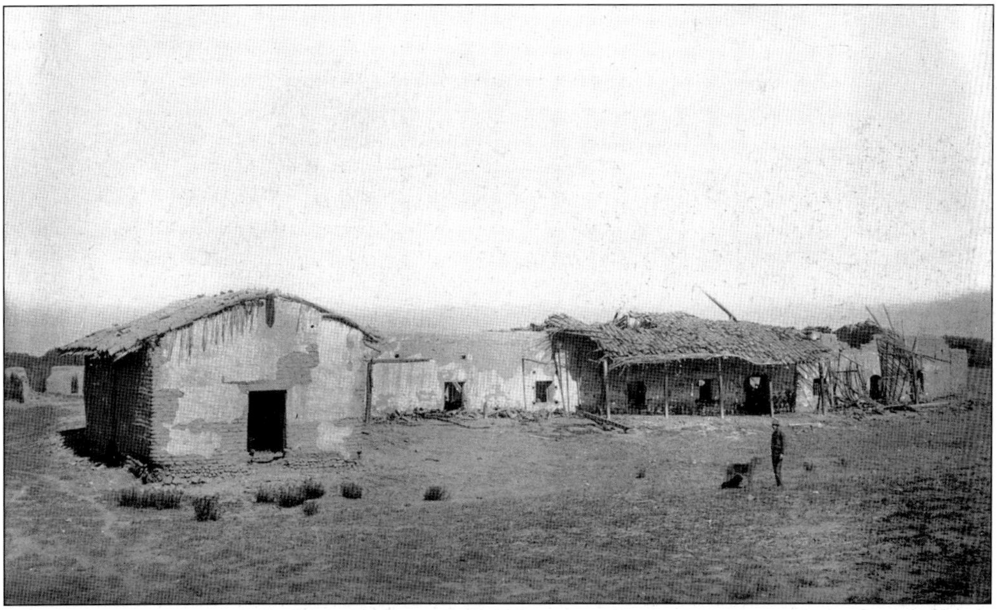

Mission Neustra Senora de la Soledad was founded on October 9, 1791, the 13th in the California Mission chain. Many believe it was plagued by bad luck. Crops never flourished, the first two friars in charge had bad reputations, and a massive epidemic in 1802 killed many Native Americans. After the missions were secularized, the buildings fell into ruin, as seen here in 1880. Notice the standing "ghost" dog due to the lengthy exposure time of this photograph. (Courtesy of the Monterey County Library.)

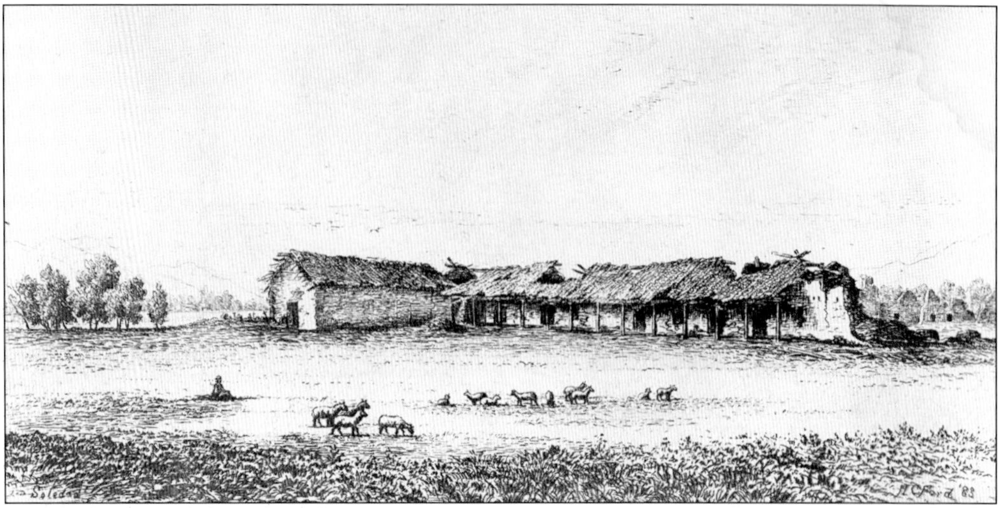

In 1856, artist Henry Miller set out from San Francisco to draw each of the California missions. He braved wild animals, slept in fields, and survived with little money, selling his sketches along the way. His drawing of Mission Soledad shows collapsed walls and roofing. At this time, the mission belonged to Feliciano Soberanes. Soberanes took mission tiles and timbers to his Alisal ranch in order to build two structures, hastening the deterioration of the mission. (Courtesy of the Monterey County Library.)

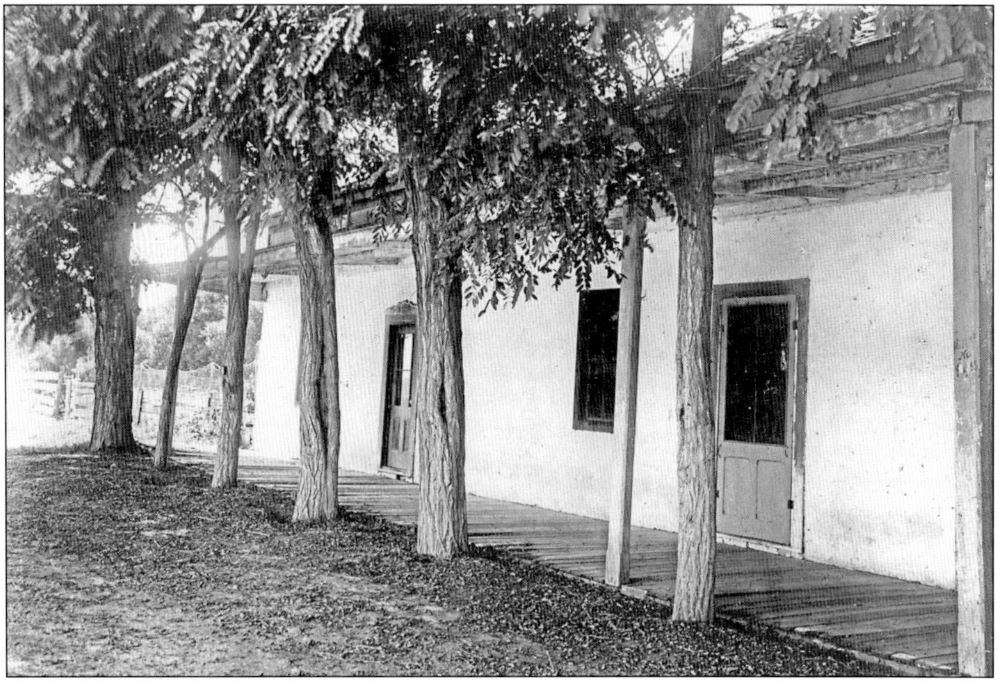

Jose Maria Soberanes, a young soldier, accompanied Portola on his famous trek from Mexico to find Monterey Bay. He left military service in 1795 and was granted, along with his father-in-law, Joaquin Castro, Rancho Buena Vista in the Soledad area. Jose's granddaughter Josefa received a portion of the rancho known as Rancho Los Coches. Josefa and her husband, William Brenner Richardson, built the Los Coches adobe, which stands today just off Highway 101 and Arroyo Seco Road. Richardson planted the locust trees pictured here.

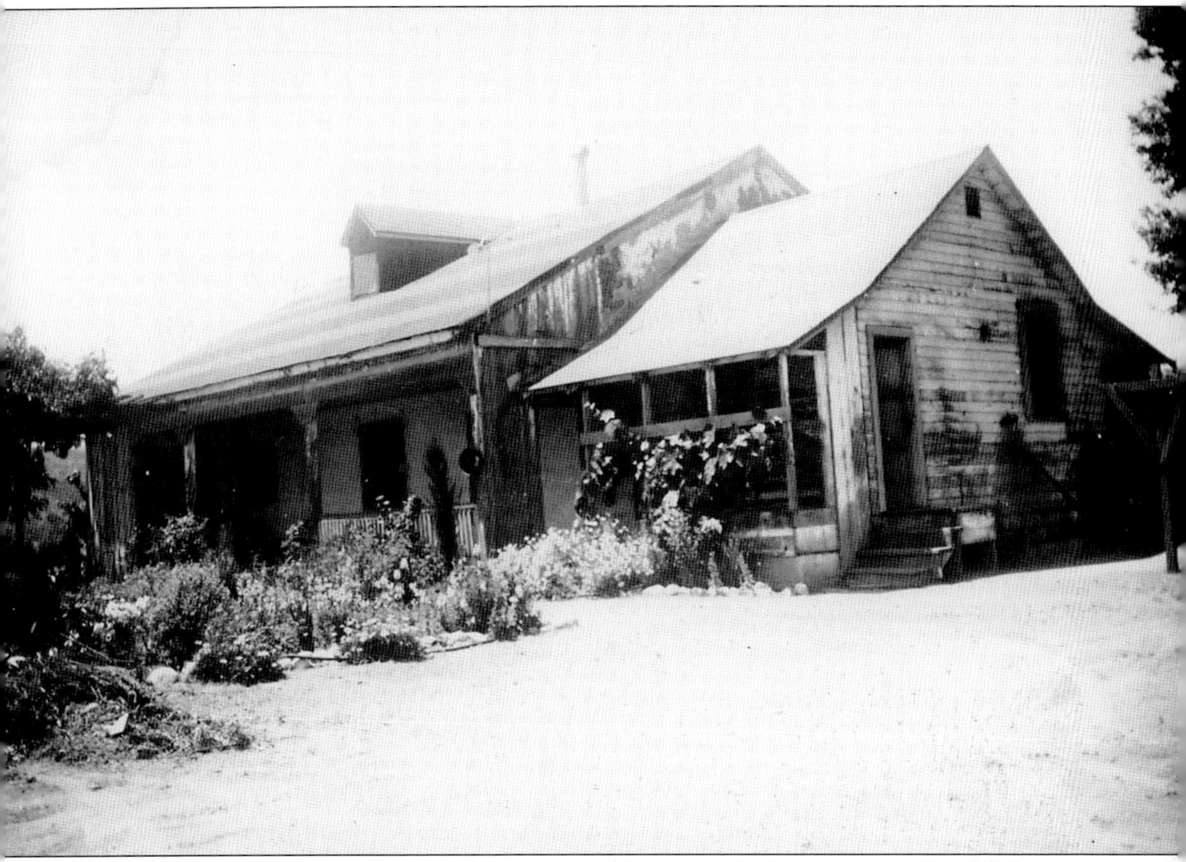

In May 1841, Governor Alvarado gave the Soledad Mission land to his cousin's husband, Feliciano Soberanes. The Soberanes family became the administrator of the property and built this home nearby the mission. In *Crusoe's Island*, published in 1864, J. Ross Brown wrote about his visit to the Soberanes's home. "Notwithstanding the fleas, which abounded in overwhelming numbers, I contrived to sleep soundly. Next morning, after a good breakfast of coffee, tortillas, jerked beef, etc., as before, I mounted my mule and proceeded on my journey, much to the regret of Soberanes, who positively refused to accept a cent for the accommodations he had afforded me." (Courtesy of the Monterey Public Library, California History Room.)

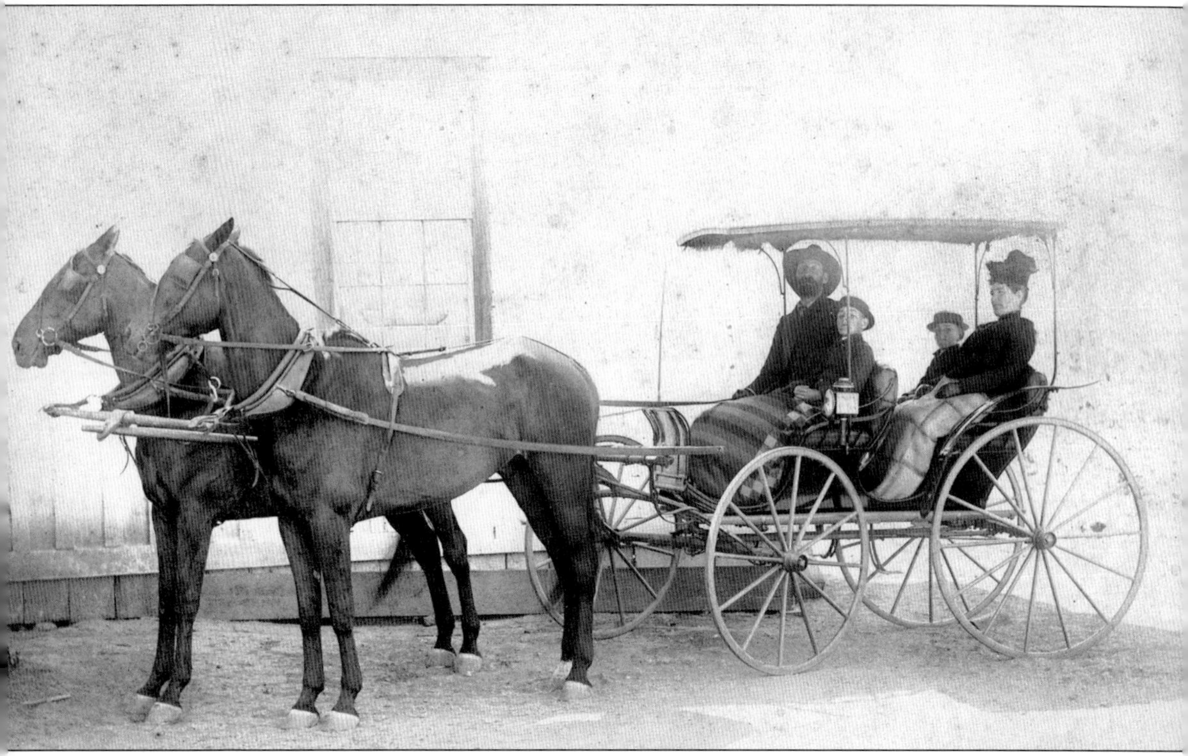

Benito Soberanes steadied his team of horses while a photograph was taken of his wife, Ada, and two sons, Benny and Nathaniel, on a sunny day in Gonzales in 1887. Benito was the great grandson of Jose Maria Soberanes who traveled with the Portola expedition to California. Between 1863 and 1864, his father, Feliciano, lost over 2,000 head of cattle when a devastating drought plagued the Salinas Valley. (Courtesy of the Monterey County Historical Society.)

Two

CHUALAR

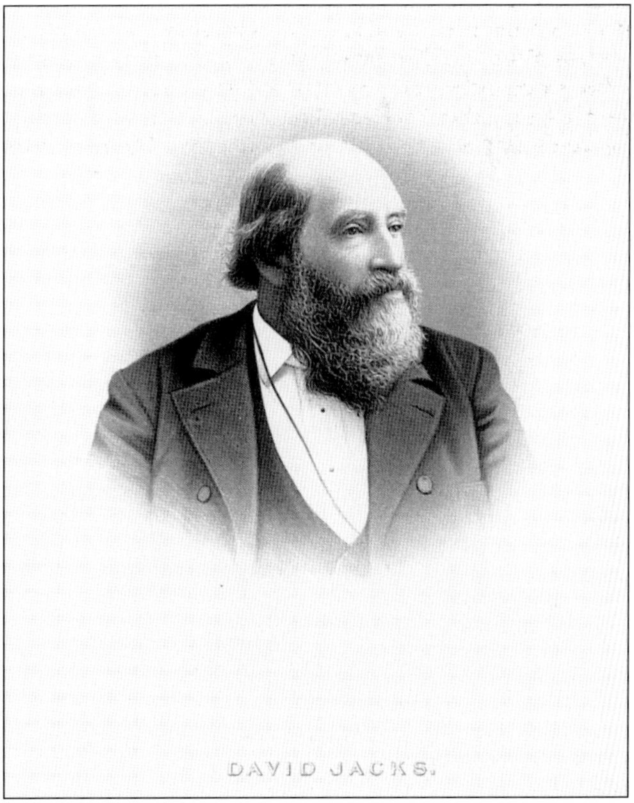

Pictured is land baron David Jacks, who laid out the town of Chualar in 1874 near the western boundary of his Rancho Chualar. The name comes from a Spanish adaptation of an Indian word meaning "place where the chual [pigweed] grows." Just one year later, L. L. Paulson wrote that "everything argues well for the ultimate success of this little hamlet. Its situation is attractive and advantageous, its contiguous lands fertile and well tilled, and its people industrious, enterprising and correspondingly prosperous." (Courtesy of the Monterey Public Library, California History Room.)

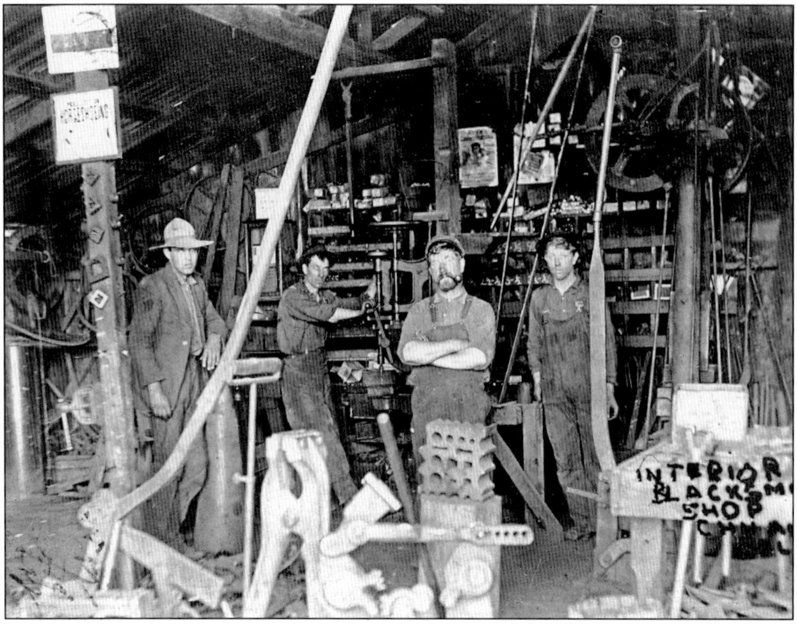

Like all blacksmith shops, this establishment in Chualar offered a variety of services, from farm equipment repair to horseshoeing. Shops were crammed with machinery, spare parts, and wrought iron—all critical to keeping rural communities up and running.

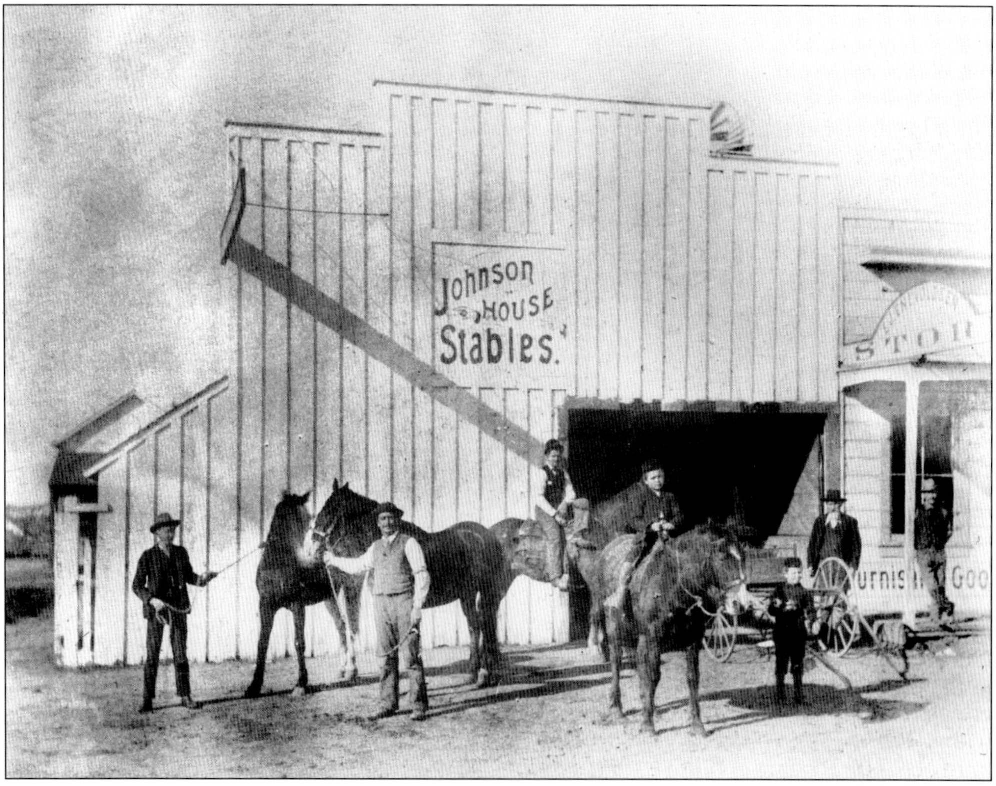

In addition to farming, Charles W. Johnson ran the Johnson House hotel and livery stable. The livery stable was considered first-class, offering the "best of turn-outs at the shortest notice." (Courtesy of the Monterey County Historical Society.)

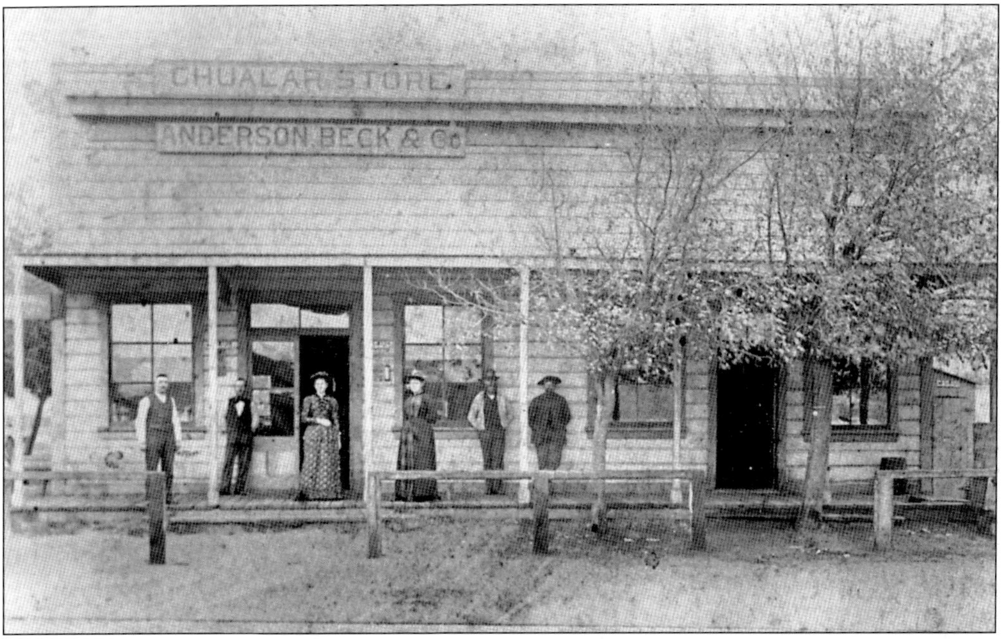

Anderson, Beck, and Company was the principal general store in Chualar. They were noted for their "well-selected stock of general merchandise, including clothing, dry goods, hardware, groceries and provisions . . . they keep a large stock of agricultural implements such as wagons, buggies, plows, harrows, reapers, leaders, etc."

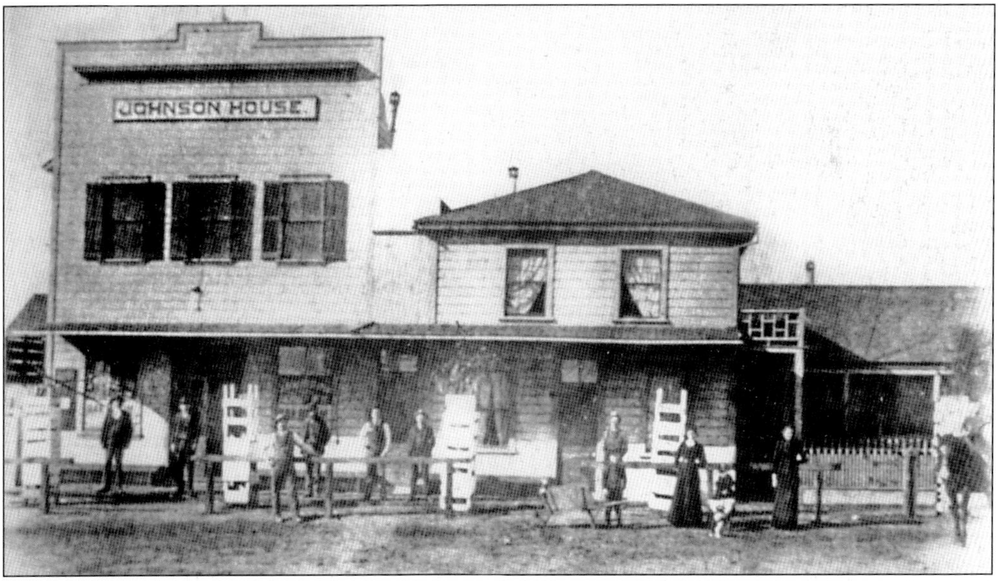

Charles W. Johnson arrived in Chualar from Sweden in 1876. He leased and farmed several hundred acres from David Jacks. In addition, he purchased a hotel in town. The *Gonzales Tribune* wrote, "It is no exaggeration to say that the Johnson House is one of the best hotels in the interior of the county. His table is always supplied with the best and choicest viands and his rooms are second to none found in any country hotel. His bar-room is handsomely and tastily decorated and furnished and in it can be found the best and choicest brands of foreign and domestic wines, liquors and cigars."

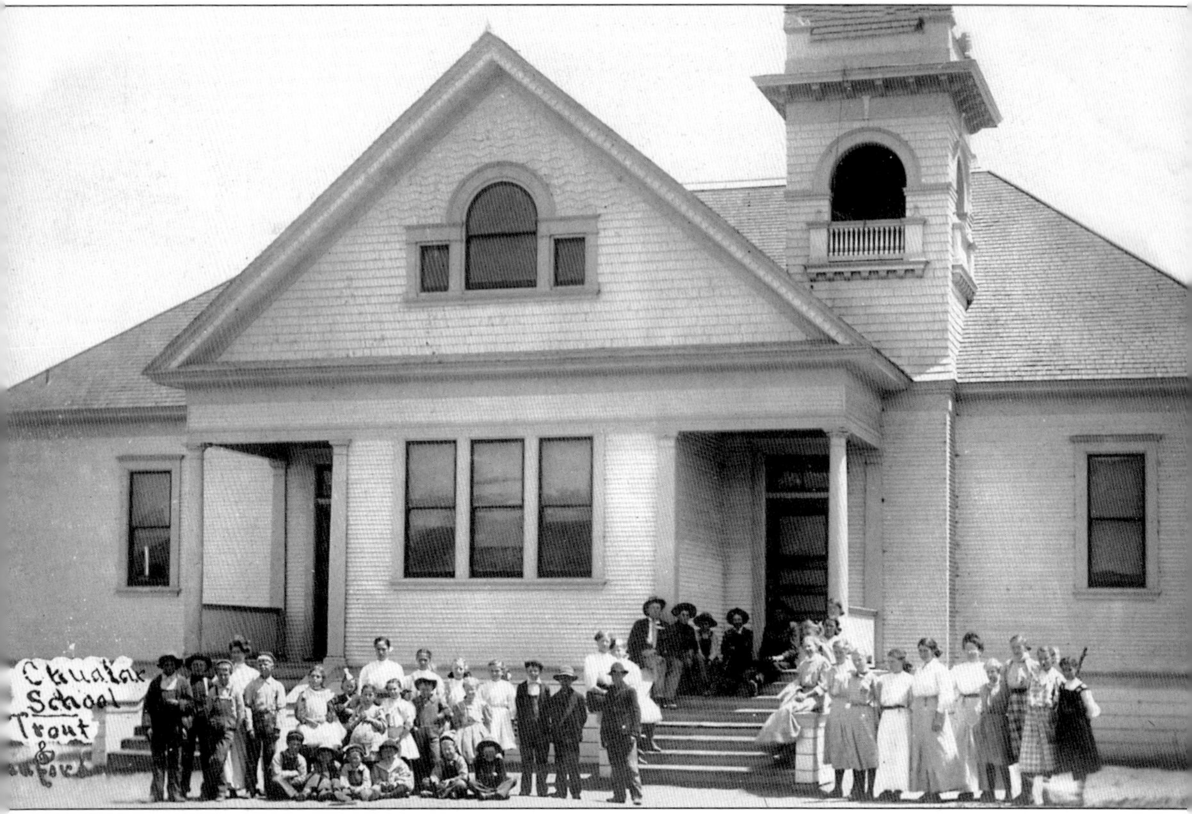

In 1894, the *Gonzales Tribune* noted that, educationally, Chualar "has kept pace with its rapid growth and now enjoys the distinction of possessing school facilities second to no town of its size in the west." (Courtesy of Pat Hathaway, California Views.)

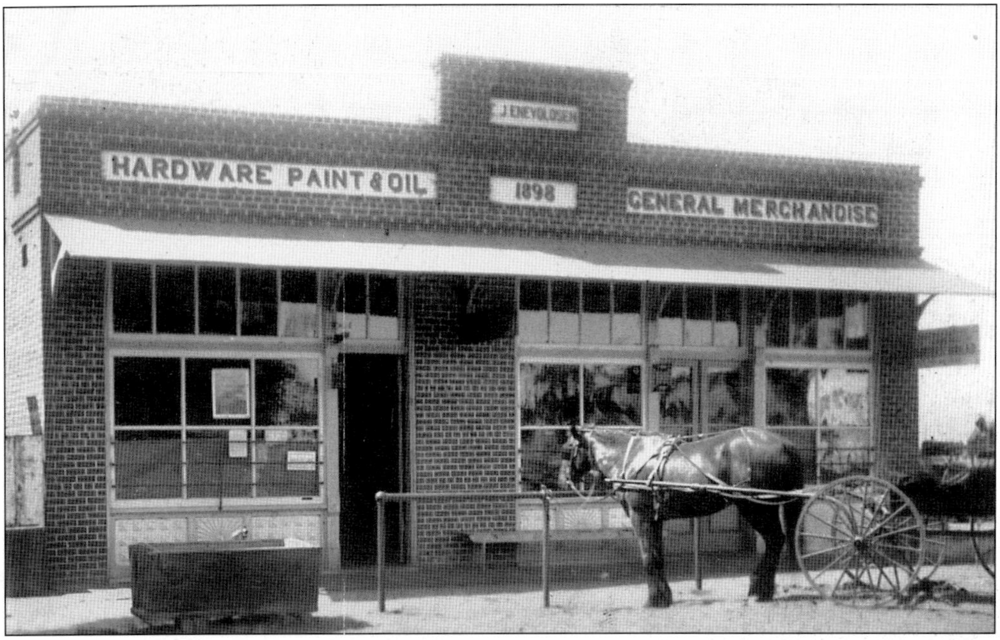

Enevold Jorgen Enevoldsen left his native Denmark at age 19 and arrived in Chualar in November 1882. He opened the hardware and general merchandise store pictured here. The *Gonzales Tribune* noted that "his genial disposition has won for him many friends and he is now considered one of the prominent business men of that town." (Courtesy of Pat Hathaway, California Views.)

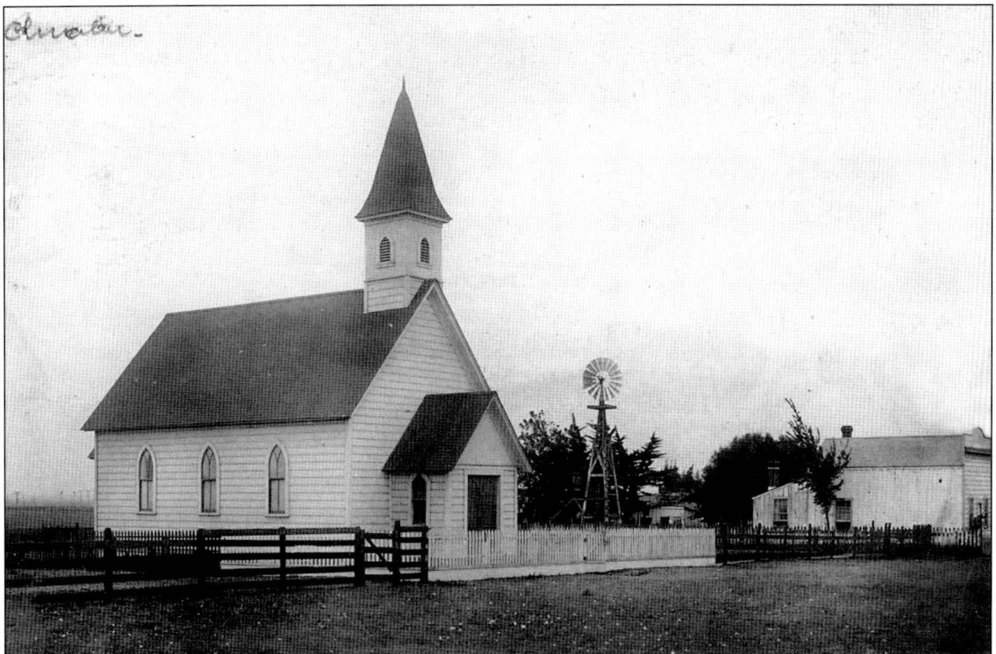

Chualar's Lutheran church served the town's principally Scandinavian population, but Methodists also held services in this building every other week. (Courtesy of Pat Hathaway, California Views.)

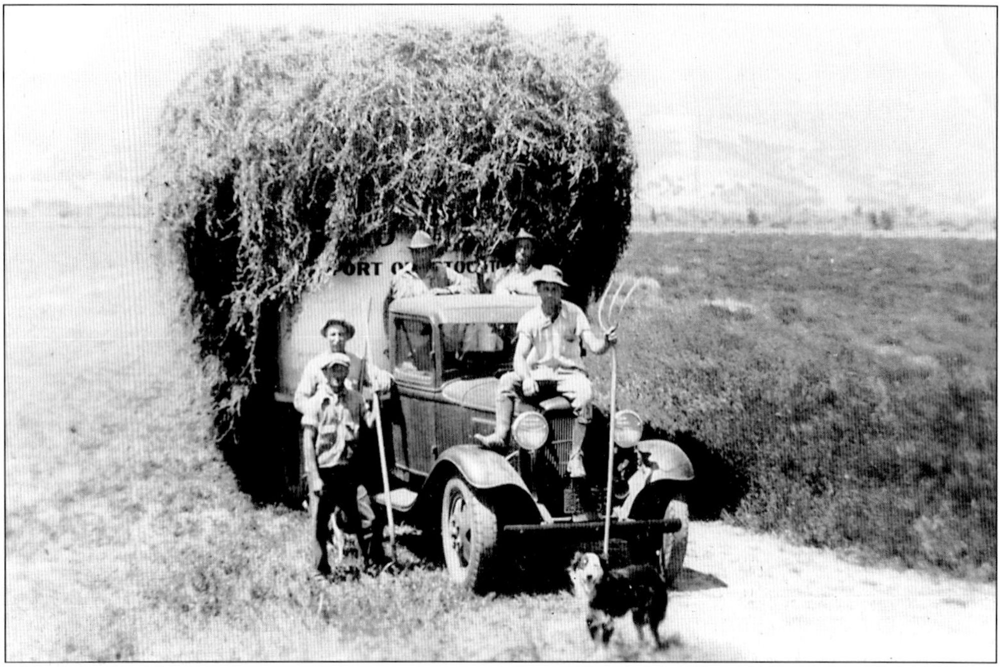

Emilio Pasque (seated on truck) is pictured on his way to Aptos to deliver a load of hay. Hay sold for $5 a ton, loaded. Pasque operated a dairy one mile southwest of Chualar that he leased from Mary Jacks Thomas.

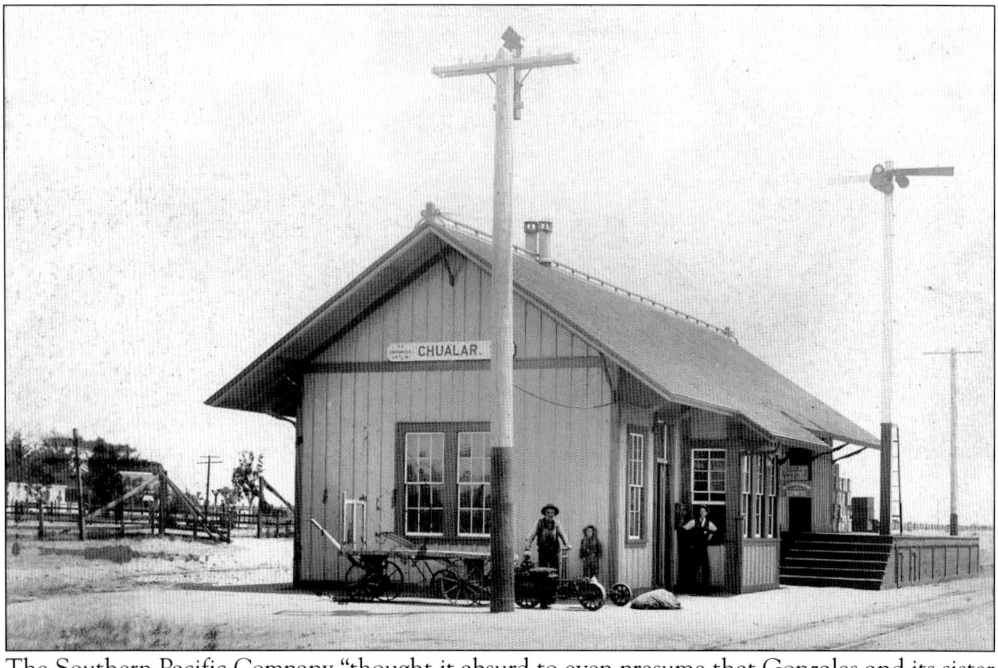

The Southern Pacific Company "thought it absurd to even presume that Gonzales and its sister town Chualar would ever be of sufficient importance to justify erecting depots." Brothers Thomas and George Faw stepped in, and their Salinas Valley Warehouse Association footed the bill for both depots and took over their management. (Courtesy of Pat Hathaway, California Views.)

Three

GONZALES

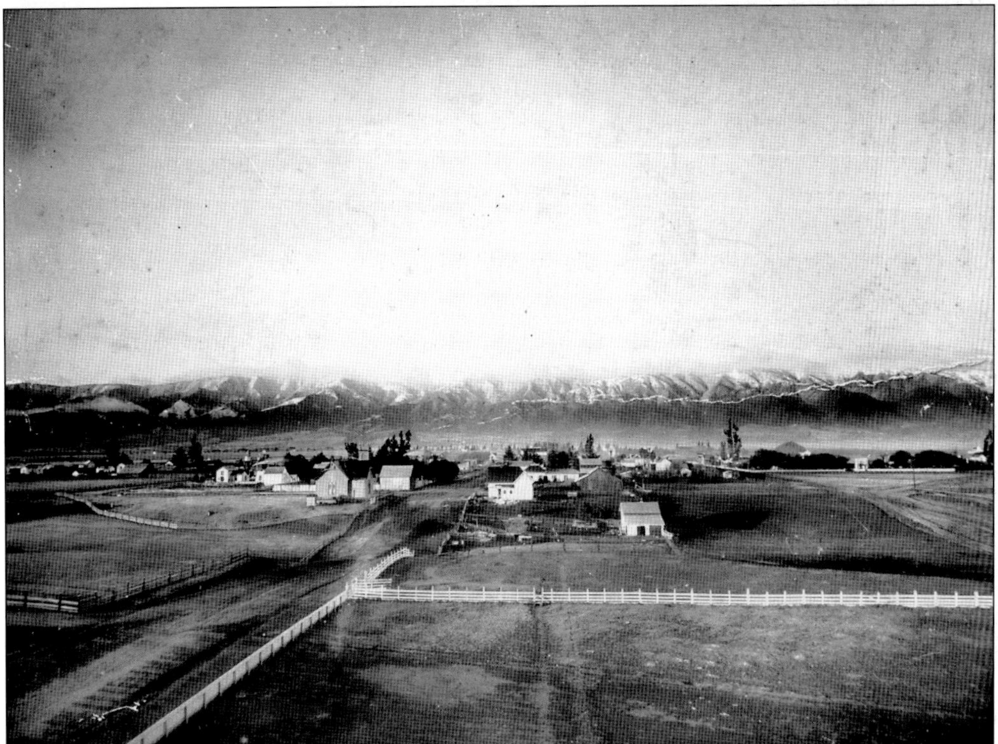

Teodoro Gonzalez was granted the Rancho Rincon de la Puente del Monte in 1836. His sons, Dr. Mariano and Alfredo Gonzalez, founded the town in 1874—the same year the Southern Pacific Railroad began to extend its line down the Salinas Valley. Fifty blocks were surveyed, and people started to lease or purchase lots from the brothers. The town was named after the Gonzalez family, although at some point in time the ending "z" was replaced with an "s." (Courtesy of Edward Whalen.)

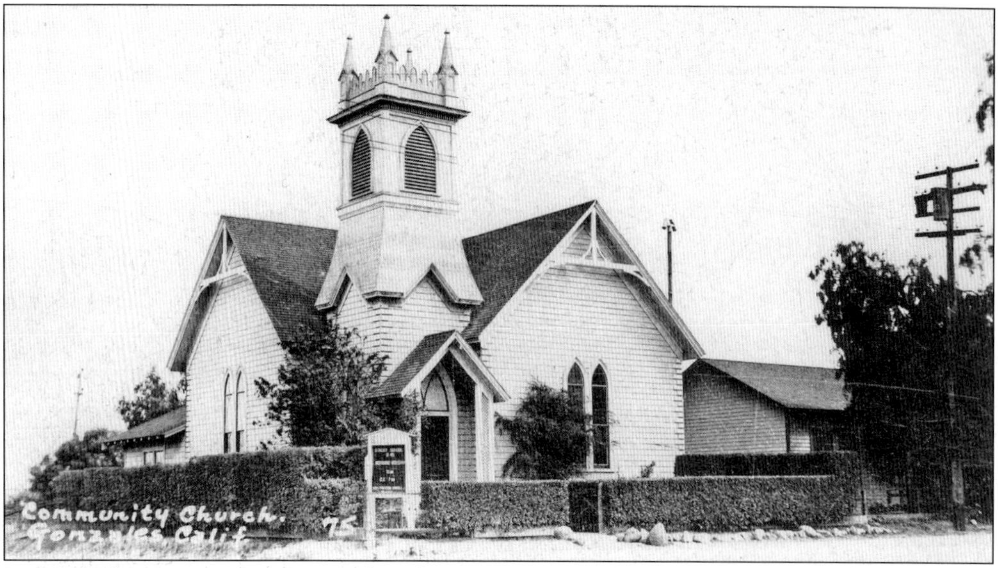

In 1874, Thomas Faw and D. K. Edwards organized a Sunday school that met in the Gonzales schoolhouse on Fifth and Day Streets. Nine years later, the Baptist Church of Gonzales was officially organized, and the congregation began to build a church. When the church was dedicated on July 14, 1884, the local paper wrote that "the walls and ceilings are beautifully frescoed and present a very attractive appearance. The style of the building is Gothic. It has a tower sixty feet high, containing a bell, the tones of which have been heard six miles distant." (Courtesy of the Monterey County Historical Society.)

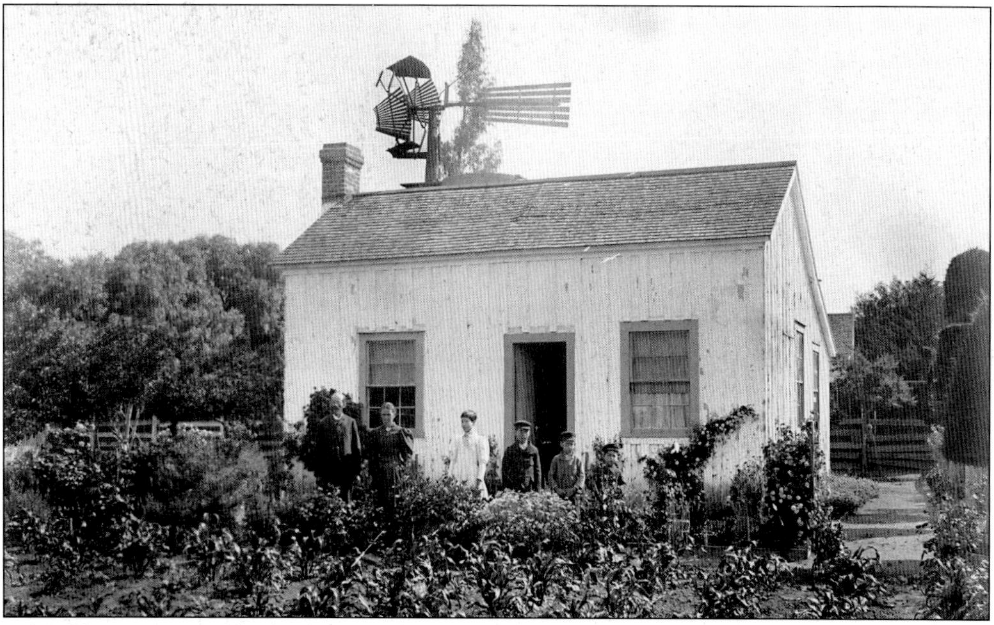

A healthy corn crop fills the front yard of Frank Mojica's house on the corner of Day and Sixth Streets in Gonzales. In 1849, Frank and his brother traveled from Mexico to California, lured by the gold discovery in the Sierra foothills. Both invested their mining money in property near Gonzales and started a hog ranch. This house was built in 1876, one of the earliest homes in Gonzales. (Courtesy of Edward Whalen.)

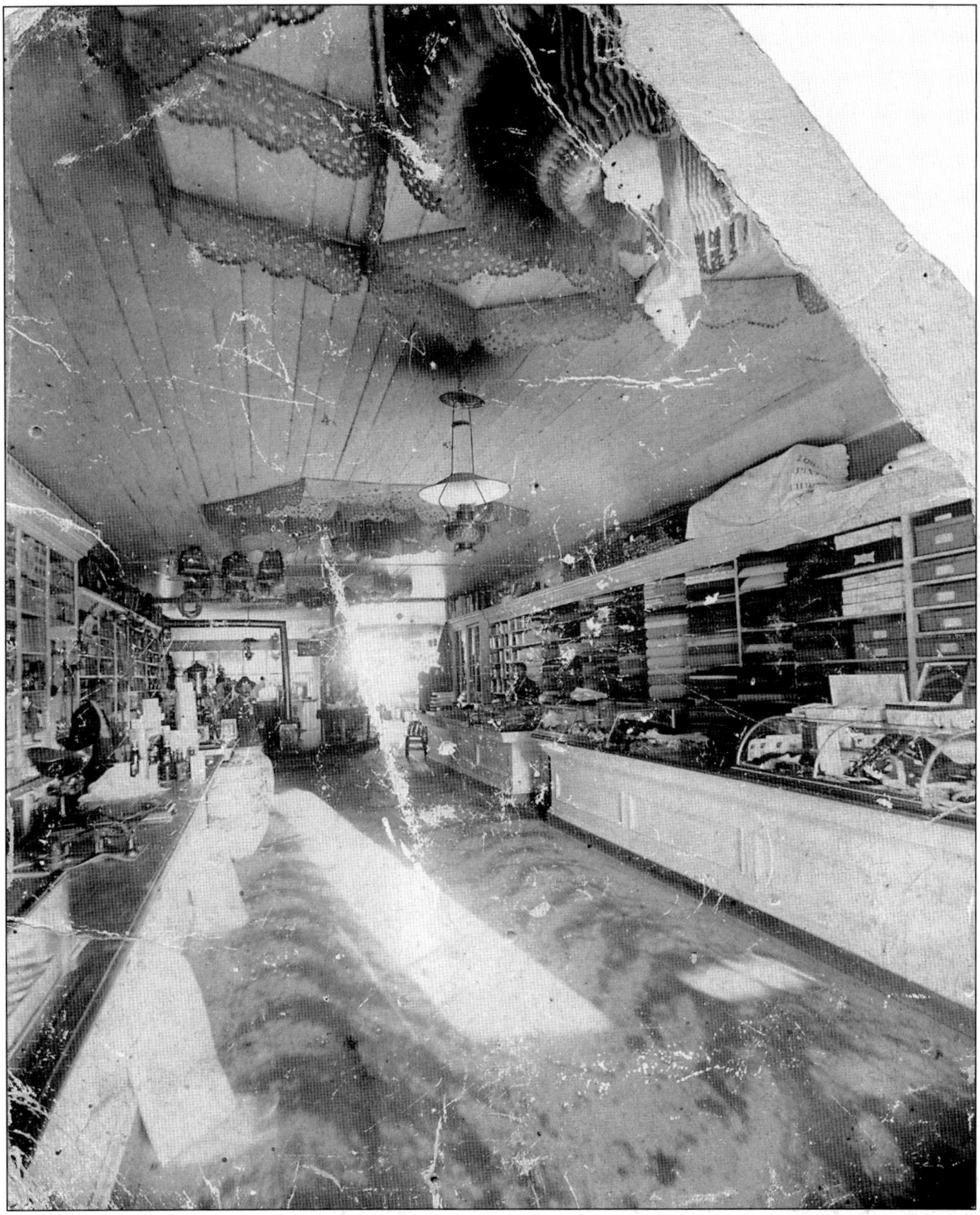

In 1874, A. Widemann and William Sarles opened the first mercantile business in Gonzales. Twenty years later, the *Gonzales Tribune* noted that "the firm of Sarles and Widemann is known as one of the most prosperous mercantile firms in Monterey County. They . . . transact the largest business of any firm outside the county seat. Their store is filled with a well-selected stock of dry goods, clothing, groceries, hardware and provisions and is by far the largest in the town . . . in fact, everything necessary to supply the wants of their numerous customers, from a needle to a threshing machine." Note the decorative "papel picado" on the ceiling—decorative tissue paper garlands used for Mexican fiestas. (Courtesy of Edward Whalen.)

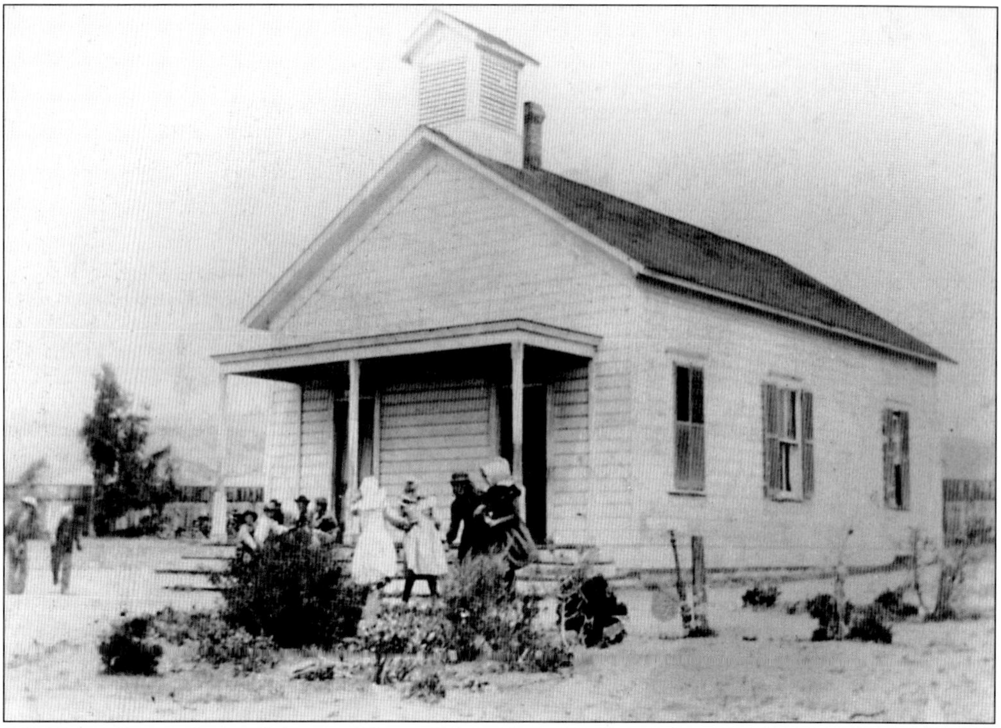

Children play in front of the La Gloria School located five miles southeast of Gonzales. The school was built for $1,325 in 1887. In 1896, teacher Jennie E. Hall wrote, "Gloria school is one of the best equipped in Monterey County. Both pupils and teacher aim to have it ranked among the best, if not the best one in the County."

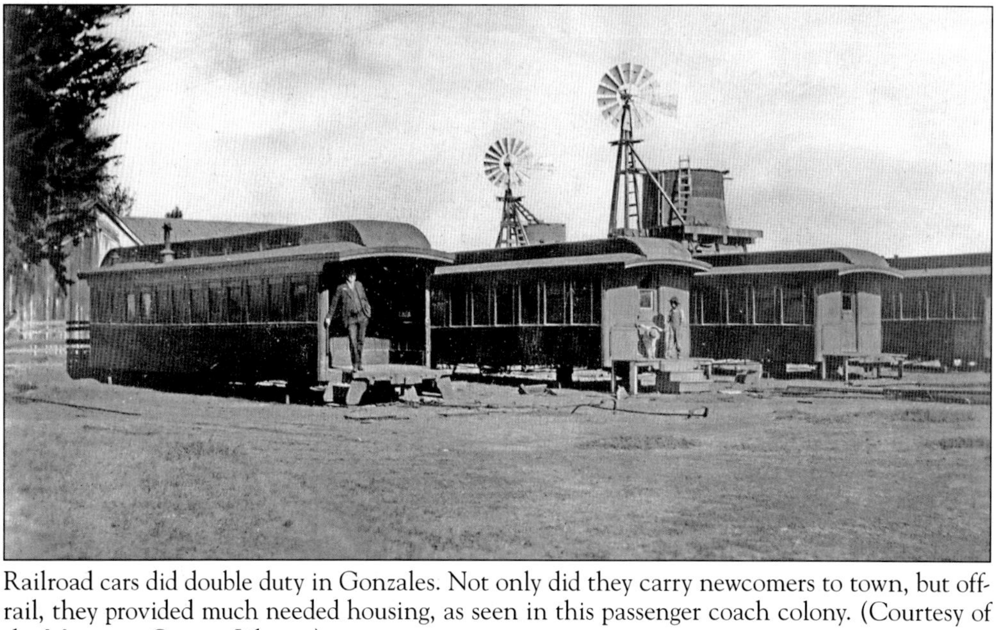

Railroad cars did double duty in Gonzales. Not only did they carry newcomers to town, but off-rail, they provided much needed housing, as seen in this passenger coach colony. (Courtesy of the Monterey County Library.)

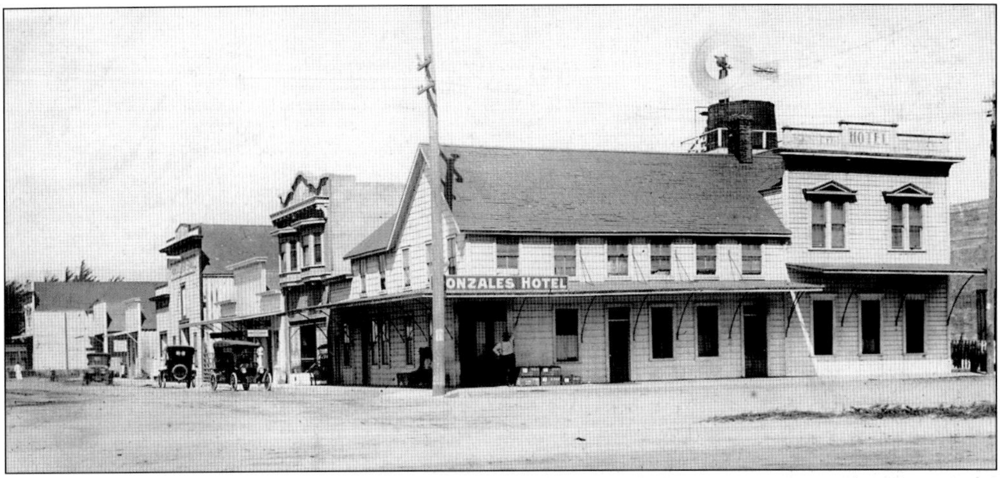

The Gonzales Hotel, located on the corner of Alta and Fourth Streets, was owned and operated by Chris Twisselmann, a German native. The *Gonzales Tribune* noted that "the rooms of the hotel are all large, cozy and comfortable, and the table is supplied with all the delicacies the market affords." It continued that if Mr. Twisselman was "placed upon a barren rock with both hands tied behind him he would by some manner of means contrive to make money." (Courtesy of Pat Hathaway, California Views.)

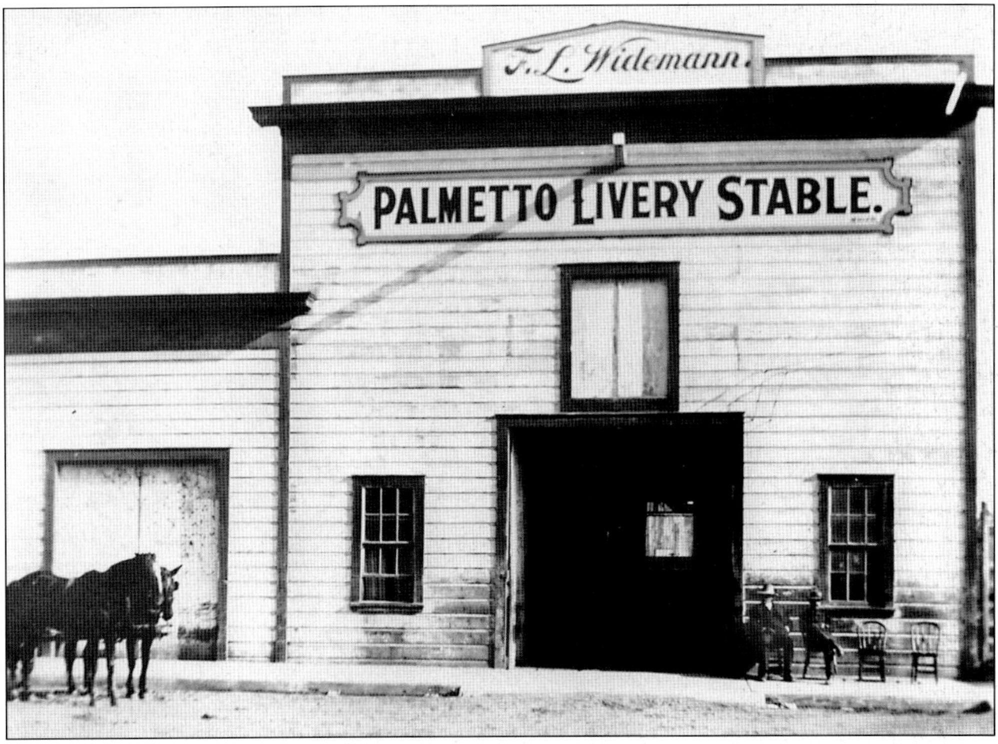

In 1911, Eugene Tavernetti bought the Palmetto Livery Stable in Gonzales from Fred L. Widemann. The *Salinas Morning Democrat* reported, "Eugene Tavernetti is a young man born and raised in this vicinity and was formerly engaged in the livery business at Soledad. He takes charge of the business today and may feel like an old cat in a new garret for a day or so, but will then be accustomed to his new haunt." (Courtesy of the Monterey County Historical Society.)

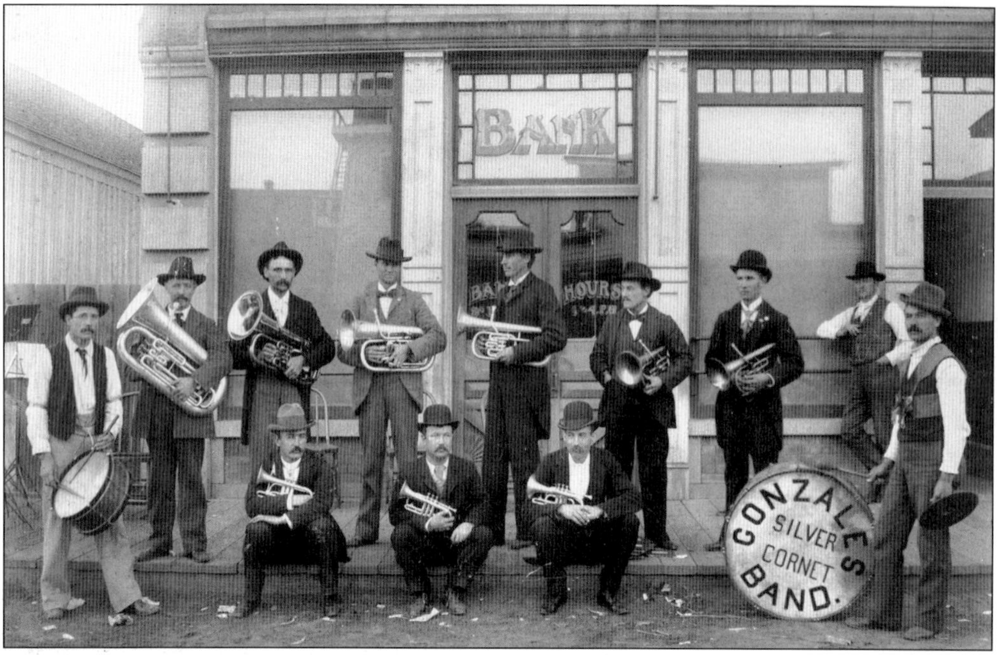

Using the sidewalk as a stage, the Gonzales Silver Coronet Band is ready to strike up a popular late-19th-century tune. Pictured, from left to right, are (sitting) unidentified, Mr. Delholm, and George Hifskish; (standing) Harry Mitchell, Jack Platz, Herman Danningberg, Bob Mann, Olli Perry, Mr. Theirett, Larkin Smith, and Militone Alvizo. (Courtesy of Edward Whalen.)

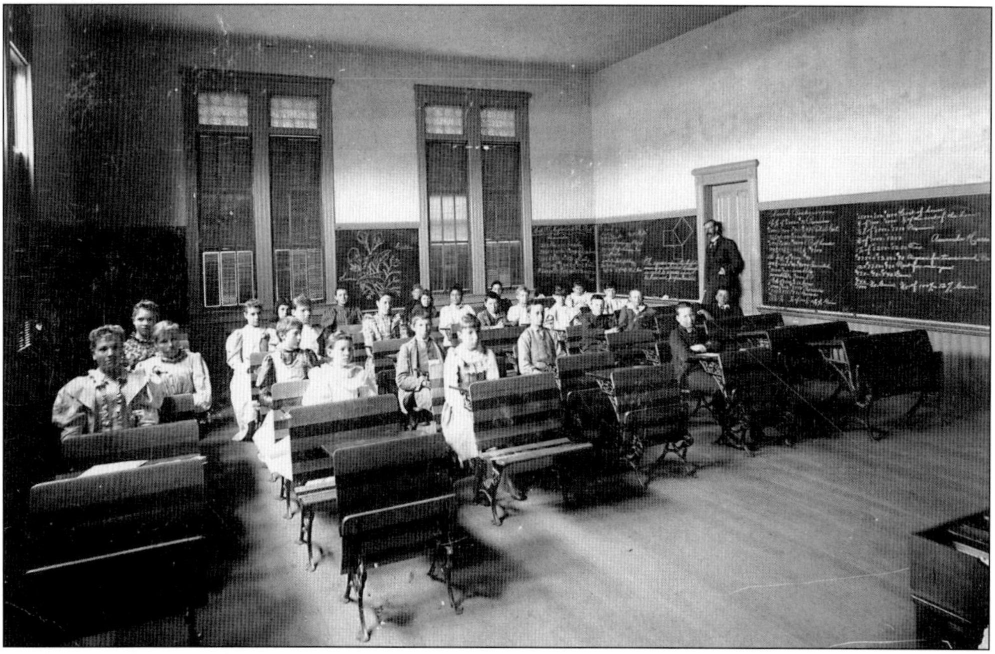

Students at the Gonzales Grammar School are on their best behavior as seen here in 1896. Teacher Mr. Burnett stands ready to start the lesson once the photographer has snapped his photograph. This school was built in 1893, was two stories tall, and had four rooms—three for grammar school and one for high school. (Courtesy of Edward Whalen.)

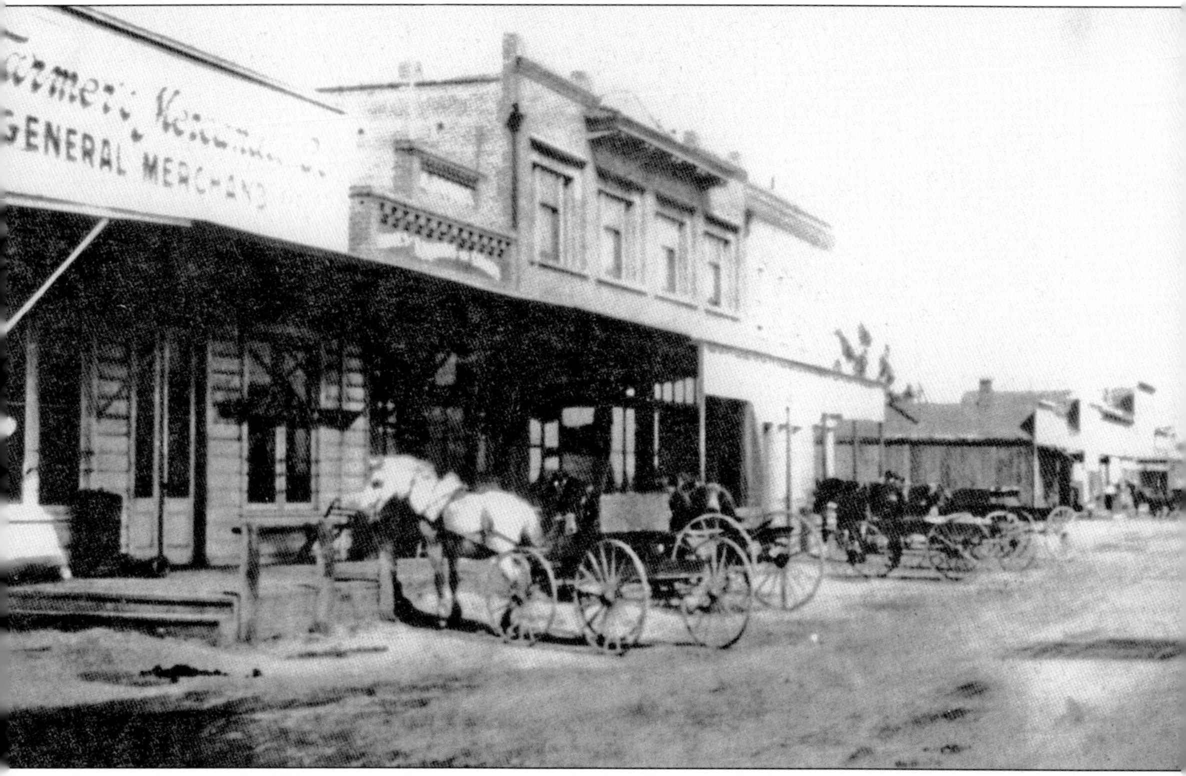

Pictured around 1900, patient horses wait at the hitching rails that lined Gonzales's Fourth Street. At the time, the town was described as having "a good hotel, also a restaurant, a general merchandise store and blacksmithing establishment, together with those undoubted evidences of advanced civilization, the saloon and schoolhouse; however, here as elsewhere in California, the saloons predominate." (Courtesy of the Monterey County Historical Society.)

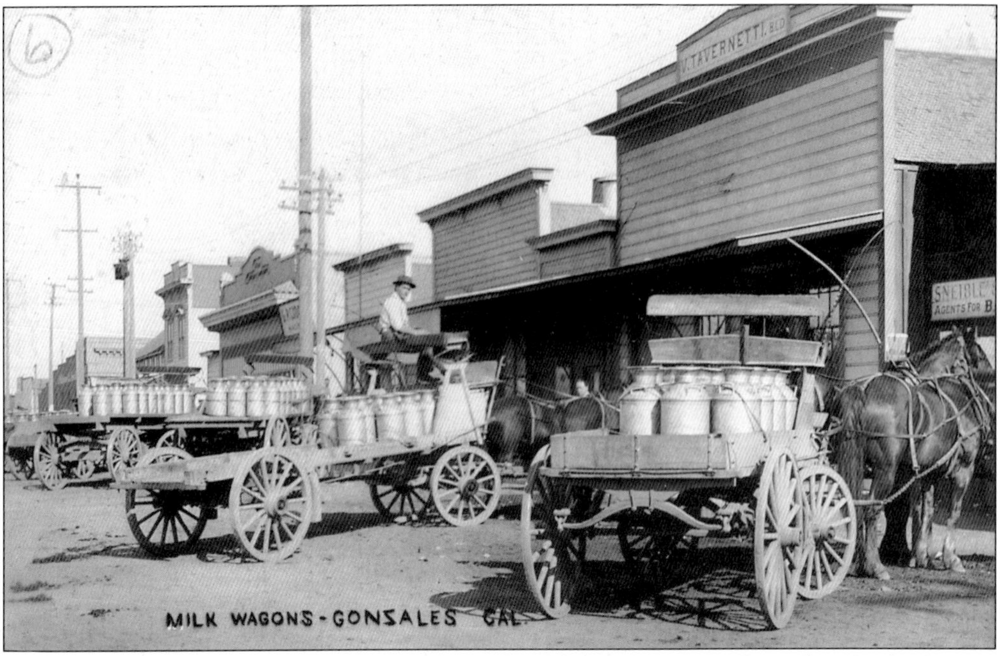

Farmers delivered wagonloads of fresh milk to the Alpine Factory in Gonzales. Emilio Pasque recalled that "in Gonzales the Swiss ran the hotel and the bank. The garage was Swiss, the store was Swiss and there were pretty near all Swiss around there. If you talked Swiss everybody would understand you." (Courtesy of Edward Whalen.)

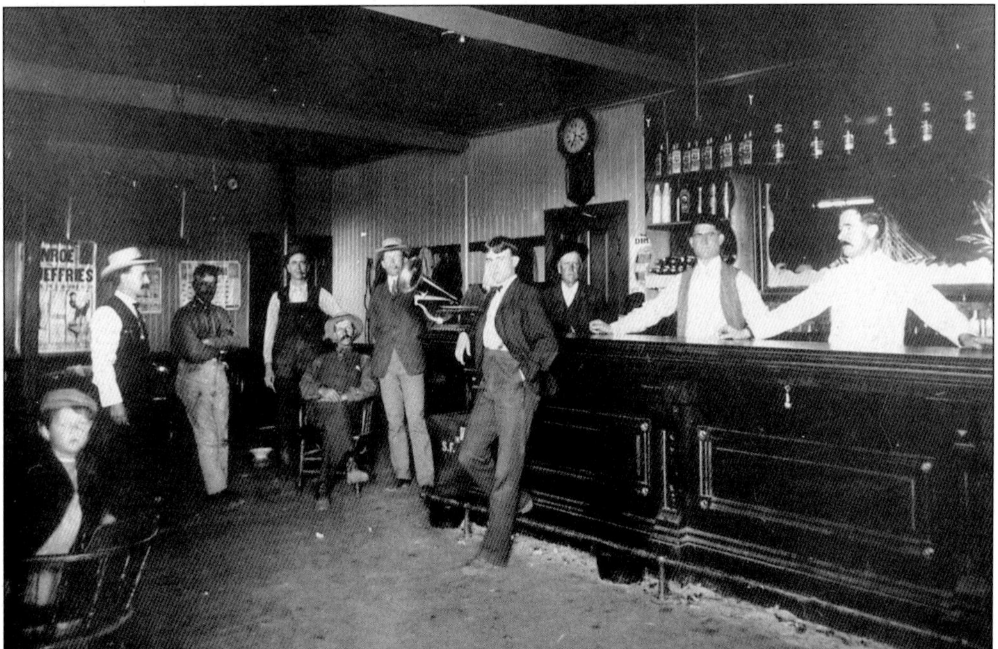

Patrons of the Gonzales Hotel bar pose for a casual portrait in 1904. Pictured, from left to right, are Otis McKinsey, John Gould, unidentified, Fred Sneible, Fred Widemann, Dan Mills, Dr. Ned Gould, Bill Graves, Loren McKinsey, and William Pettitt. (Courtesy of Edward Whalen.)

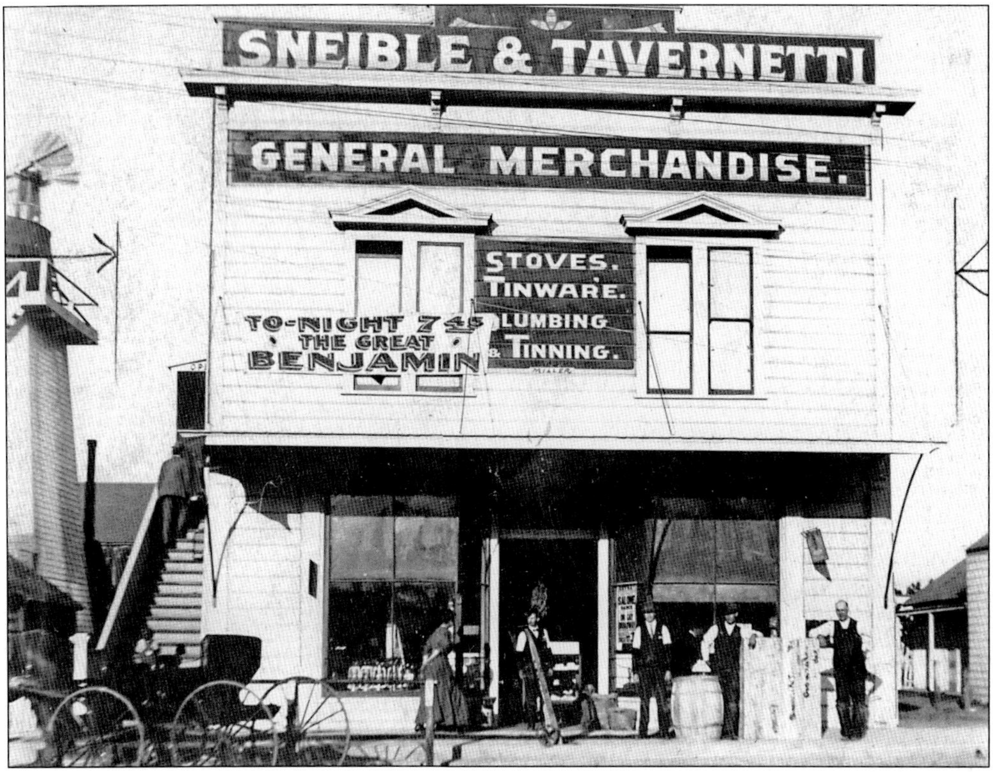

Sneible and Tavernetti's General Merchandise store in Gonzales, known as the S&T, is pictured here in 1908. Mr. Sneible leans against a crate at the extreme right while Mr. Tavernetti stands in the doorway. They built a new store in 1913, and one year later, Mr. Sneible was killed in an explosion. (Courtesy of Edward Whalen.)

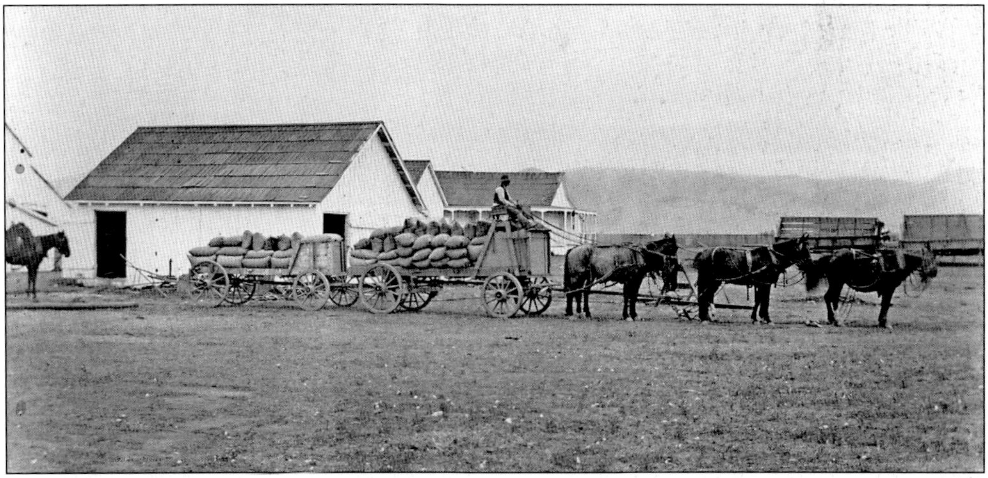

A Gonzales farmer leaves for town with sacks of grain piled high on his wagons. The typical grain wagon had two rear wheels that were five feet high and two front wheels, four feet high. The wheels were made of hardwood spokes banded with steel. The wheel hubs had a built-in oil container with a snap-on lid. Sheep wool in the container soaked up the oil and kept it from running out. The heat from the turning axle determined how much of the oil was used. Generally there was enough oil for a day's work. (Courtesy of the Monterey County Historical Society.)

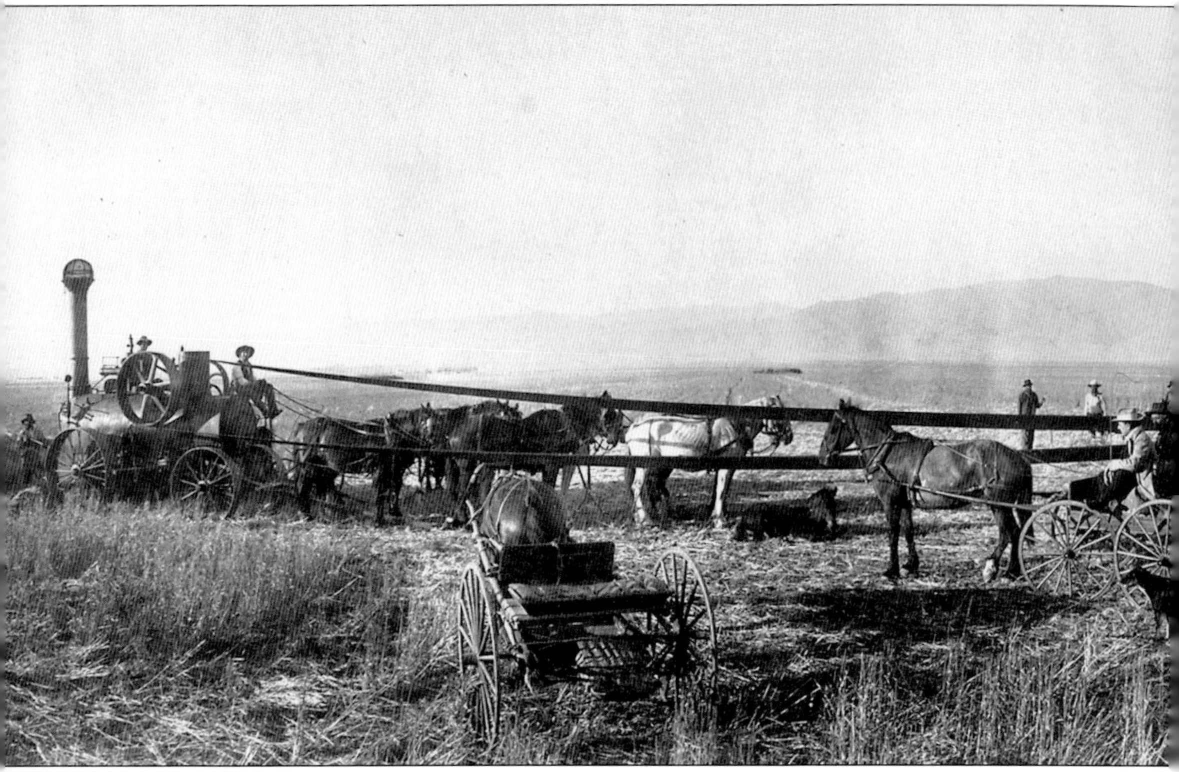

The Salinas Valley's wheat and barley crops were harvested by threshing crews up until World War I. Vincent Tavernetti's Pitt-engine grain harvester and Bronson-Pitt separator, pictured here, worked in fields around Gonzales and Soledad. Paul Tavernetti, the boss, supervised an engineer, fireman, separator man, sack tender, two sack

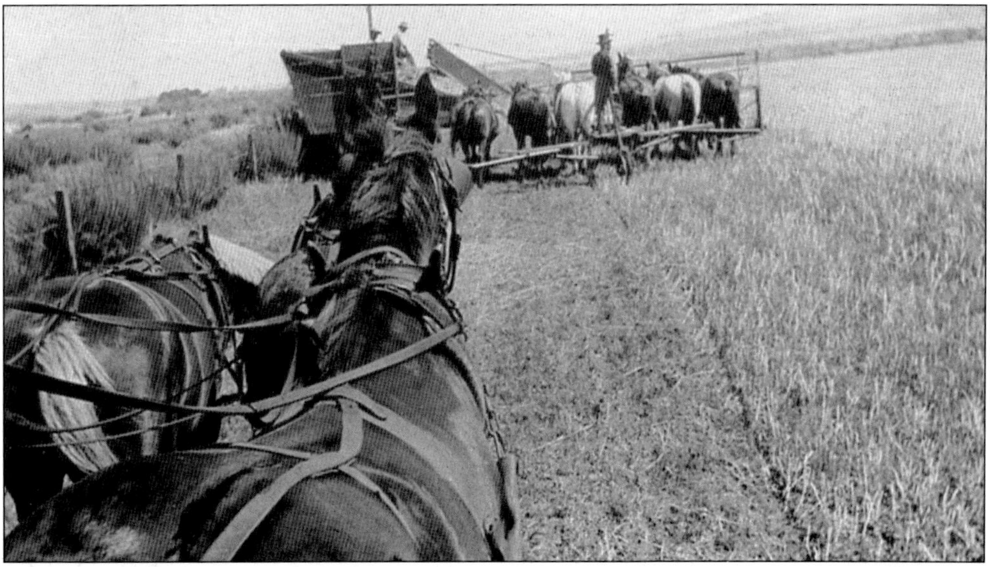

This photograph captures a bird's-eye view of heading barley on the Franscioni Ranch. A. C. Franscioni is driving the wagon in the foreground, while Silvio controls the header. Headers literally put the cart before the horse, and were pushed through the fields by horse teams.

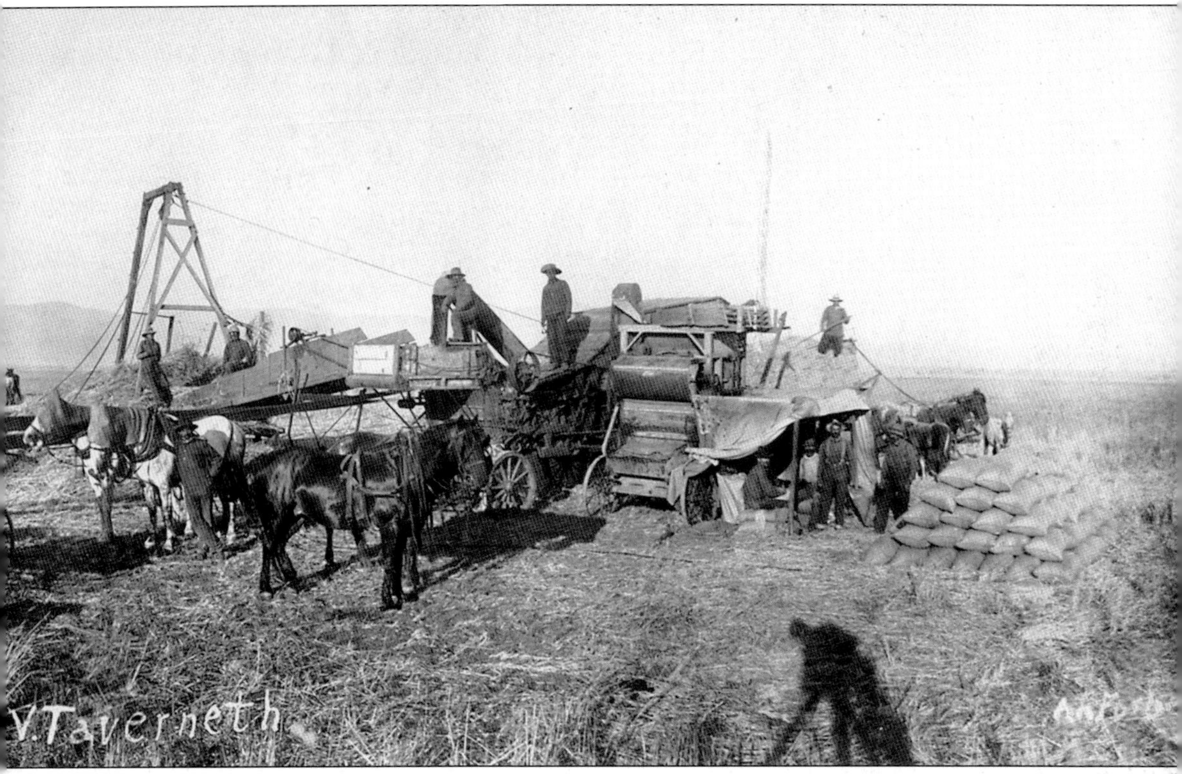

sewers, two hoedowns, straw buck, waterbuck, derrick man, roustabout, and cook. They earned $1.50 per day plus meals and a bed of straw. Tavernetti is seated in the buckboard with Tilden Tognazzini. (Courtesy of Edward Whalen.)

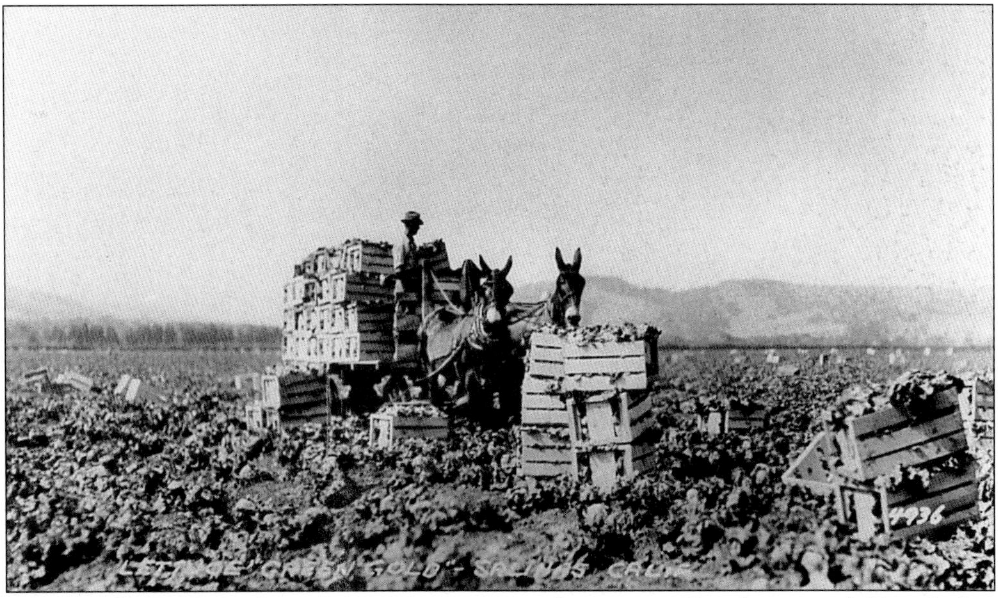

After World War I, dry farming gave way to irrigated row crops. Here lettuce is field-packed in pine crates.

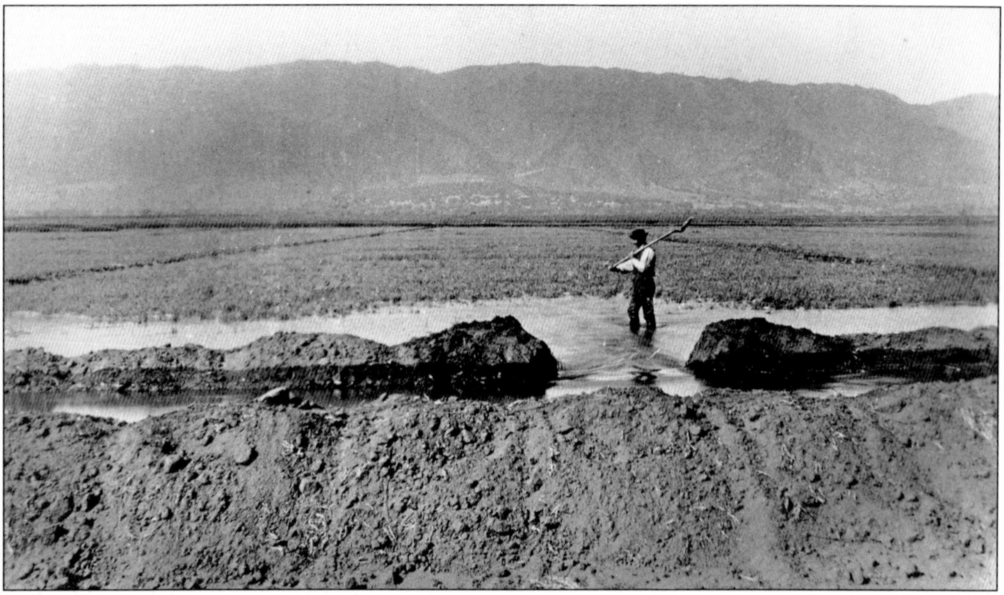

In 1899, rancho owners Mariano and Alfredo Gonzalez filed a claim for water from the Salinas River. A dam and headgate were built on the Field ranch, along with a 7.5-mile canal that ran south to the Jack's Ranch. A portion of that canal is shown above. At the same time, the Gonzalez brothers subdivided their vast holdings into 100-acre dairies. Farmers jumped at the chance to own watered land, having recently suffered a spate of drought years. In a particularly dry year, 1898, many farmers lost everything. The Gonzales Water Company, organized by the Gonzalez brothers and Matt Williams in July 1899, helped boost the population of the town of Gonzales and the valley's dairy industry. Pictured below is the headgate of the Gonzales Irrigation Canal. (Photograph below courtesy of the Monterey County Historical Society.)

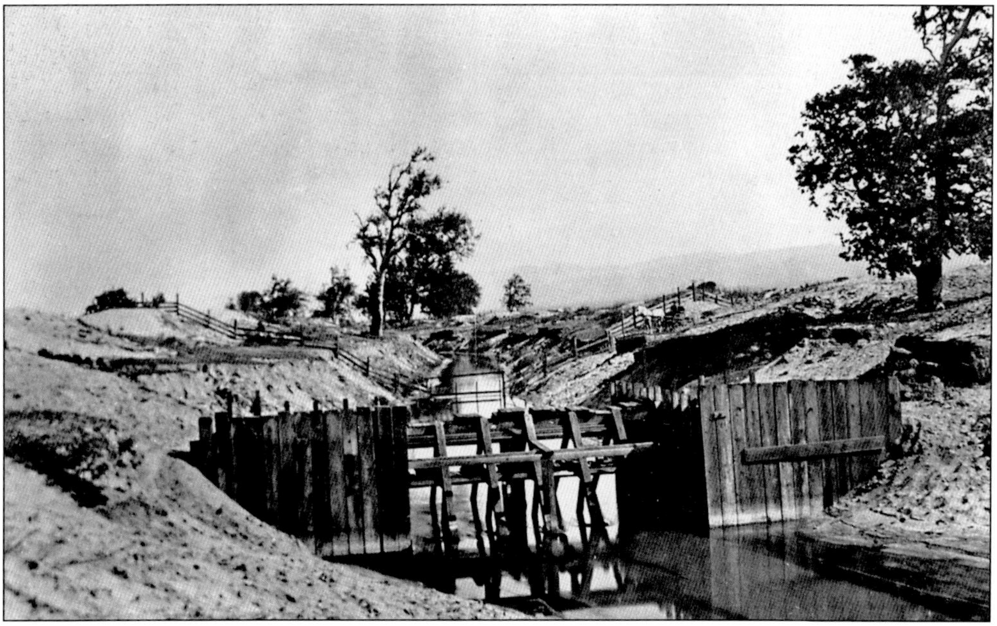

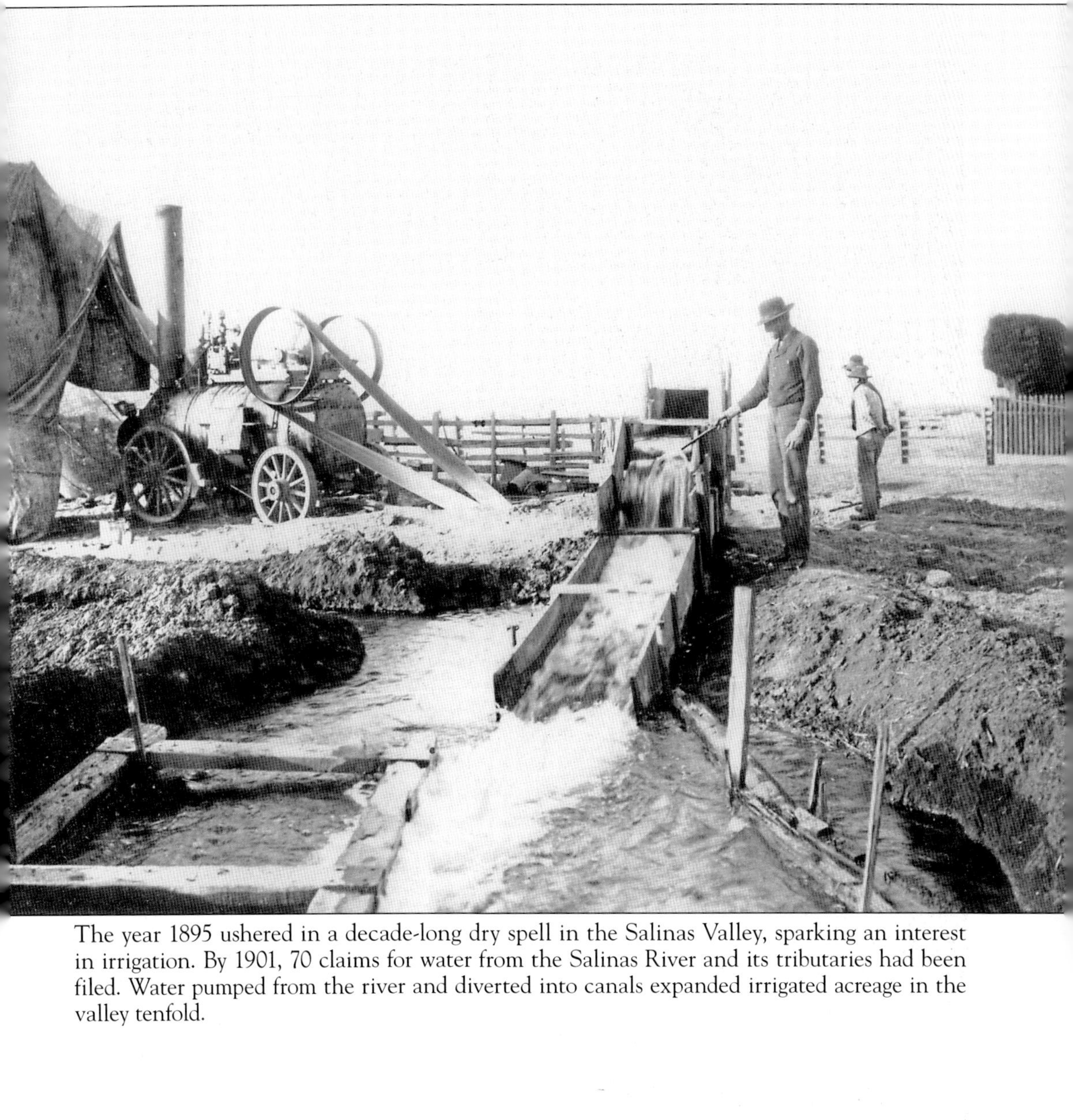

The year 1895 ushered in a decade-long dry spell in the Salinas Valley, sparking an interest in irrigation. By 1901, 70 claims for water from the Salinas River and its tributaries had been filed. Water pumped from the river and diverted into canals expanded irrigated acreage in the valley tenfold.

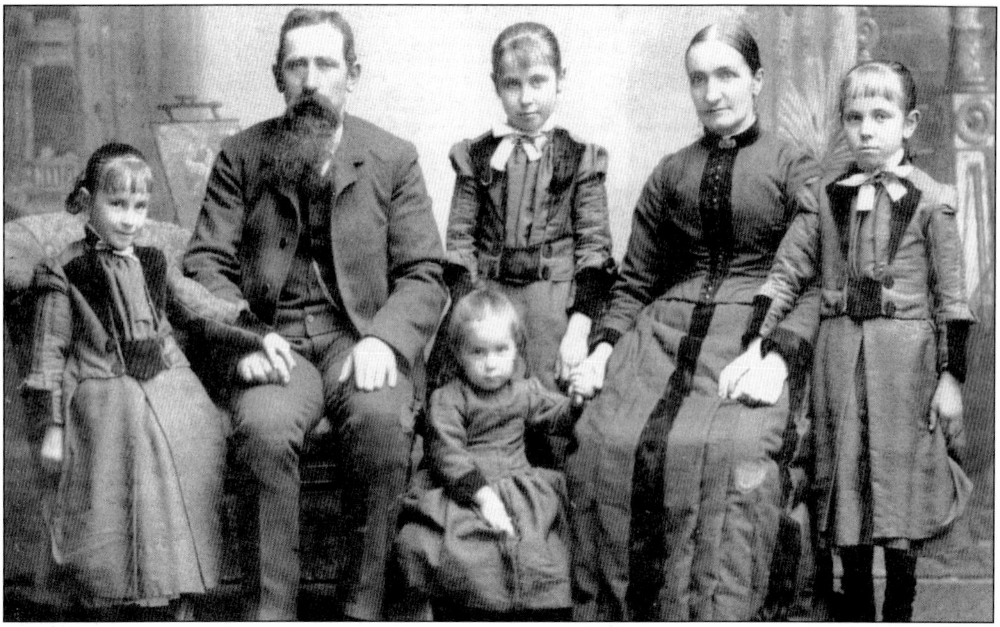

Leopoldo "Guy" Giacometti is pictured with his family. He married his wife, Laura Rianda, in 1880, and they had six children. In 1867, Mr. Giacometti left Ticino, Switzerland, when he was 20 years old. He raised barley on 800 acres near Camphora and later purchased a dairy near Gonzales. Mr. Giacometti was known for his "willingness to contribute heartily of his time and means" and served as a trustee of the Camphora school district. (Courtesy of the Soledad Historical Society.)

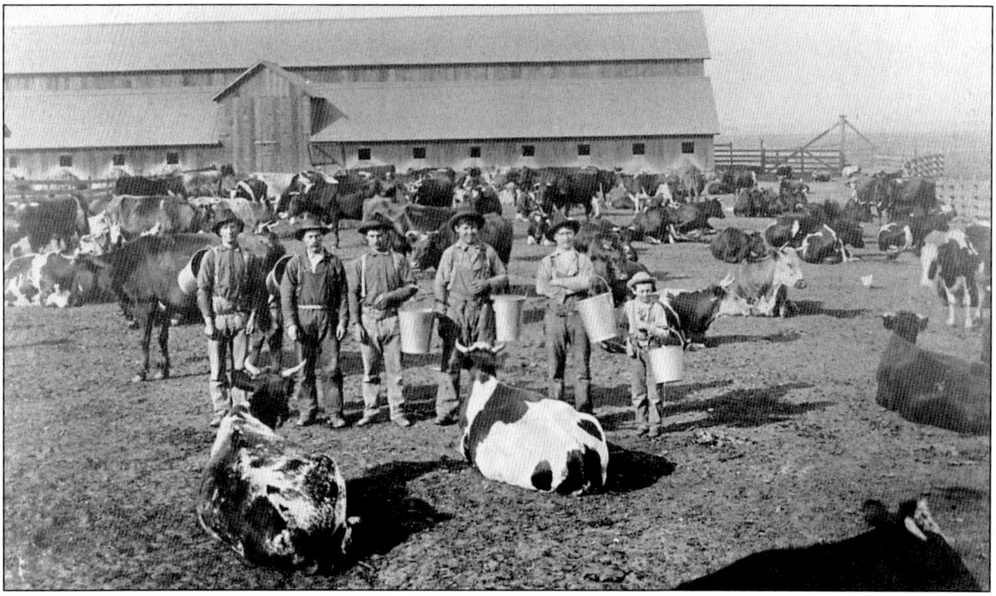

In 1903, milkers posed midst Holstein cows at the John Foletta dairy near Gonzales. The dairy was "one of the largest and best established enterprises of the kind in this part of Monterey County. Here he cares for and milks 160 cows, the milk from which he manufactures into cheese in a factory on the ranch." The little boy is John's son Ed Foletta, and next to him is Severino Foletta, John's brother.

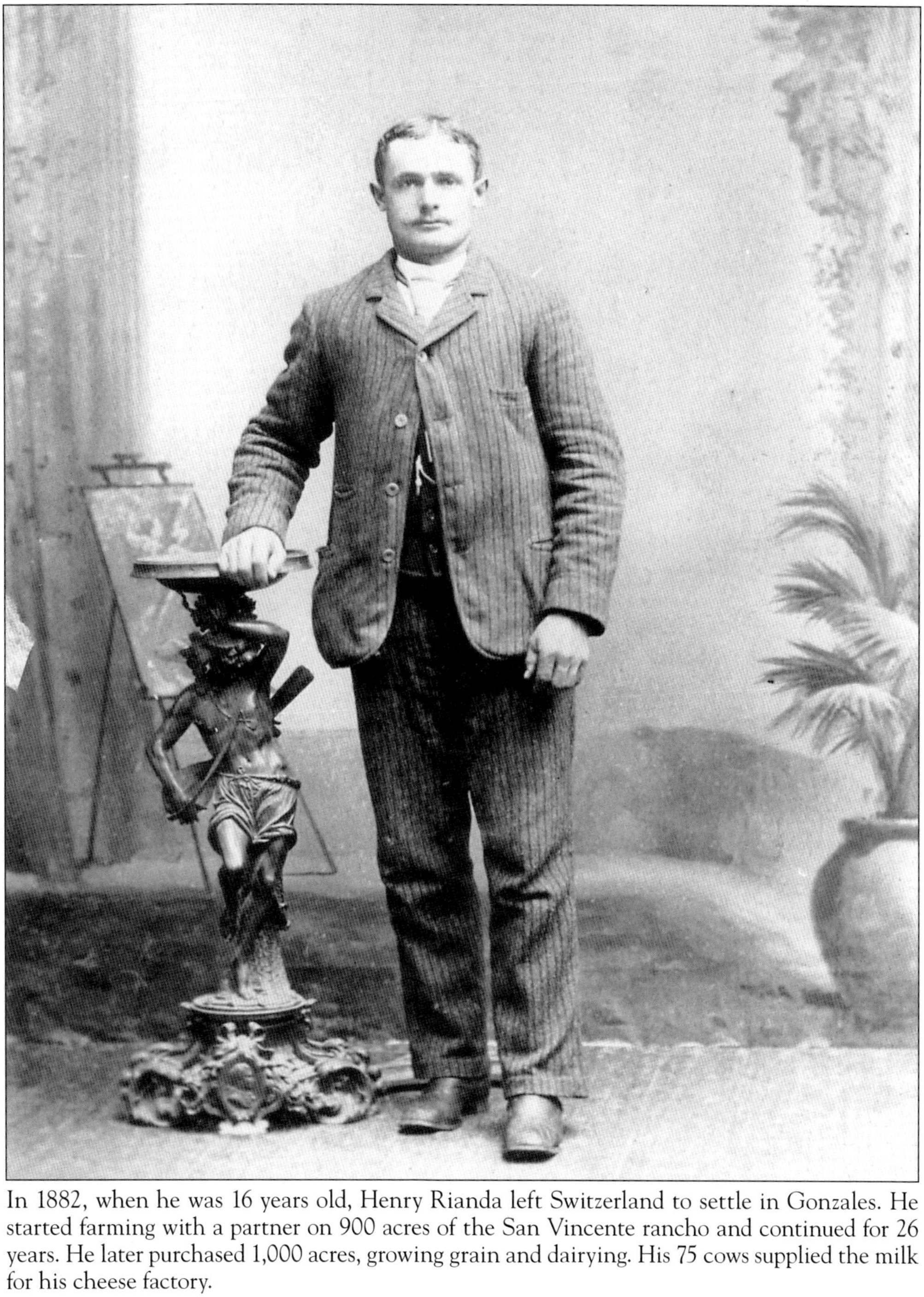

In 1882, when he was 16 years old, Henry Rianda left Switzerland to settle in Gonzales. He started farming with a partner on 900 acres of the San Vincente rancho and continued for 26 years. He later purchased 1,000 acres, growing grain and dairying. His 75 cows supplied the milk for his cheese factory.

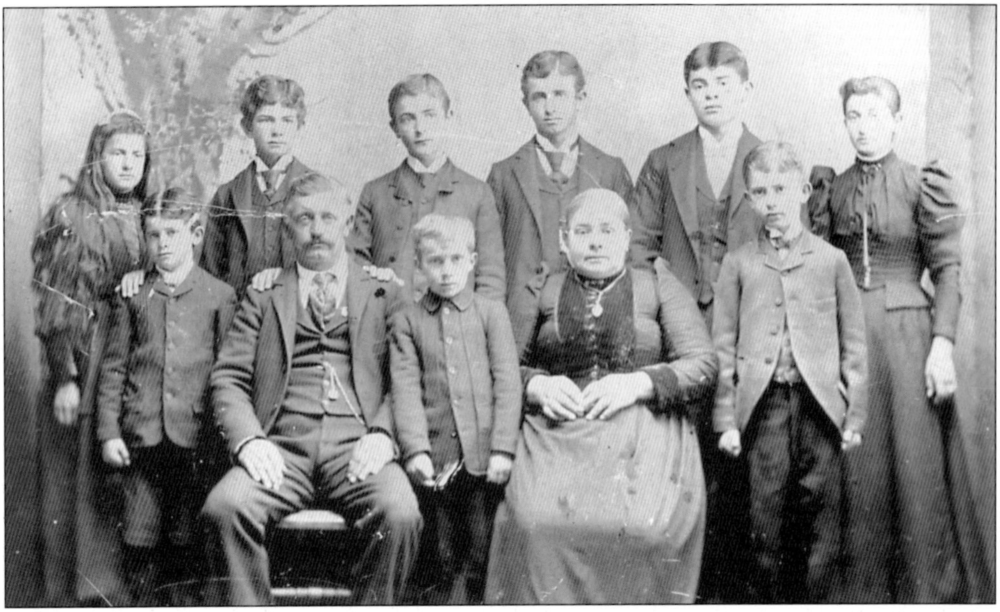

Vincent Tavernetti settled near Gonzales in 1876, raising grain and making a specialty of the dairy business. In 1898, he built the first pumping plant in the area to irrigate alfalfa and potatoes. Vincent Tavernetti is seen here with his wife, Paulina, and his children, pictured, from left to right, are (first row) Eugene, Attilio, and Joe; (second row) Della, Walter, Paul, William, Henry, and Aurelia.

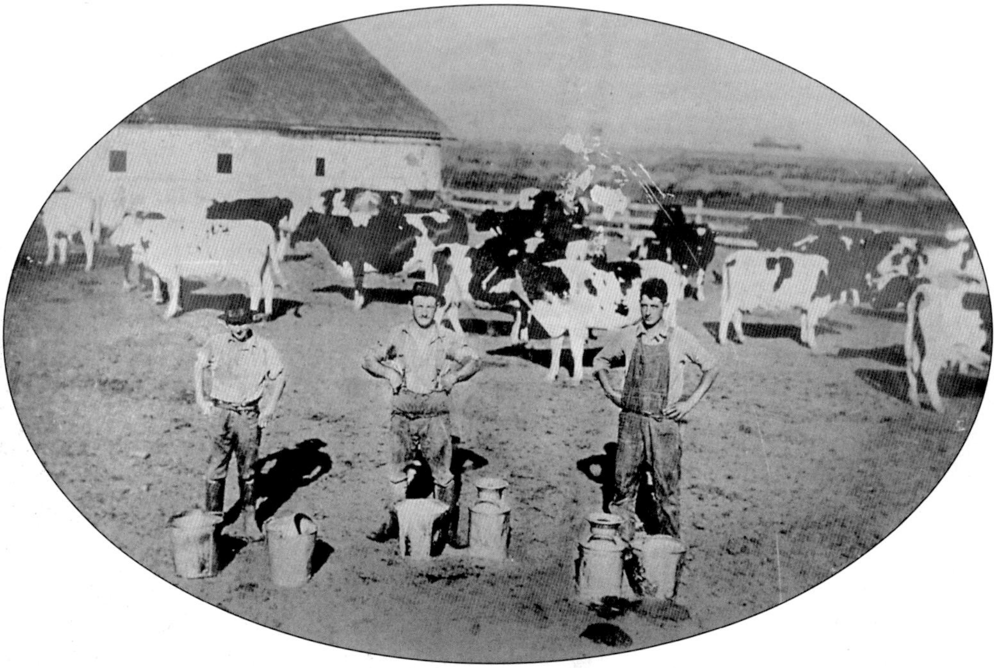

Pictured, from left to right, are milkers Clem Franscioni, Joe Passelli, and Emilio Pasque at a dairy near Gonzales. Pasque recalled, "I still have what they call Swiss Diamonds. You'd get calluses from milking and they used to shine. So when you went to the bank, if you had Swiss Diamonds on and a little mud on your shoes, the banker would loan you more money."

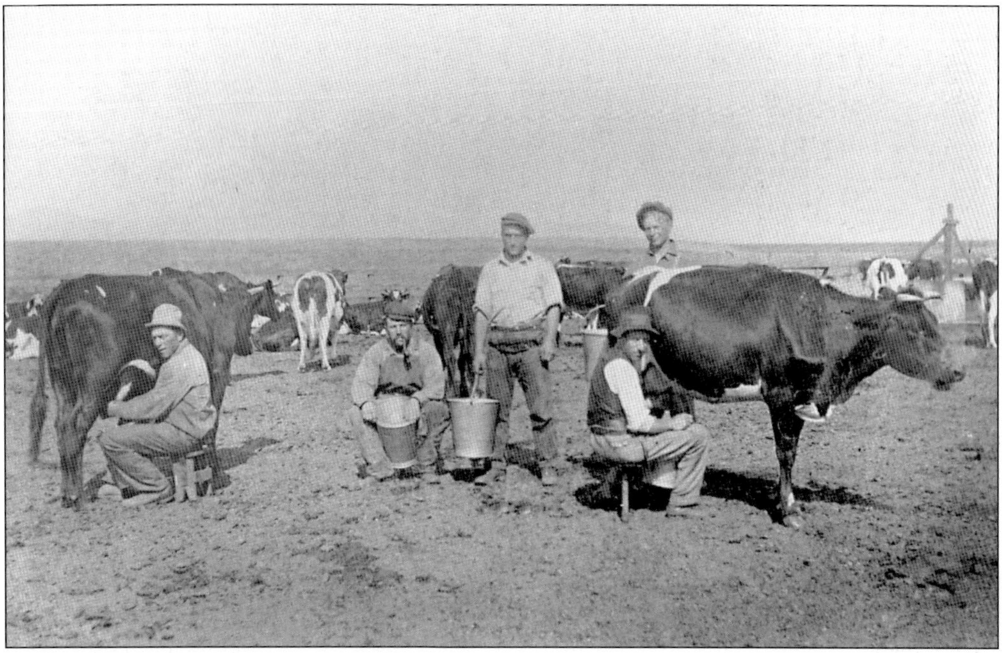

Lorio Verzasconi remembers that "We'd get up at 3:30 in the morning, milk cows, then, work in the field 'til 12 o'clock. At noon we'd take a little rest 'til about 3 o'clock. Then we'd start milking again—it went on forever. I tell you I worked for 14 months without a day off." Notice the one-legged milking stool on the left. These stools were strapped around the waist so milkers could move easily from cow to cow while milking.

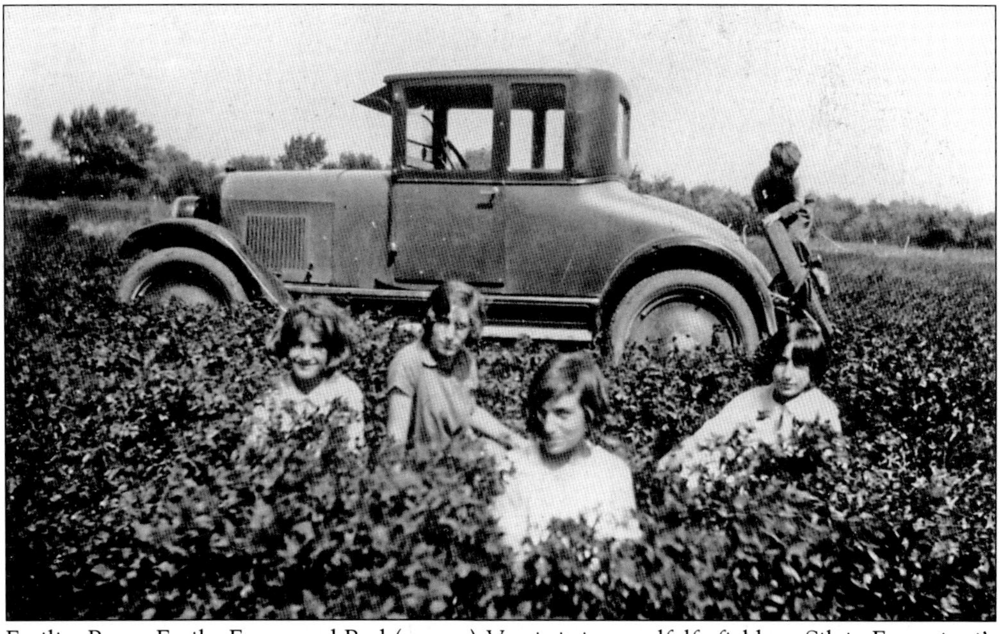

Emilia, Rena, Emily, Erma, and Red (on car) Vosti sit in an alfalfa field on Silvio Franscioni's ranch near Gonzales. Franscioni came to the United States from Switzerland in 1888. After working on dairy farms, he was able to partner with his brother Aquilino to purchase part of the Soberanes Ranch.

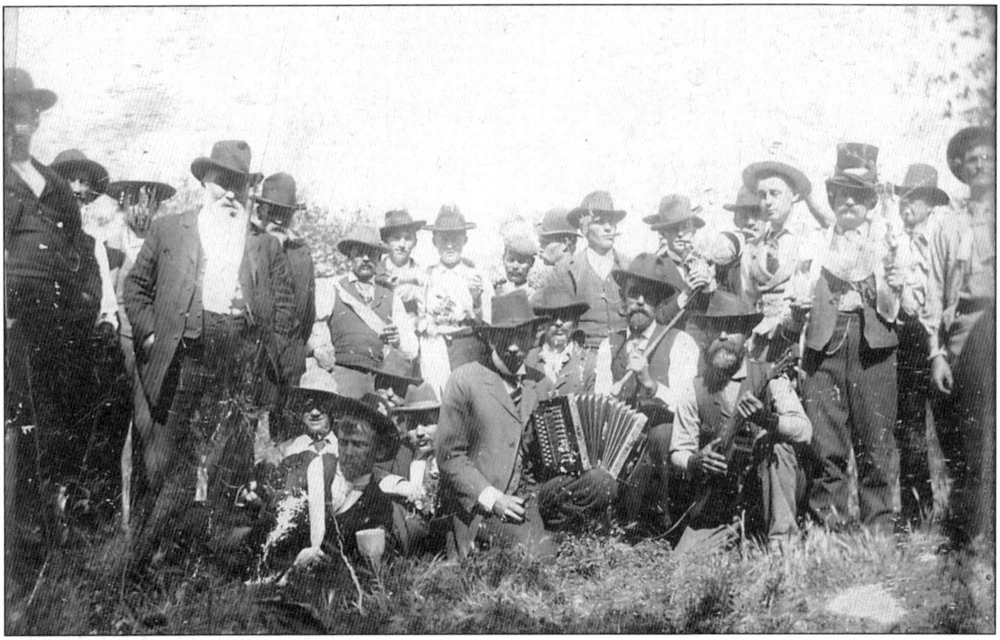

Frank Corda remembers that in Gonzales, "We really got together. The neighbors used to come over and they'd cook chestnuts, sing, drink wine and sit by the fireplace. Almost every Saturday night there was a dance at one ranch or another. Usually there was an accordion and we'd dance until 2 o'clock. Then we'd go home and milk cows—no sleep." Here the accordion is played by Charles Espinosa. (Courtesy of Edward Whalen.)

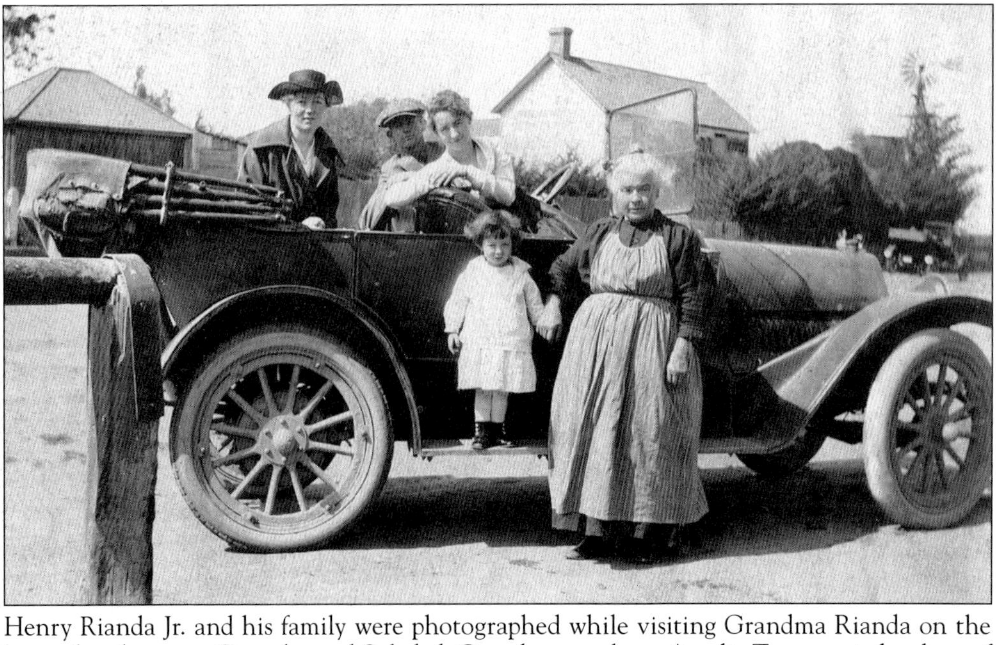

Henry Rianda Jr. and his family were photographed while visiting Grandma Rianda on the homeplace between Gonzales and Soledad. Grandma was born Aurelia Tavernetti, daughter of well-known Gonzales resident Vincent Tavernetti. She married Henry Senior, who had come to Gonzales in 1882. In just two years, he leased 900 acres, raising wheat, barley, and hay. He later went into the dairy business and operated a cheese factory.

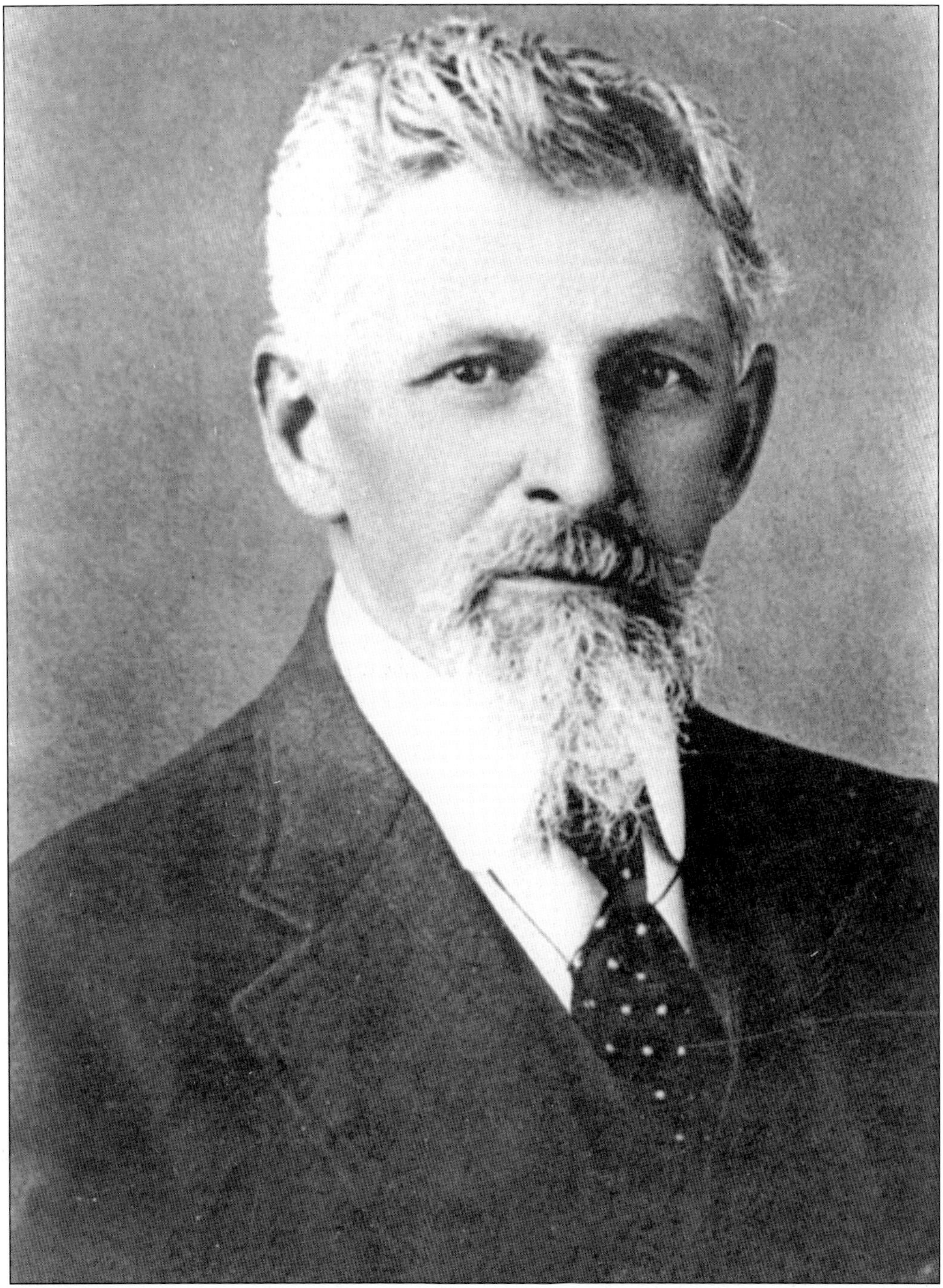

After years of experimentation, John B. Meyenberg perfected the process of preserving evaporated milk. He left his native Switzerland in 1883 and traveled to the United States. That same year, he was granted patents on his preserving process and began to establish milk plants across the country. He came to Gonzales in 1904 to establish his last factory. Named after his beloved Alps, production started on his "Alpine" brand. In 1923, the *San Francisco Call* wrote that "the history of the Salinas Valley cannot be written" without the name of John B. Meyenberg.

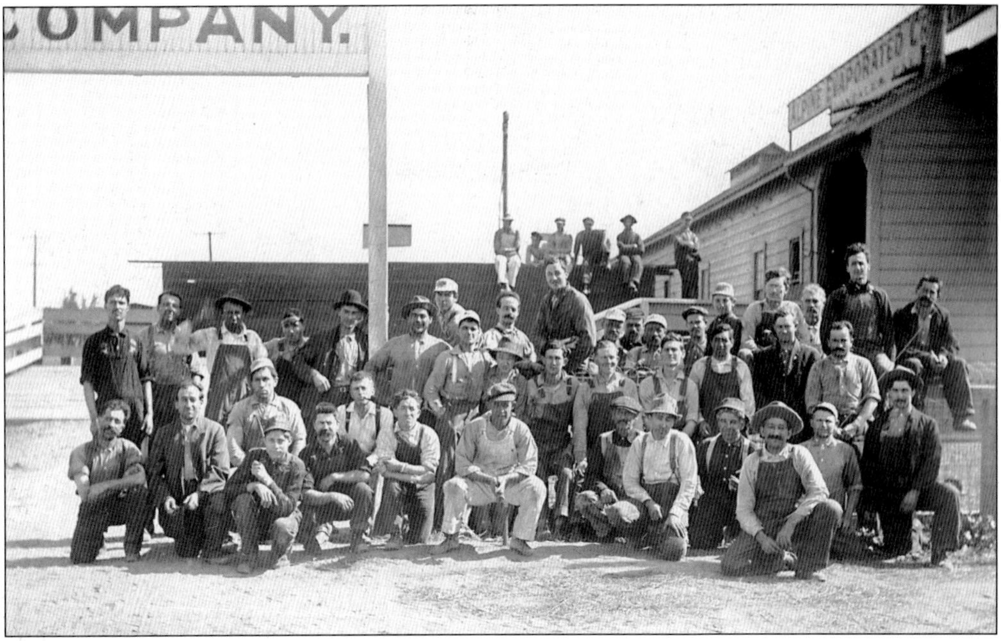

Alpine Evaporated Cream Company workers gather in front of the factory buildings about 1910. John B. Meyenberg built the company near Gonzales in 1906, knowing that dairy farming was the area's principal industry. The plant had an annual output of 175,000 cases and utilized 7,000 cows, all of which were milked within a five-mile radius of Gonzales. This was one of the first and largest industrial plants in the Salinas Valley. Other plants were later built in Salinas and on Metz Road in King City. (Courtesy of Edward Whalen.)

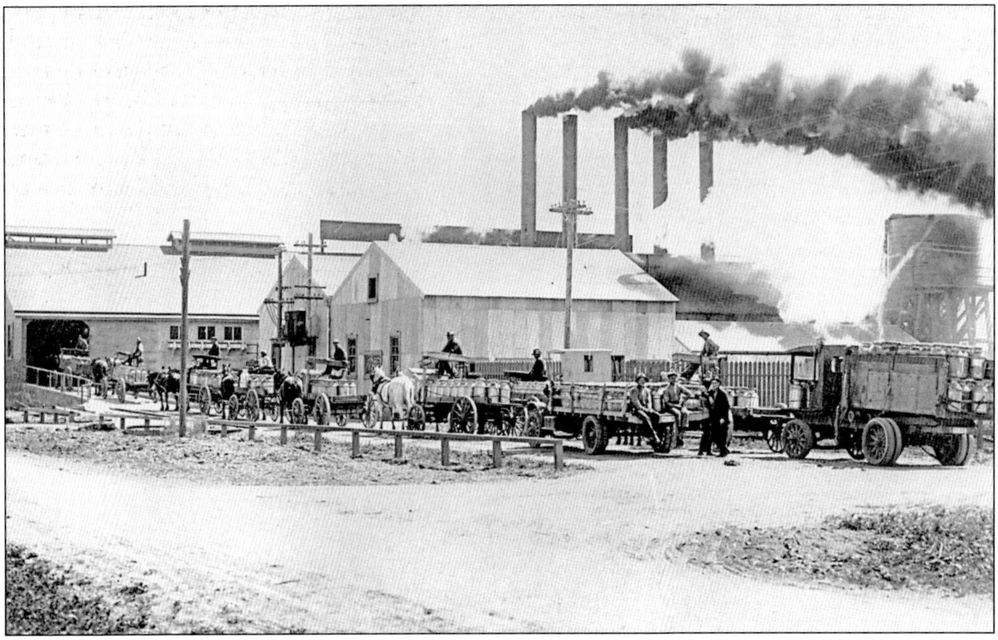

Dairy farmers line up to deliver milk to the Alpine Evaporated Cream Company in Gonzales. With the success of their first plant, the company built a plant near King City and one in Salinas. By 1915, 90 percent of the valley's milk went to Alpine.

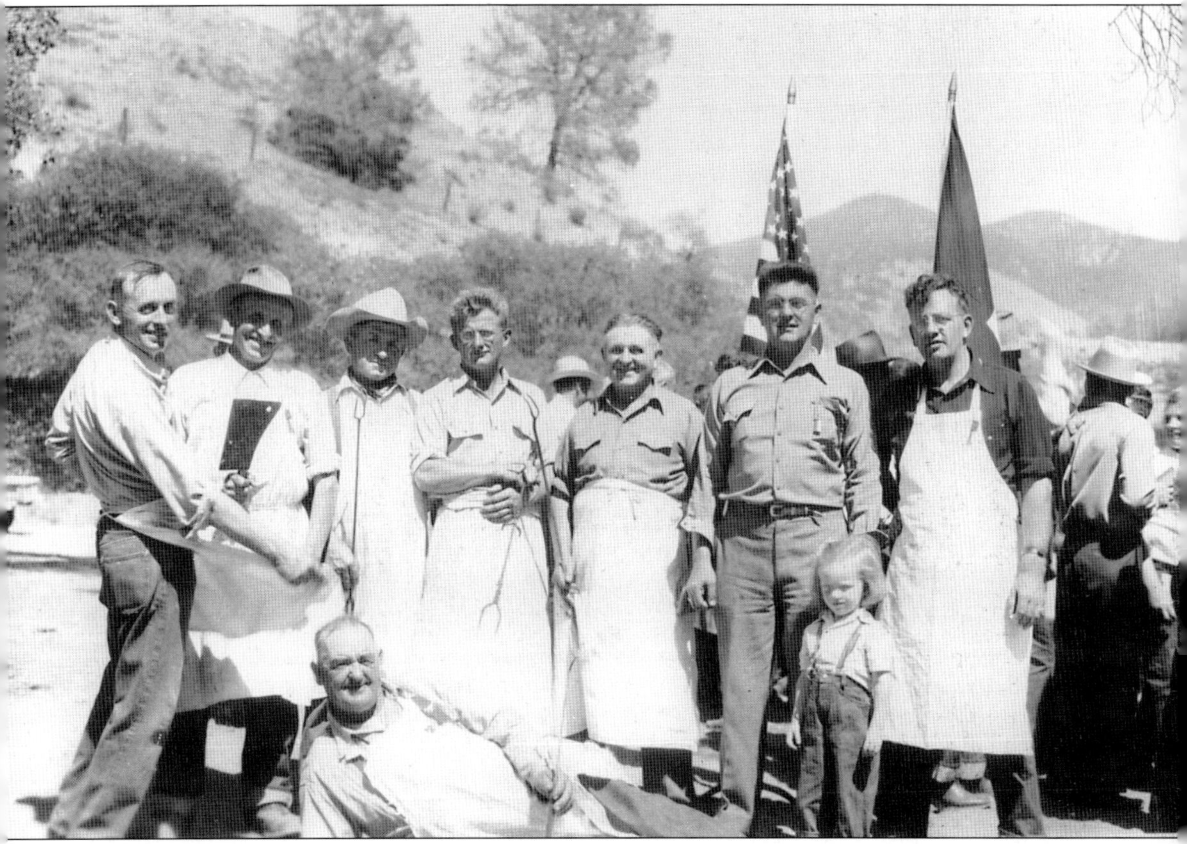

The barbeque committee takes a break during the dedication of the Swiss Rifle Club grounds on June 29, 1947. Located east of Gonzales, the club hosted target shoots and barbeques for their members. The club was founded in 1900 by a group of Swiss immigrants from Canton Ticino. Swiss tradition held that all able-bodied men should practice marksmanship in case the country was invaded. Immigrants carried this tradition with them to the Salinas Valley. Pictured, from left to right, are Elmo Borradori, Emilio Berta, Paul Migotti, Gus Sargenti, Paul Selmorini, Marcel Escher, Dick Polastro, and Lewis Pura.

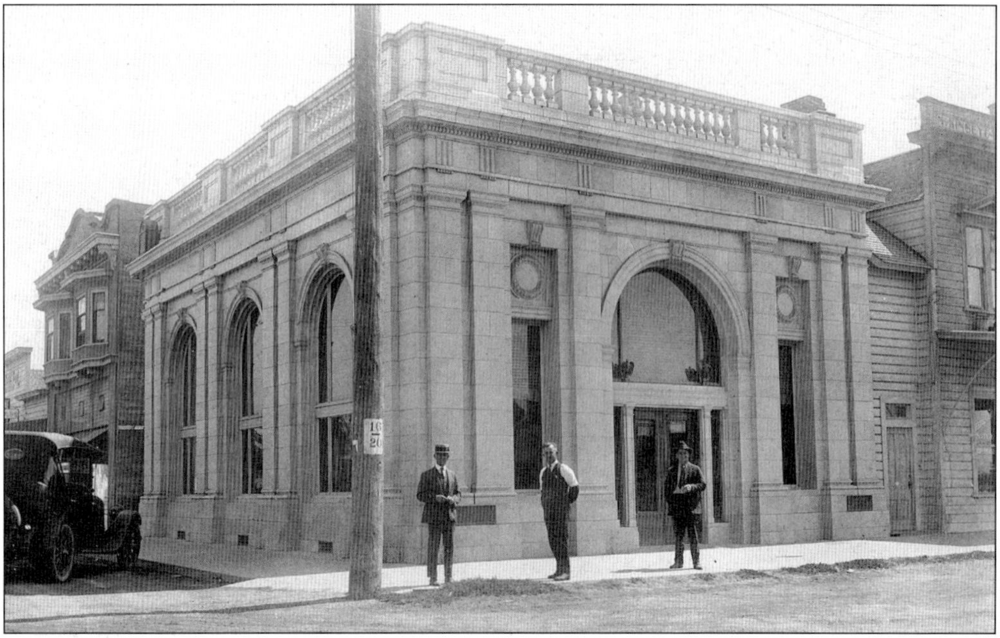

Louie Vidoroni, Bill Tavernetti, and Gene Tavernetti Sr. stand in front of the Wells Fargo Bank in Gonzales, built in 1917. The first bank in Gonzales, known as the Bank of Gonzales, was directed by Alfredo Gonzalez, one of the town founders. The bank was taken over by Monterey County Trust and Savings Bank and this, in turn, by American Trust and Savings Bank. It later became Wells Fargo Bank. (Courtesy of Edward Whalen.)

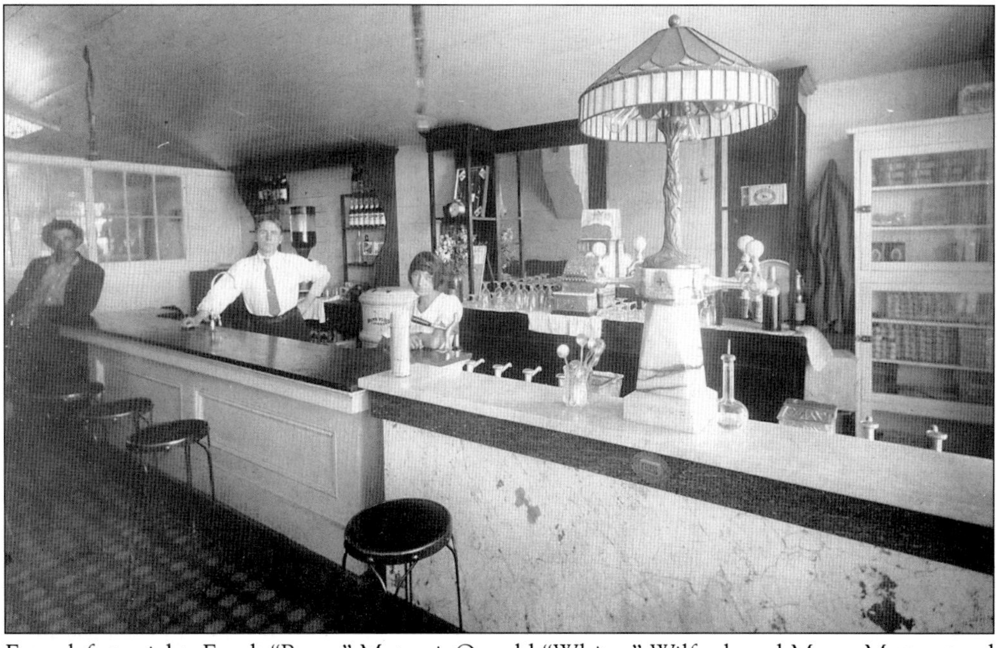

From left to right, Frank "Beans" Matasci, Oswald "Whitey" Wilford, and Mercy Motta stand behind the counter of Whitey's Ice Cream Parlor in Gonzales in this 1912 photograph. Frank Matasci was the local druggist, and Mr. Wilford also operated a cigar factory and pool parlor in town. (Courtesy of Edward Whalen.)

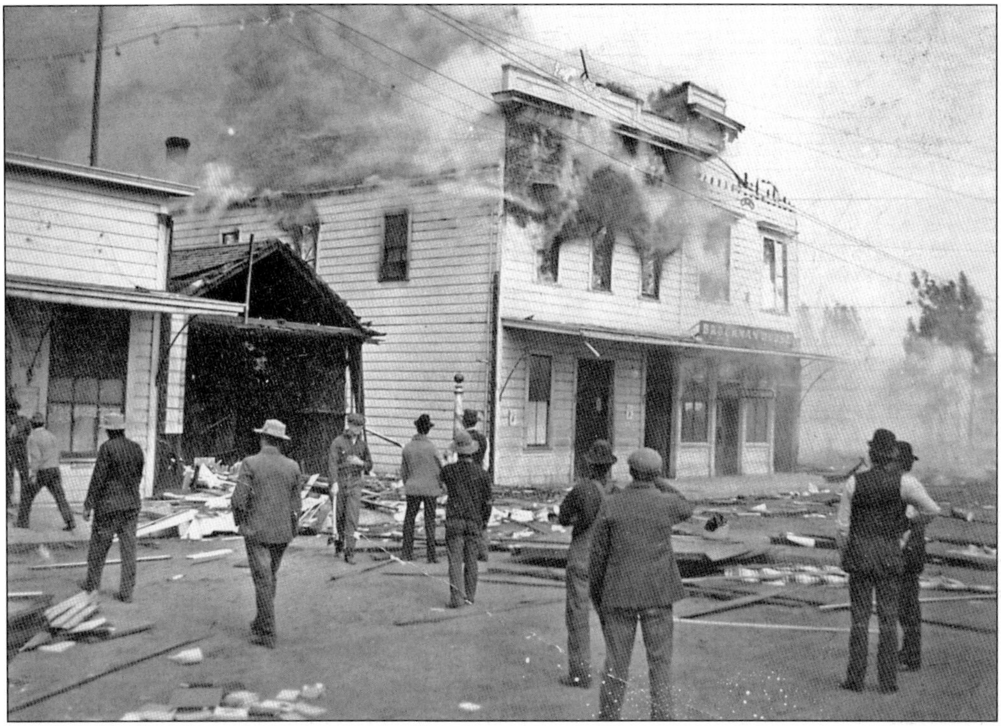

In Gonzales on September 23, 1914, a fire started in the shoemaker's shop from an overheated wood stove. Soledad's fire department was notified, and they arrived by local train, armed with hoses, but there were no hydrants. Bucket brigades could not douse the fire, which eventually burned every frame building on the north side of Fifth Street from Belden Street to the Bank of Gonzales. Here the Brockman House goes up in flames. (Courtesy of Edward Whalen.)

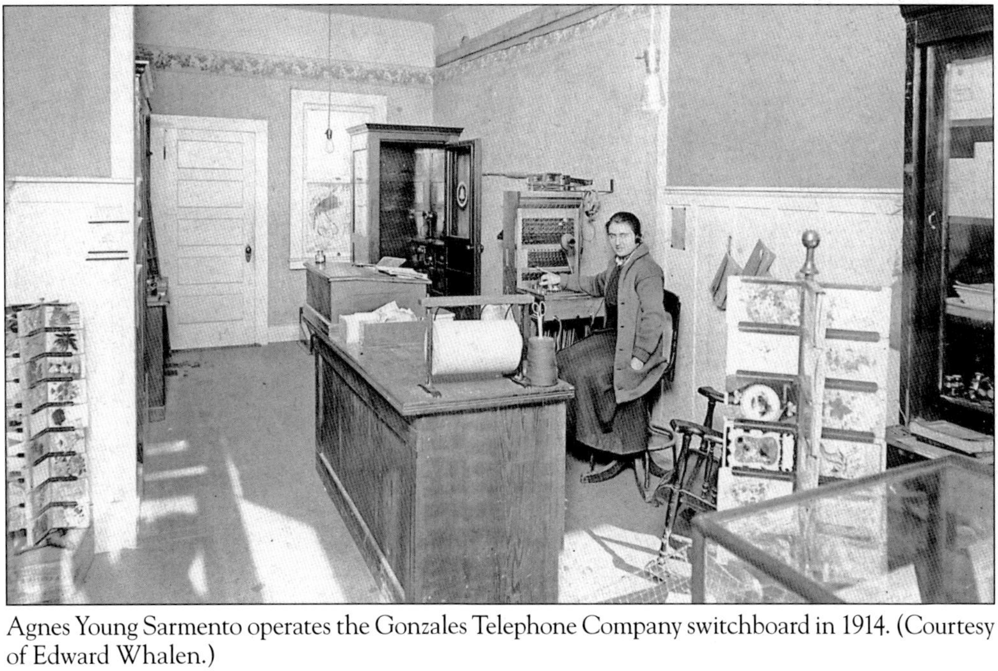

Agnes Young Sarmento operates the Gonzales Telephone Company switchboard in 1914. (Courtesy of Edward Whalen.)

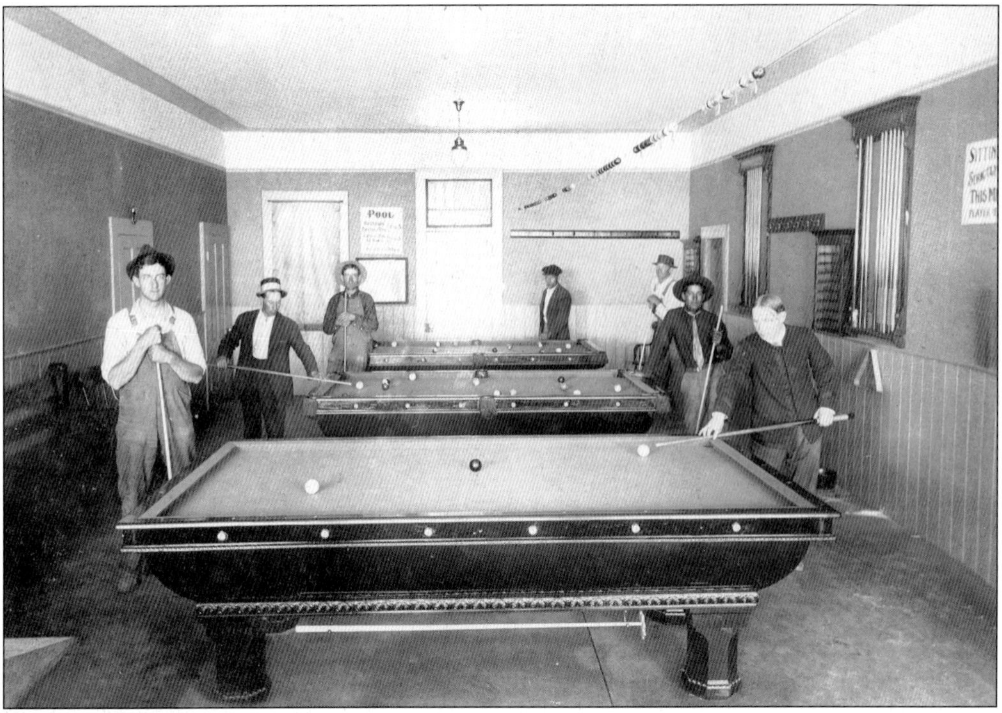

In the 1920s, Whitey Wilford, standing at the right, owned and operated a pool room at Whitey's Place in Gonzales. Carl Widemann is playing with Whitey, and Frank Mojica stands behind him. (Courtesy of the Monterey County Historical Society.)

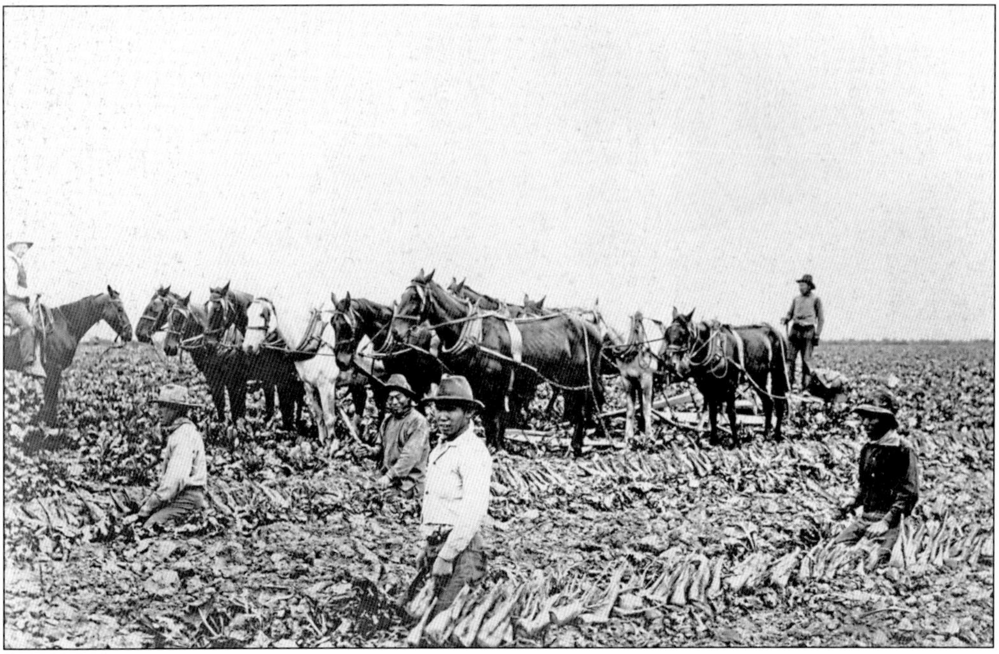

Filipino workers are pictured harvesting sugarbeets. Beets were harvested from August to November. They were pulled from the soil, then topped and tossed into wagons. The tops were used as cattle feed or left in the field to fortify the soil.

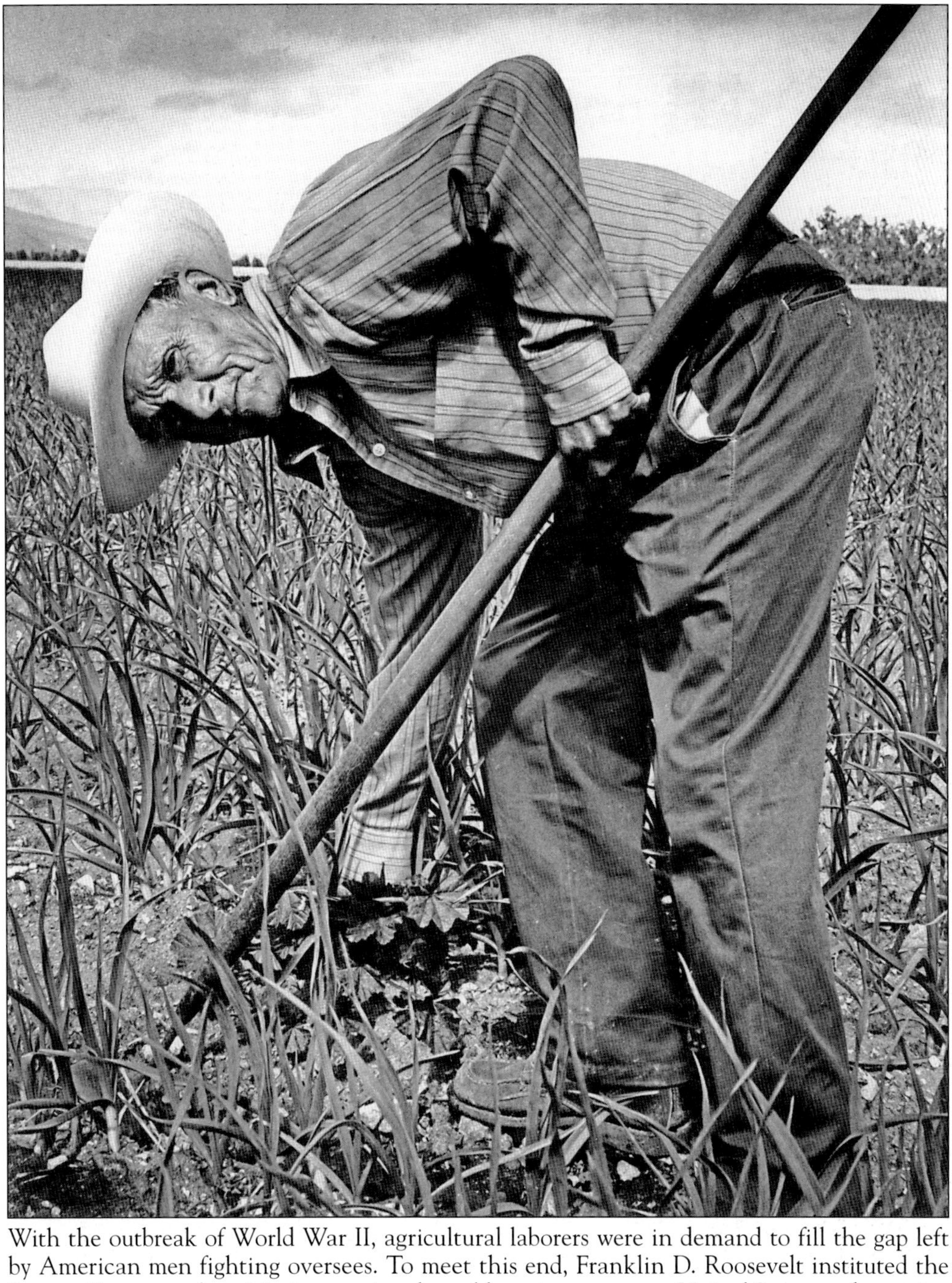

With the outbreak of World War II, agricultural laborers were in demand to fill the gap left by American men fighting oversees. To meet this end, Franklin D. Roosevelt instituted the Bracero Program, where Mexican nationals could receive temporary United States work permits. The program was successful and by 1959, 72 percent of Monterey County's seasonal labor force were braceros.

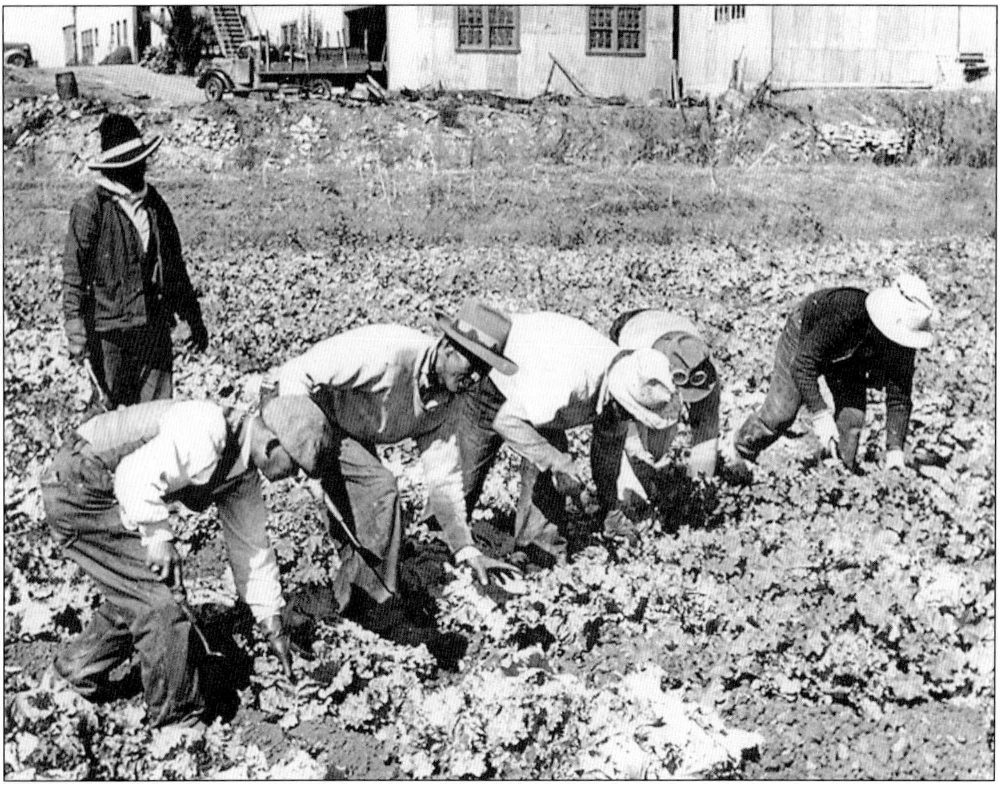

Mexican farm workers weed lettuce in the 1940s using El Cortito, "the short one"—a hoe that was only 24 inches long. This tool forced workers to stoop all day long, leading to serious back injuries. Use of this hoe was outlawed in 1975.

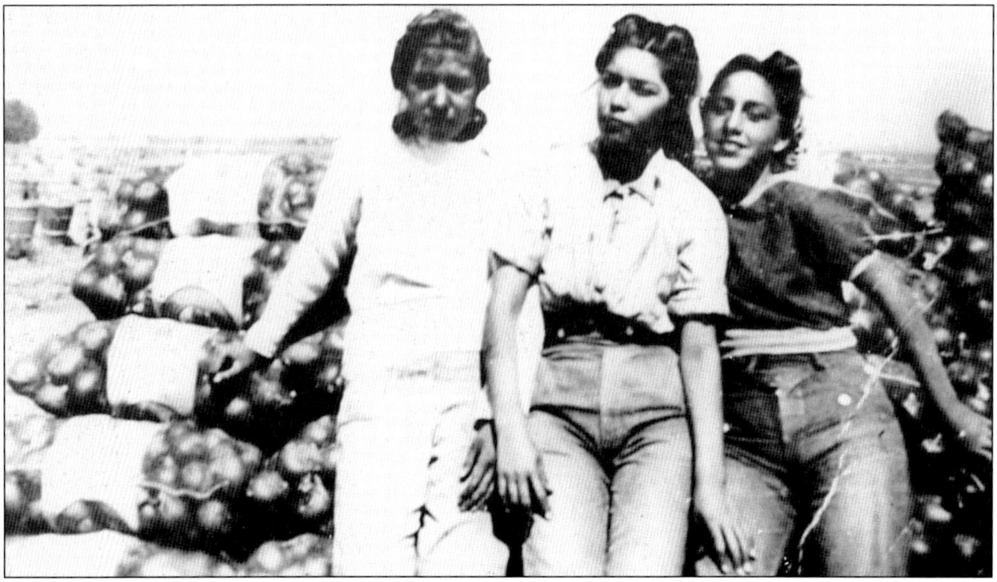

Carrie Hernandez, Carmen Rivera, and Maryon Duvan (pictured here from left to right) take a break from their work in a Salinas Valley onion field in 1941. They made 5¢ a hamper and up to $1 per day. (Courtesy of the Monterey Public Library, California History Room.)

Four

SOLEDAD

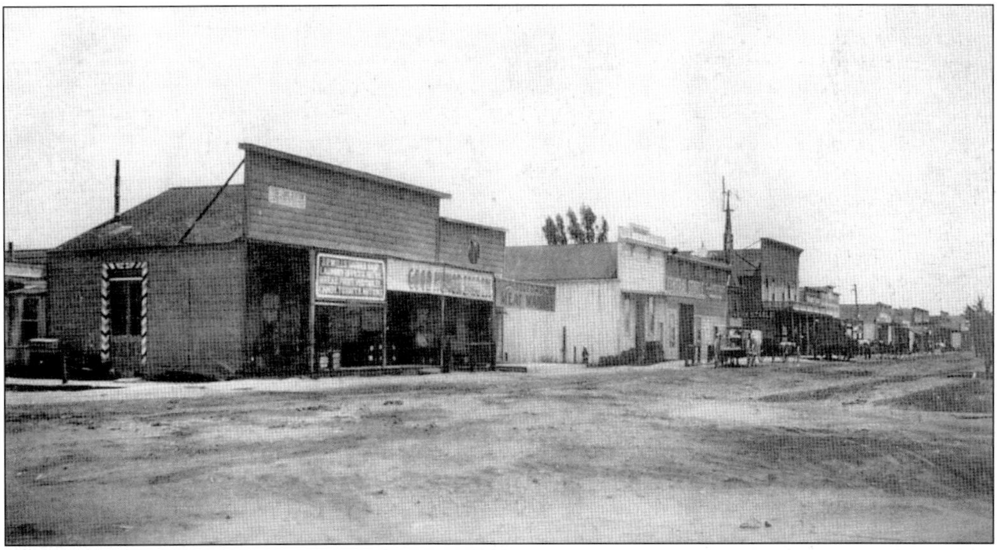

The Rancho San Vincente belonged to the Esteban Munras family. Before his death, Esteban instructed his wife, Catalina, to "hold onto the land and when the time is right, subdivide for a township. Give one lot for a church, one for a school and one for a cemetery." She also donated a right-of-way to the railroad, which arrived in December 1872. Naming the town in honor of the nearby mission, Soledad remained the Southern Pacific's terminus for the next 14 years. Pictured in 1908 is Soledad's Front Street.

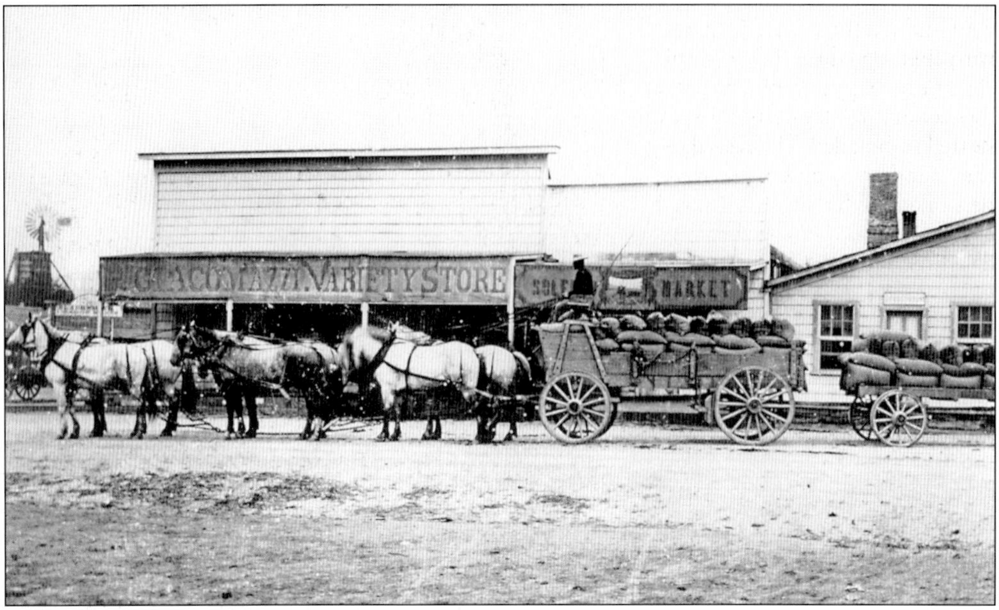

James Rianda Sr. is pictured hauling grain into Soledad. Behind him is the Variety Store owned by Peter A. Giacomazzi, and next door is the Soledad Meat Market owned by M. M. Franscioni and I. P. Gambetta. The *Salinas Daily Index* reported that "they handle the choicest and most delicious meats, as all their patrons can testify."

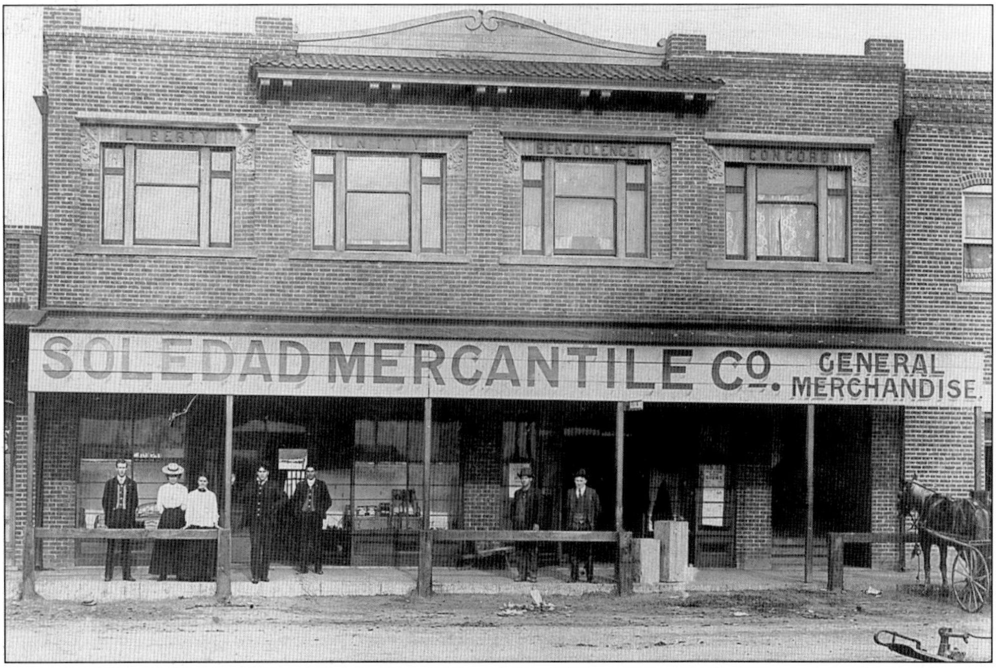

The Soledad Court of the Foresters built this brick building in 1904. Their motto, "Liberty, Unity, Benevolence, and Concord," graces each upstairs window. Meetings were held here until 1989. Downstairs the Soledad Mercantile carried a variety of wares for local townsfolk. (Courtesy of Pat Hathaway, California Views.)

Paul and Clotilde Bianchi pose with their daughter Tillie in this 1891 photograph. Paul came from Switzerland in the mid-1880s and settled in Soledad. Described as the "handsome, blue-eyed Swiss," he worked on a dairy farm and eventually married the boss's daughter, Clotilde Soberanes. (Courtesy of the Soledad Historical Society.)

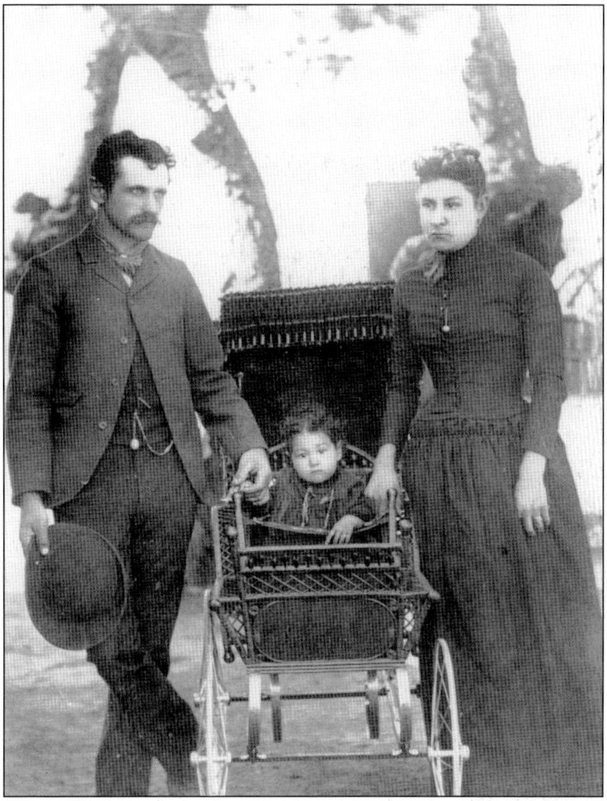

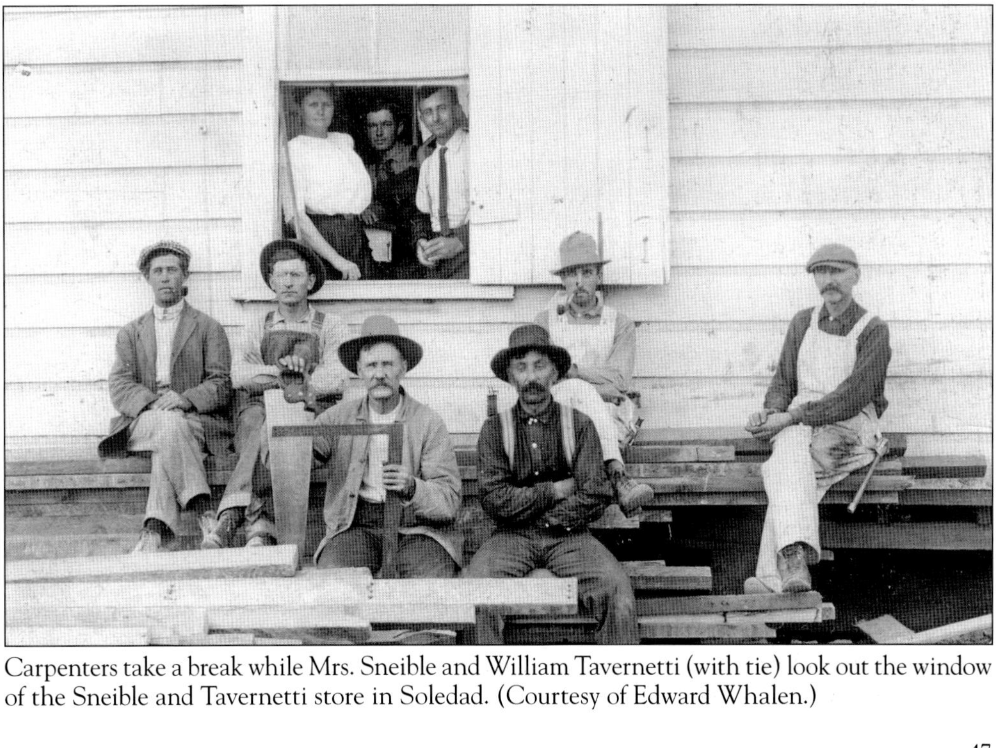

Carpenters take a break while Mrs. Sneible and William Tavernetti (with tie) look out the window of the Sneible and Tavernetti store in Soledad. (Courtesy of Edward Whalen.)

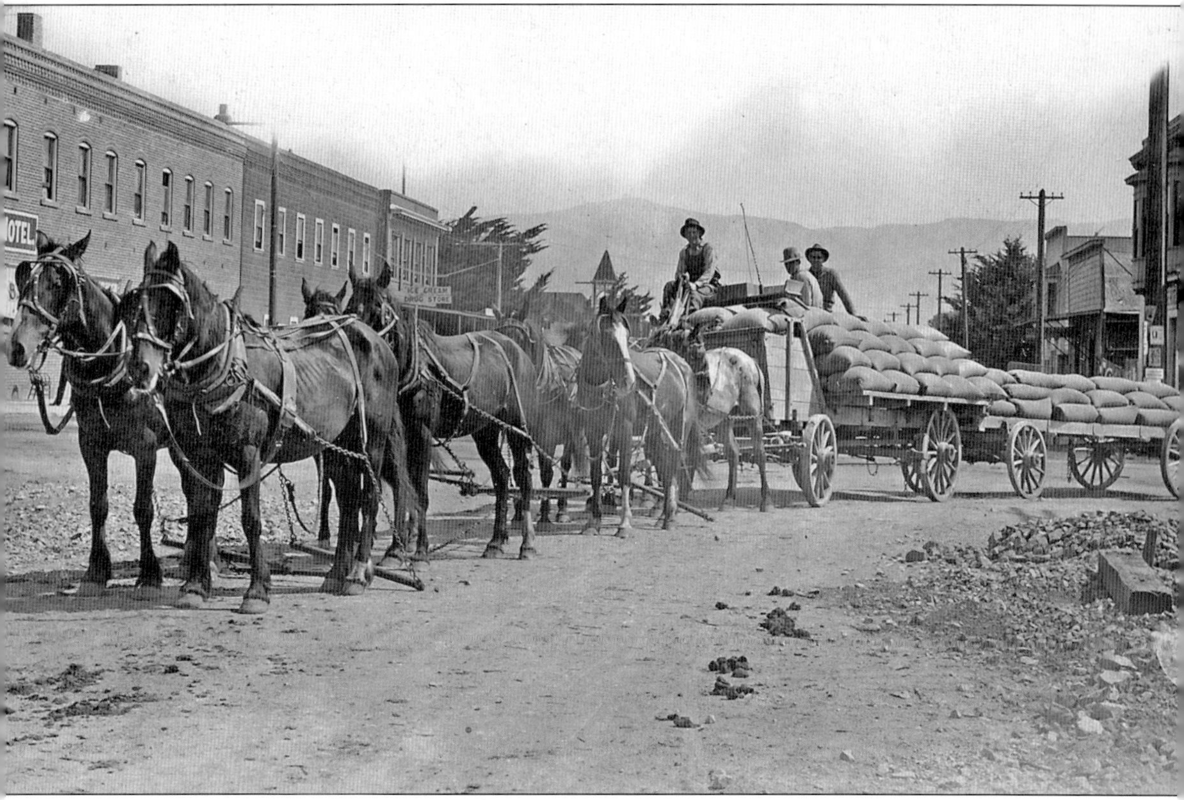

Horse teams hauling wagons stacked with burlap grain sacks were a familiar site in Soledad. The Southern Pacific railroad reached Soledad in 1872 and remained the terminus of the line for the next 14 years. Farmers as far south as Bradley hauled their grain crops to Soledad for shipment or warehouse storage. Warehouses could hold up to 10,000 tons of surplus wheat and barley. (Courtesy of the Monterey County Historical Society.)

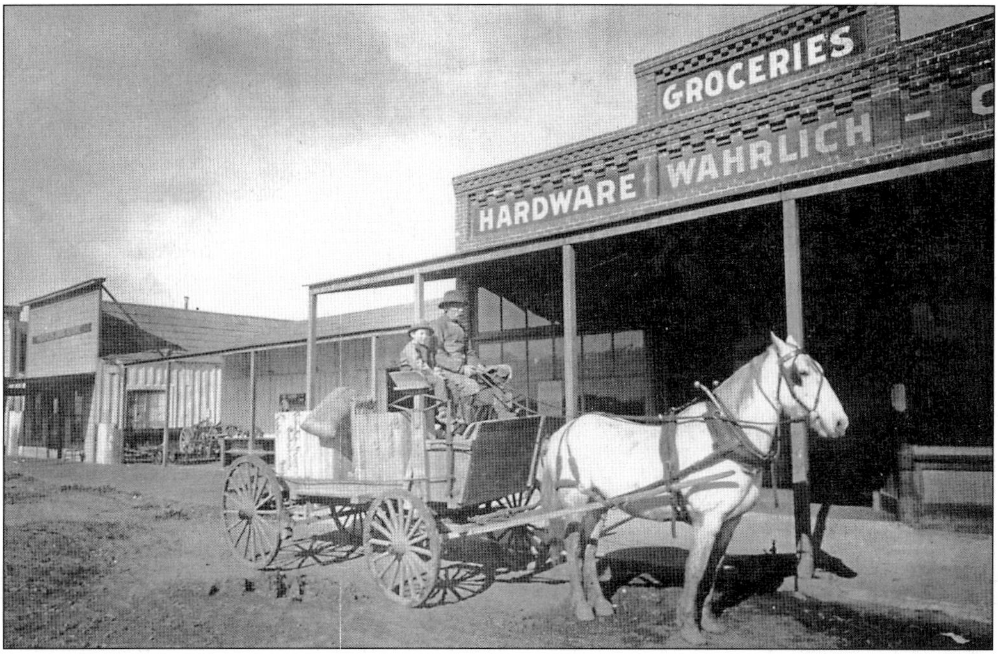

John Franscioni and his son sit in the family's buckboard in front of the Wahrlich-Cornett Company in Soledad. The store dealt in general merchandise, groceries, and agricultural equipment. Their first store burned in the fire of 1898. Pictured is their new "fireproof" building. (Courtesy of the Soledad Historical Society.)

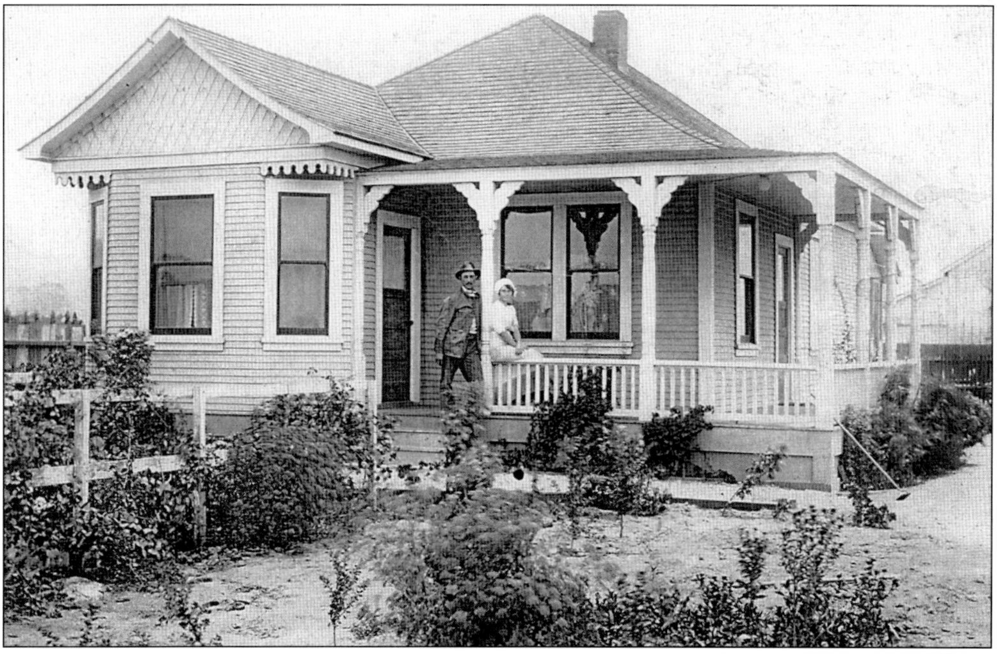
Julius and Pauline Schiekele relax on the front porch of their home on Monterey Street. Julius built the pretty Queen Anne cottage in 1913 as a wedding present for his bride. Julius manufactured concrete building blocks that were used in local buildings including the old Peverini store. The house is still standing. (Courtesy of the Soledad Historical Society.)

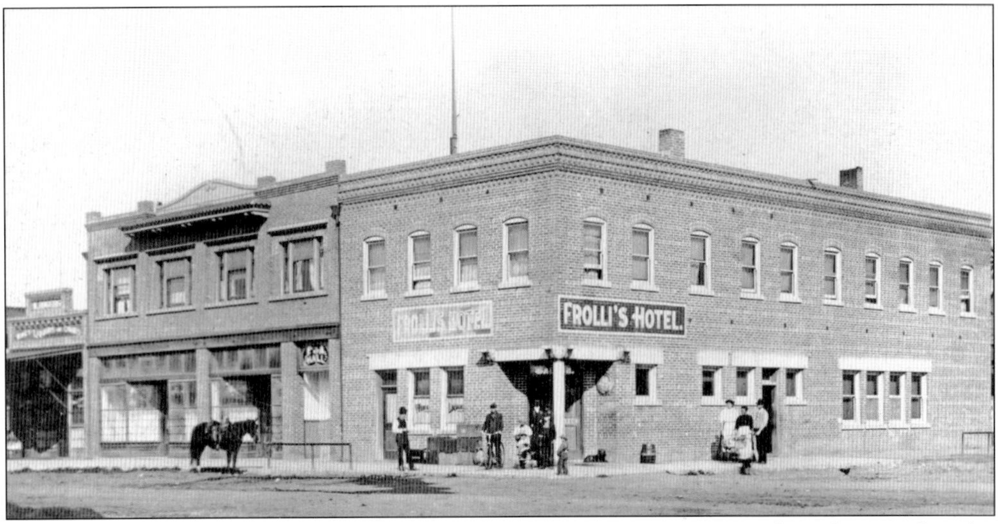

Frolli's Hotel in Soledad is pictured at the beginning of the 20th century. The *Salinas Daily Index* reported on May 28, 1901, that "S. B. Frolli, owner of the Frolli Hotel, is a resident of long standing in our community . . . In 1888 Mr. Frolli met with a severe and heavy loss by the destruction of his premises and extensive store by fire (no insurance), but arose Phoenix-like from the ruins, and with a confidence in the future of Soledad soon erected the fine, fire-proof building he now occupies."

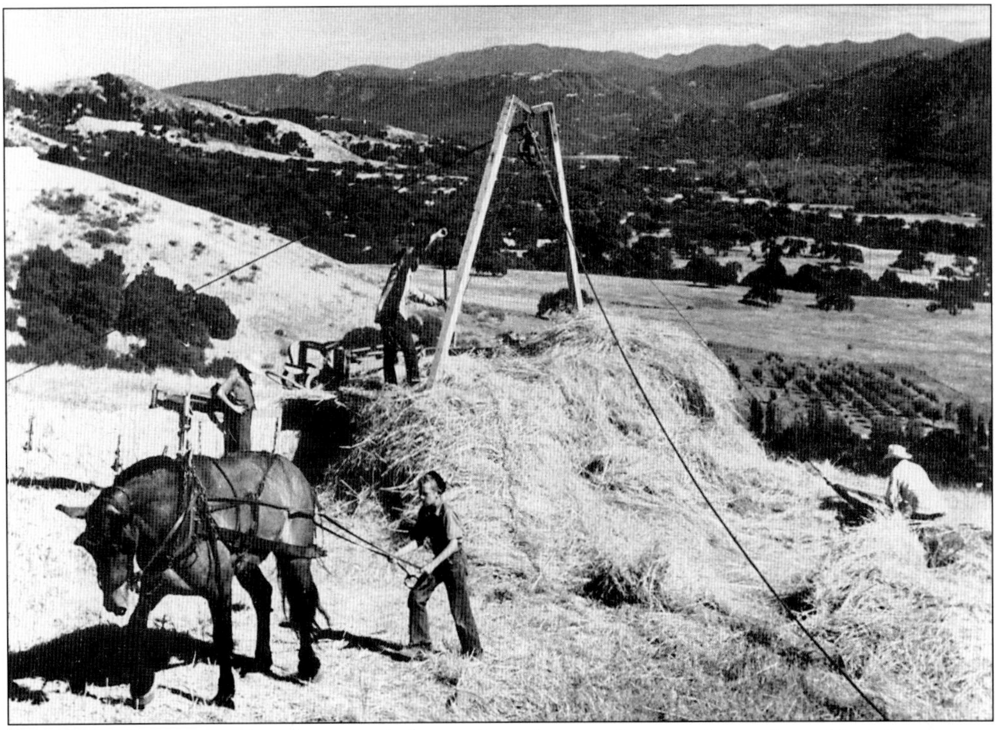

A Jackson fork suspended from an A-frame derrick is used in stacking the valley's hay crops. Stacks could reach 20 feet tall. If the hay was dry, farmers would add salt every three feet or so. As John (Bud) Vierra remembers, horses liked the salted hay better, just "like salted peanuts are better than the other ones."

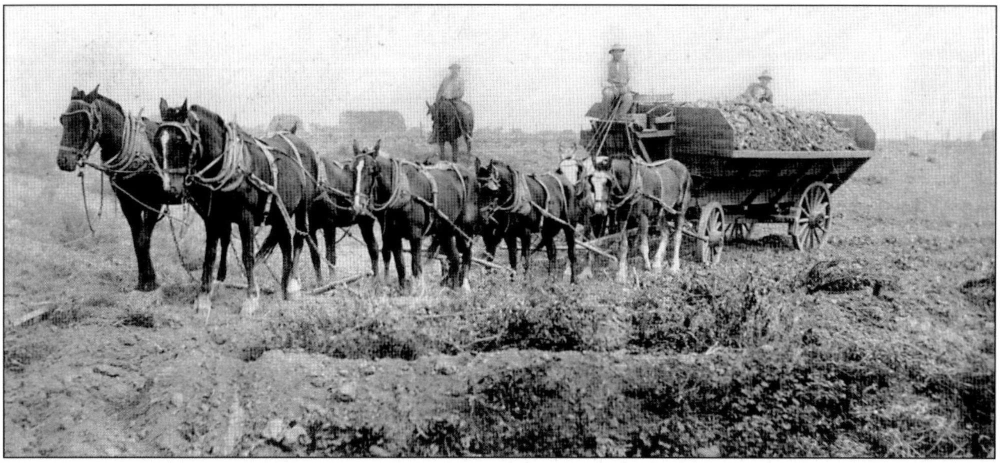

Lincoln Wiley (on horseback), John Marentes (driver), and Achille Franscioni (in wagon) are pictured with a load of sugarbeets. About 25,000 acres of Salinas Valley land were devoted to sugarbeets. Returns on beets were better than on grain for both tenant farmers and independent growers.

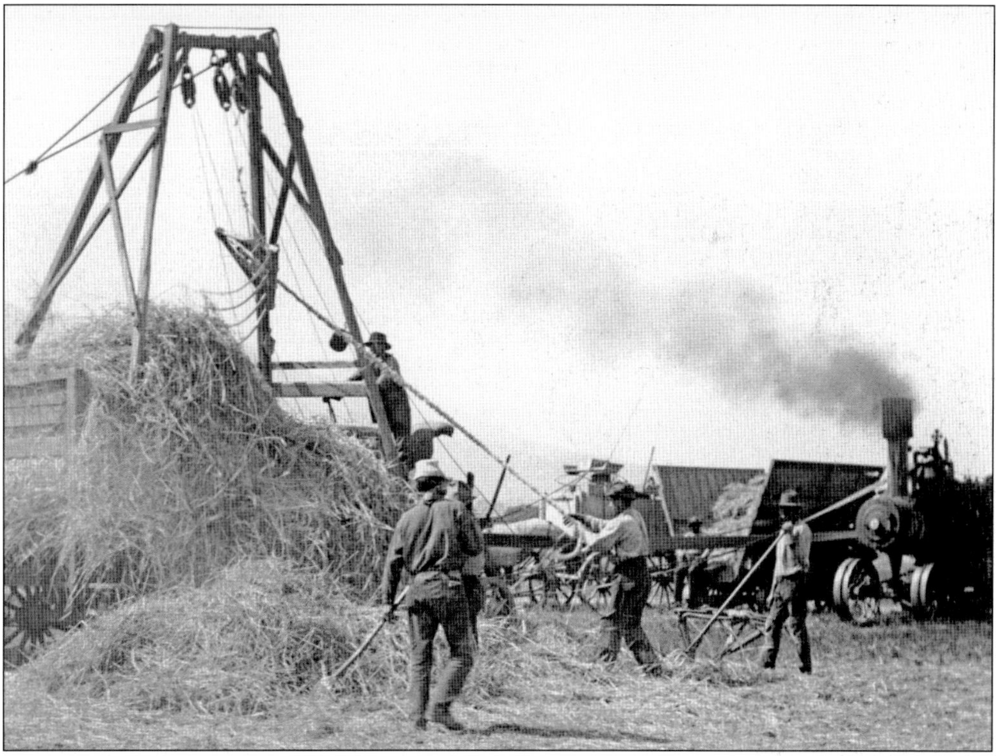

Lorentz Lorentzen, Otto Olson, and crew used a Jackson fork to load hay on the Olson ranch outside of Soledad in 1920. Haymaking started with the cutting and drying of grasses in the field. Hay cured best if it was raked into shocks or windrows. After drying, it was loaded into wagons and hauled to barns for storage. In 1888, the *Monterey Democrat* wrote, "Can you conceive the idea of riding for nearly 100 miles through a mass of waving grain, stretching away on either side almost as far as the eye can reach? Yet this is what will be seen by a traveler going through the Salinas Valley."

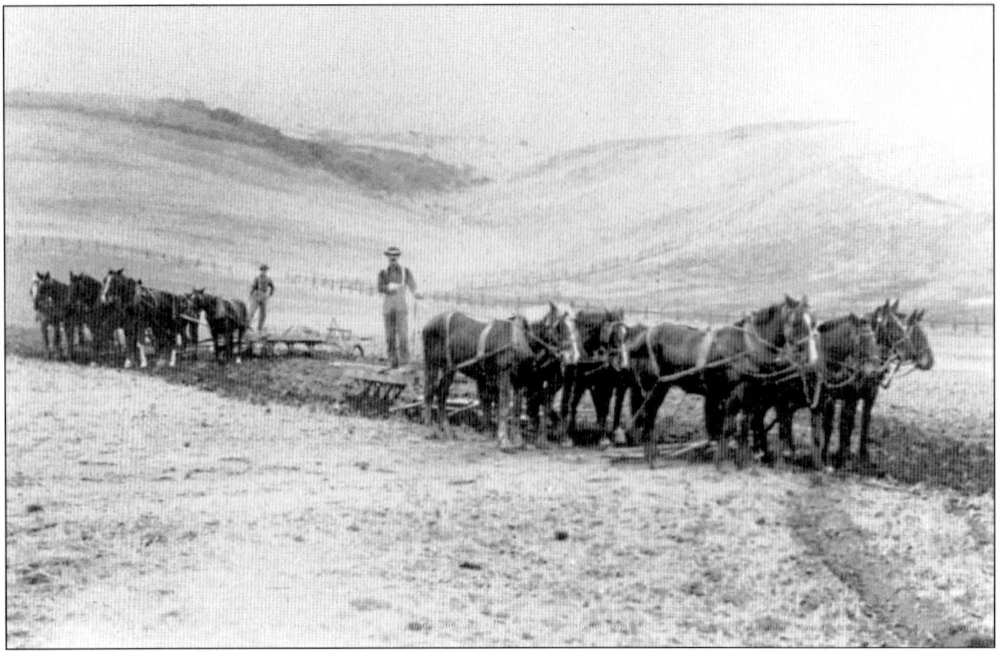

Bill Donahue (foreground) is pictured operating a gangplow pulled by eight horses on the Zabala ranch near Soledad. Gang plows made plowing easier and faster as several furrows could be made at once.

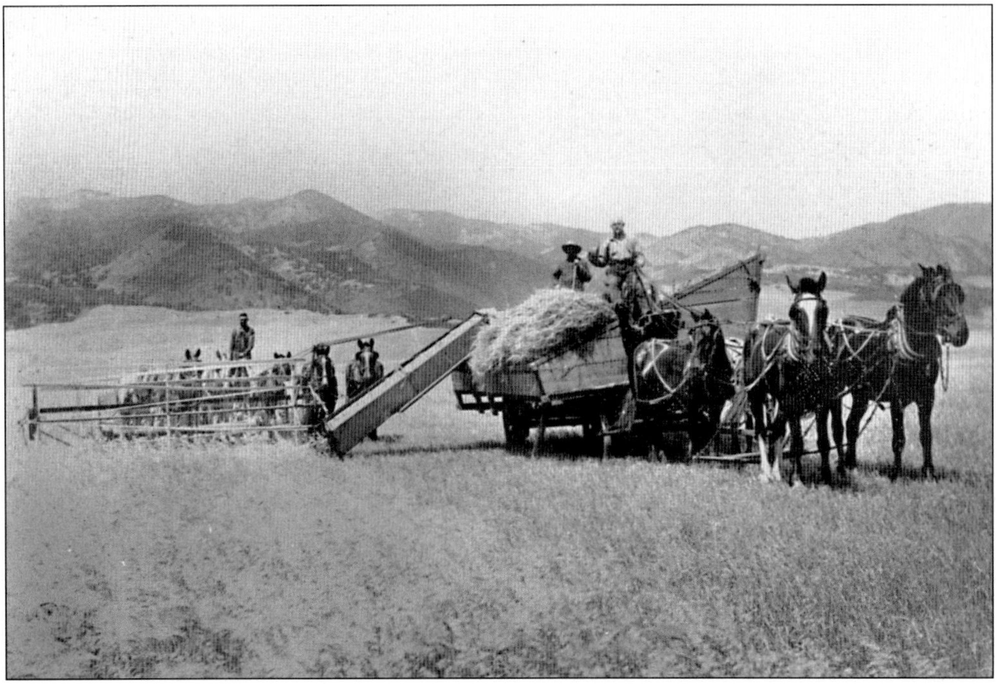

Chester Olson, Hans Peterson, and Tom Cross are pictured heading wheat with a McCormick harvester on the Olson ranch. Frank Livingston recalled that "the header was a machine which cut a swath about 12 feet wide and conveyed the un-threshed grain and straw, called heading, into the header wagon at its low side, by means of an elevator."

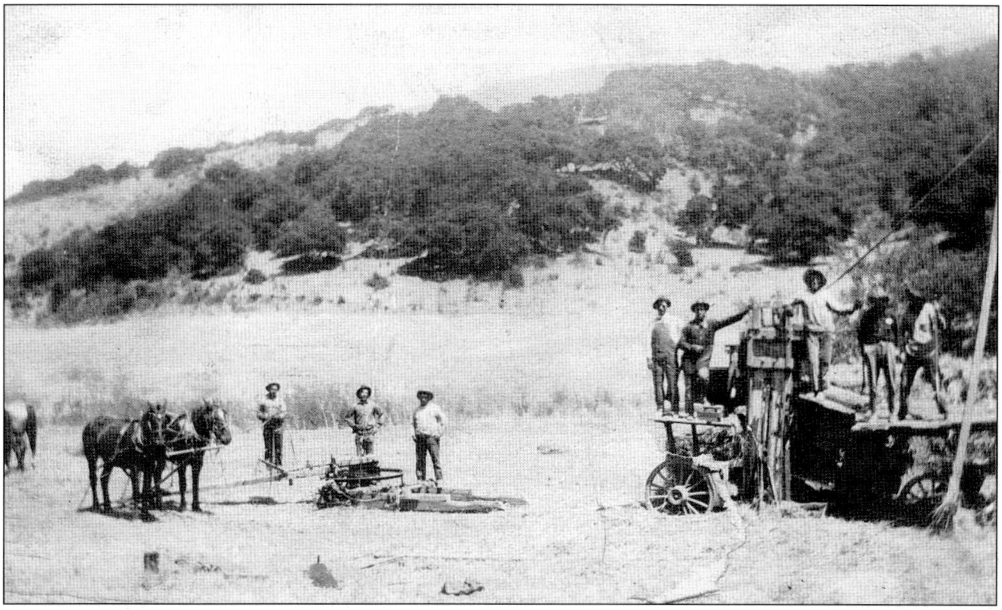

Salinas Valley hay balers are pictured in 1921. Helen McDonald remembers that "Mr. Rennie had a baling crew of nine men which came to our ranch . . . when the crew came up short a man, I would get the job of being the wire poker . . . the wire had to be shoved through the three holes in the wooden blocks that would separate one bale from another. The hay would fall down my neck and into my clothes. Oh, that made me itch!"

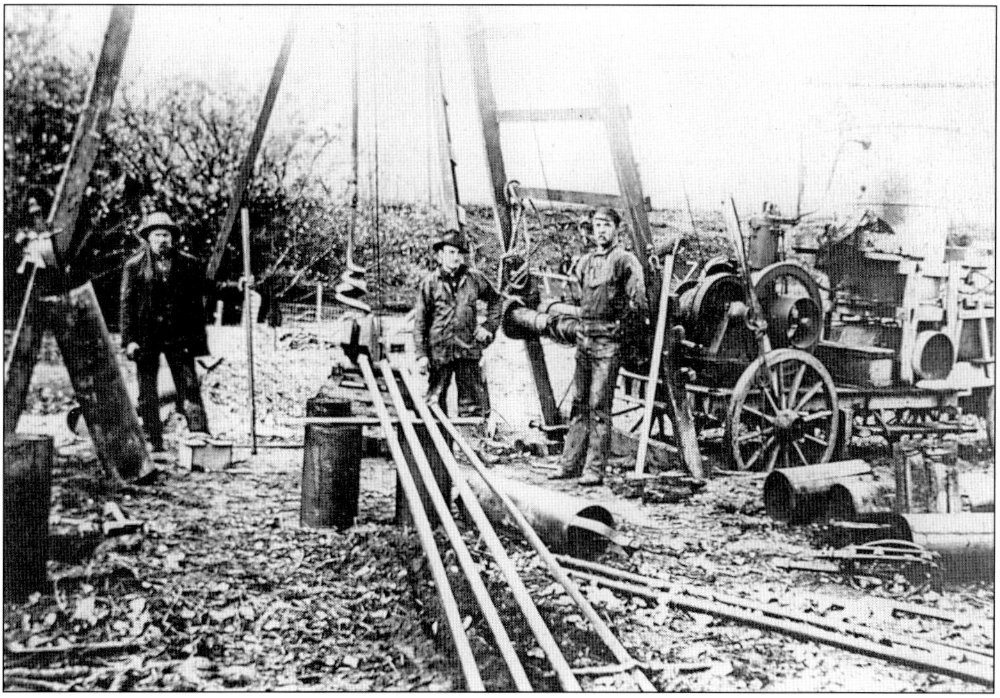

Most of the Salinas Valley's water was underground, so well drillers were important people. Pictured are drillers from the Rumley Well Driller Company, drilling a well on the Tash Ranch in the Mission District.

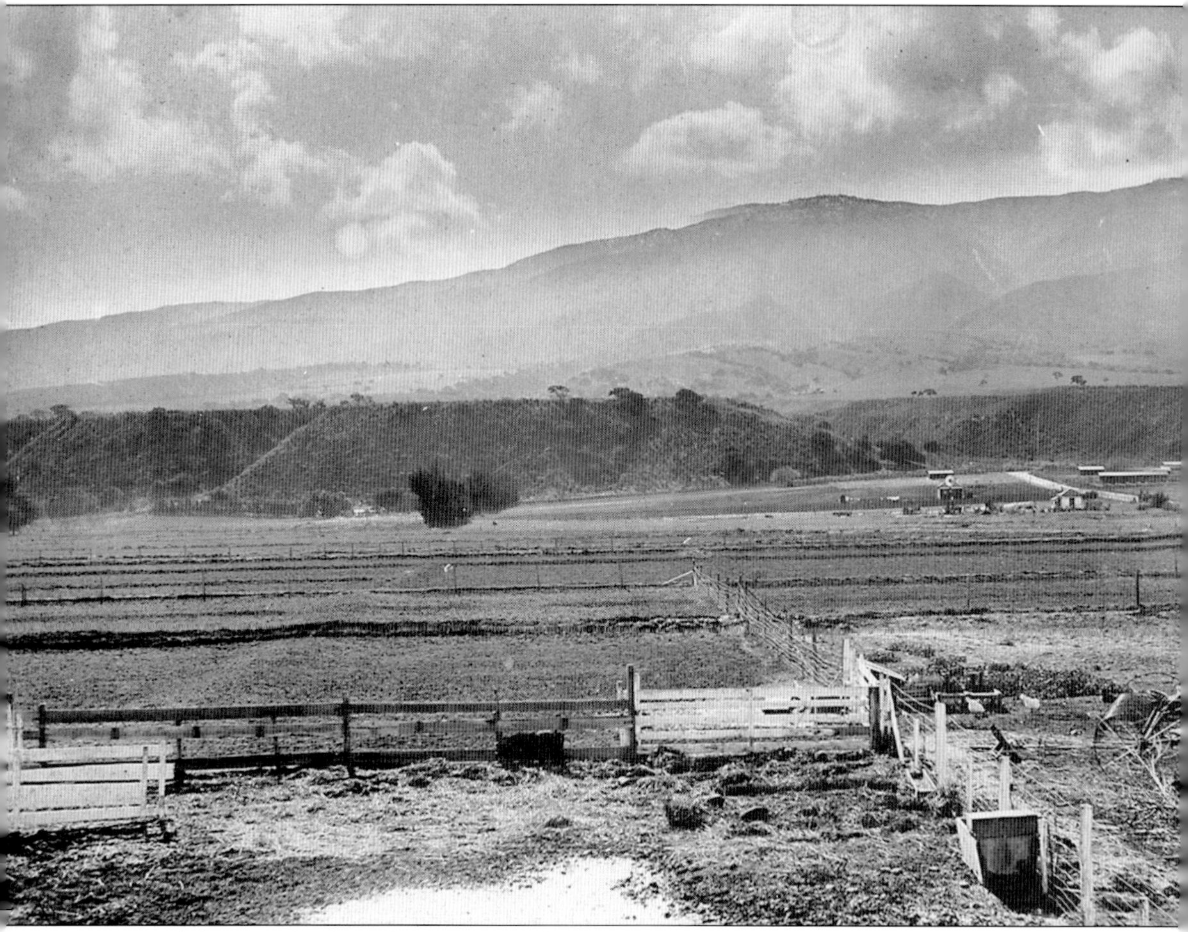

Founded in 1897 by the Salvation Army, the Fort Romie Colony was located four miles southwest of Soledad. Their slogan, "The Landless Man to the Man-less Land," drew impoverished people from across the United States looking for a fresh start. After a rough start due to drought, the

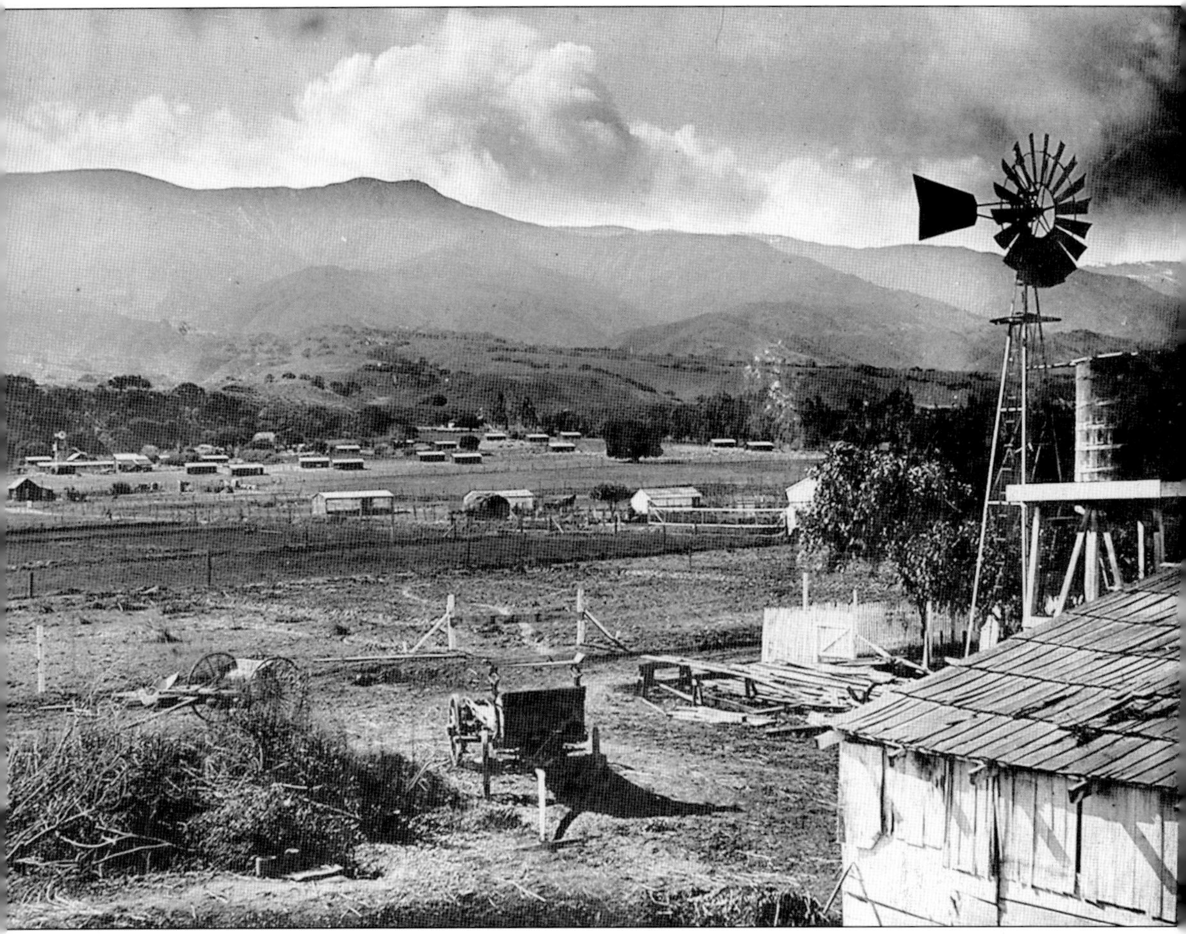

colony finally began to take hold. By 1905, 20 families were farming, raising hogs and poultry, and making butter and cheese. This photograph captures Fort Romie farmsteads looking west toward the Santa Lucia range. (Courtesy of Edward Whalen.)

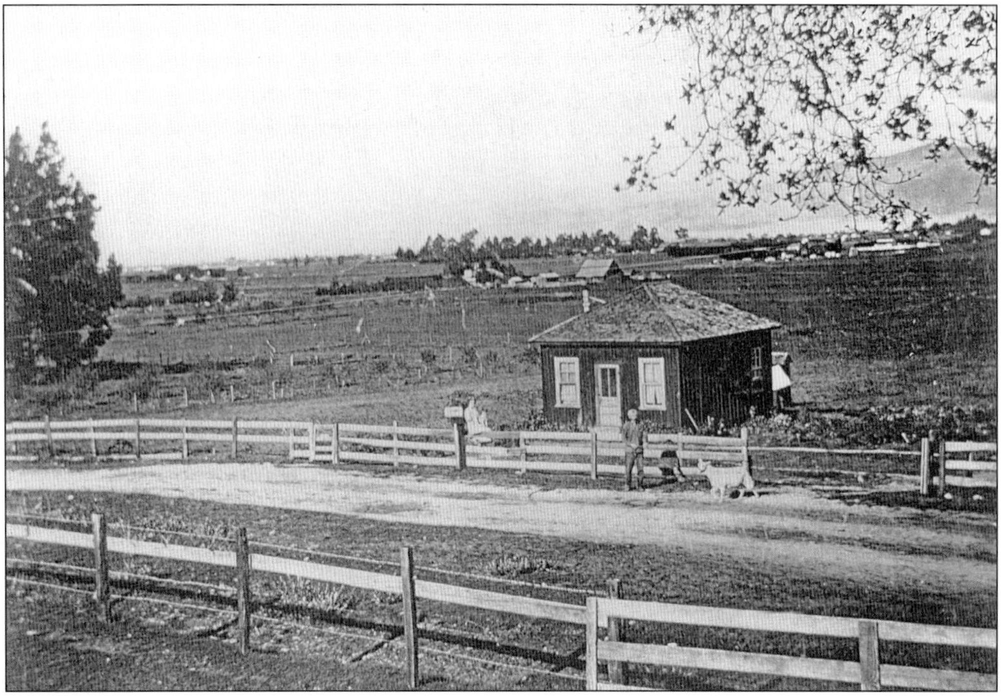

Fort Romie's original homes were either two or four rooms and cost between $110 and $120. The Salvation Army provided seed, sheds, tools, and equipment. Settlers agreed to forego "wine, spirits or objectionable drugs" and to make annual payments of $100 for 10 years. Thereafter they would own the land. This photograph was taken in 1908 and pictured are Jennie Harding James, sitting on the fence, and Ede Harding. (Courtesy of Pat Terry.)

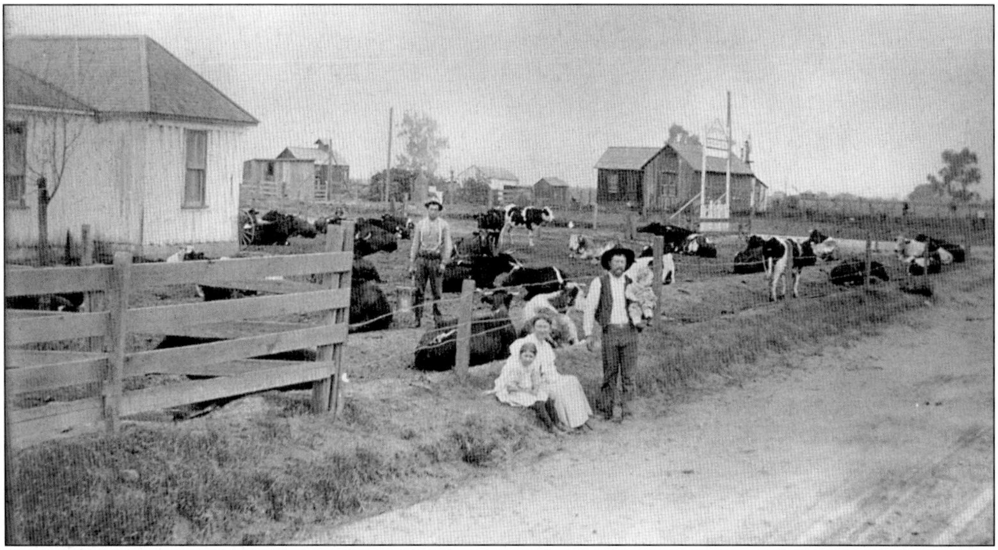

The Jerry Pura family poses in front of their Fort Romie farm in 1910. Jerry holds his son Jacob, and his wife, Electa Lyon Pura, and daughter Margaret Pura Olson are seated in the grass. Milker Ben Bernardasi holds a pail. The sign in the background reads "Fort Romie Salvation Army Colony," which was located at the intersection of Mile End Road and Fort Romie Road. (Courtesy of Pat Terry.)

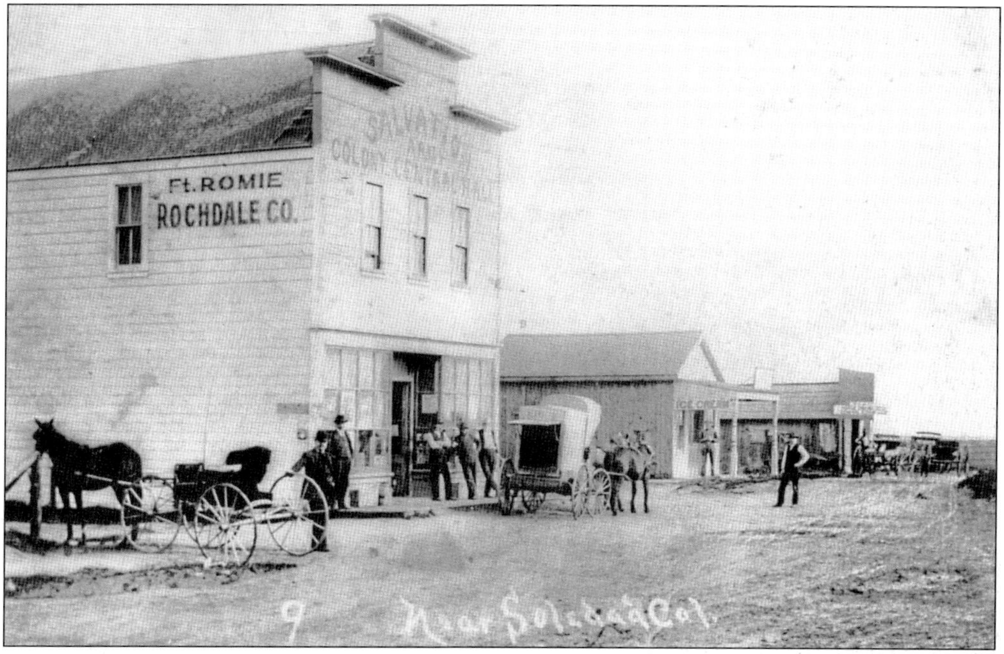

The building in the foreground housed Fort Romie's Salvation Army Central Hall. Downstairs the Rochdale Company traded general merchandise. It advertised "an up-to-date stock of fresh, clean and new merchandise at prices that are right." The store's butcher wagon delivered meat to colony residents. Down the street was Gilkey's Ice Cream parlor and Gilkey's Blacksmith shop. (Courtesy of Pat Terry.)

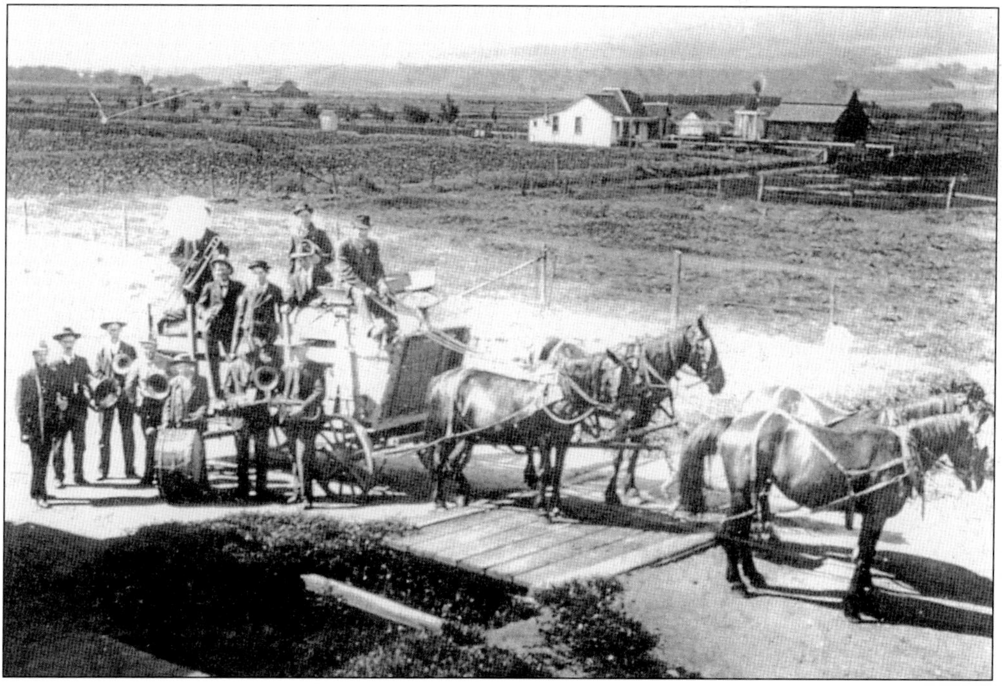

The Fort Romie Grange Band poses with their instruments. They played at baseball games and gave concerts on Sundays. Dave Binsacca drives the wagon. (Courtesy of Pat Terry.)

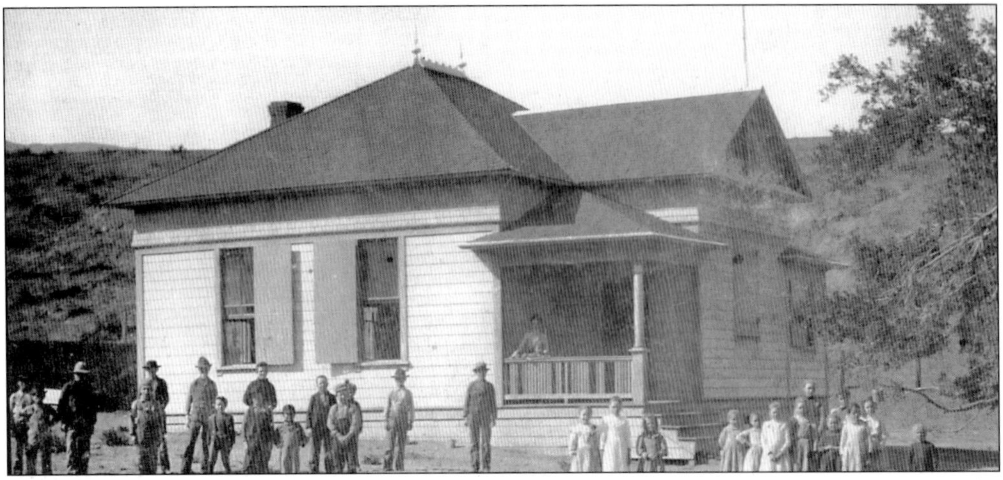

Students at the Mission School near Soledad pose for their portrait in 1914. (Courtesy of the Soledad Historical Society.)

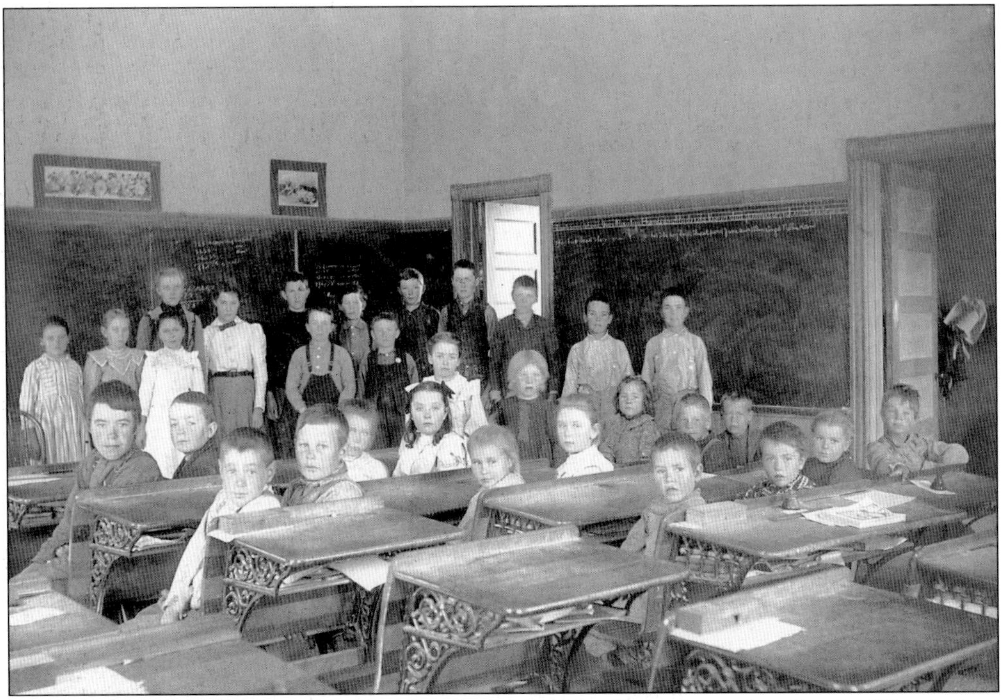

The first Mission School at Fort Romie was built in 1895 and was located on Foothill Road when this photograph was taken. William Livingston remembers that "the Romie School was taught by a girl who rode horseback to school and she used her quirt on recalcitrant students. In 1903, parents started planning for a new school. Some families wanted the school closer to Fort Romie's center and the heated debate almost led to fisticuffs. When the Ober family donated land for the school on Foothill Road, the argument was settled."

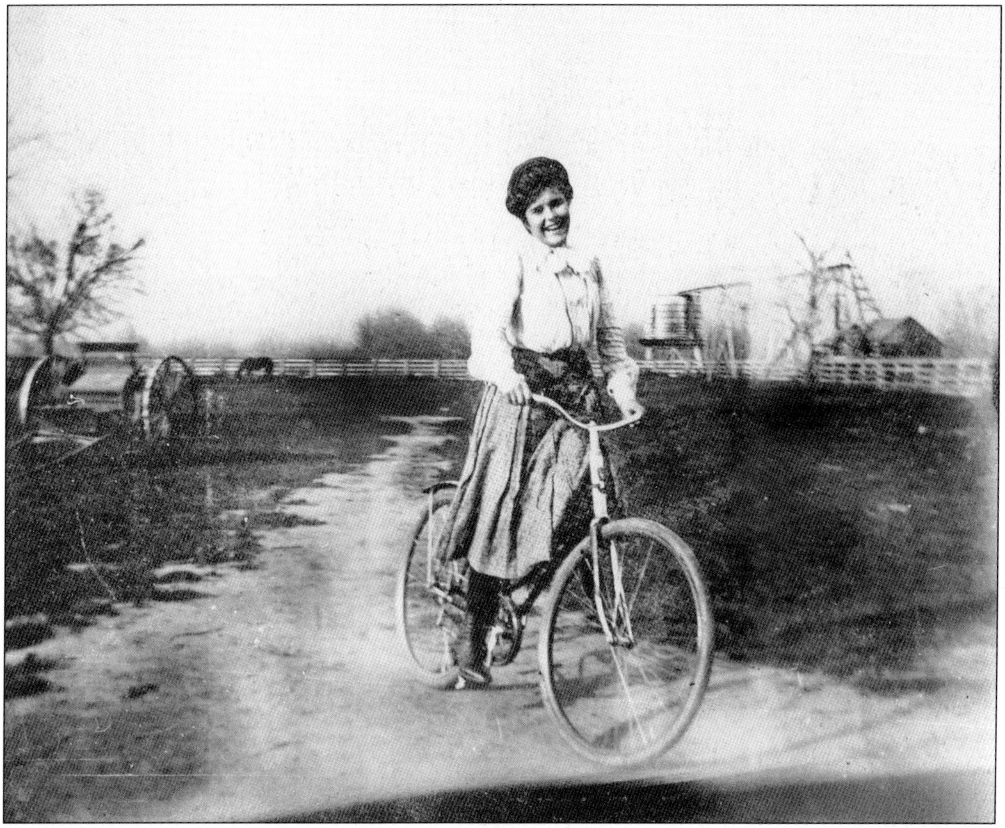

Pictured is a Mission school teacher who rode her bike to the school and boarded with a local family.

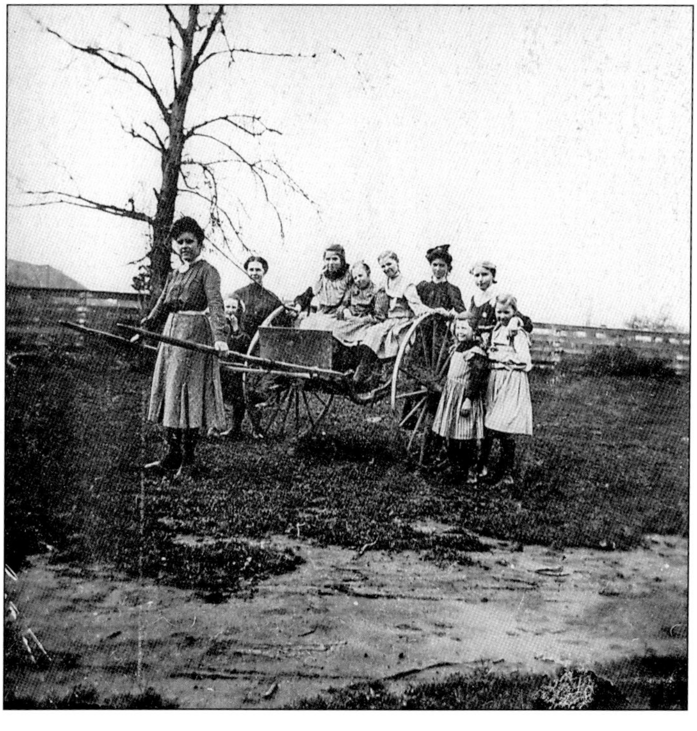

Mission school children get a ride in a two-wheel cart courtesy of their teacher.

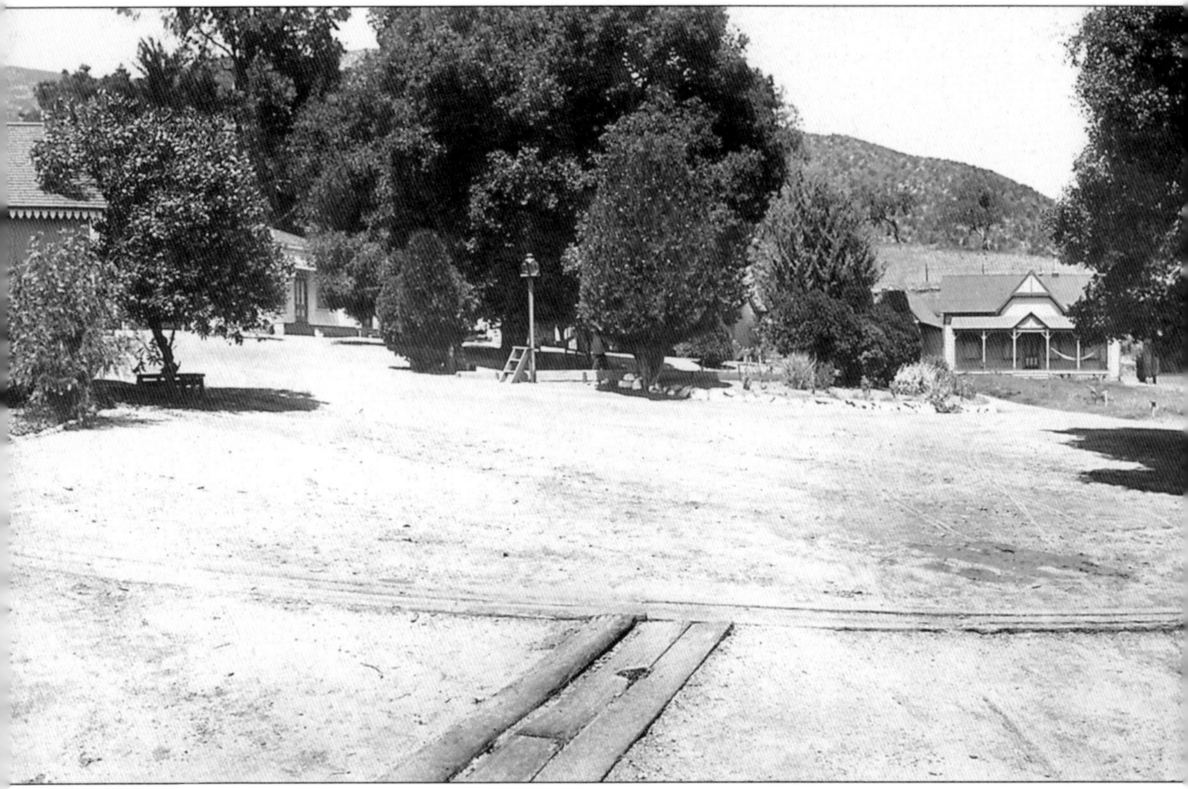

Guests at Paraiso Springs resort wait beneath a shady oak tree to board the stage to Soledad. Manager H. C. Shannon advertised the following in 1905, "Hot soda and sulfur plunge and tub baths with first class masseurs in attendance. Charming climate, grand scenery, and flowers in

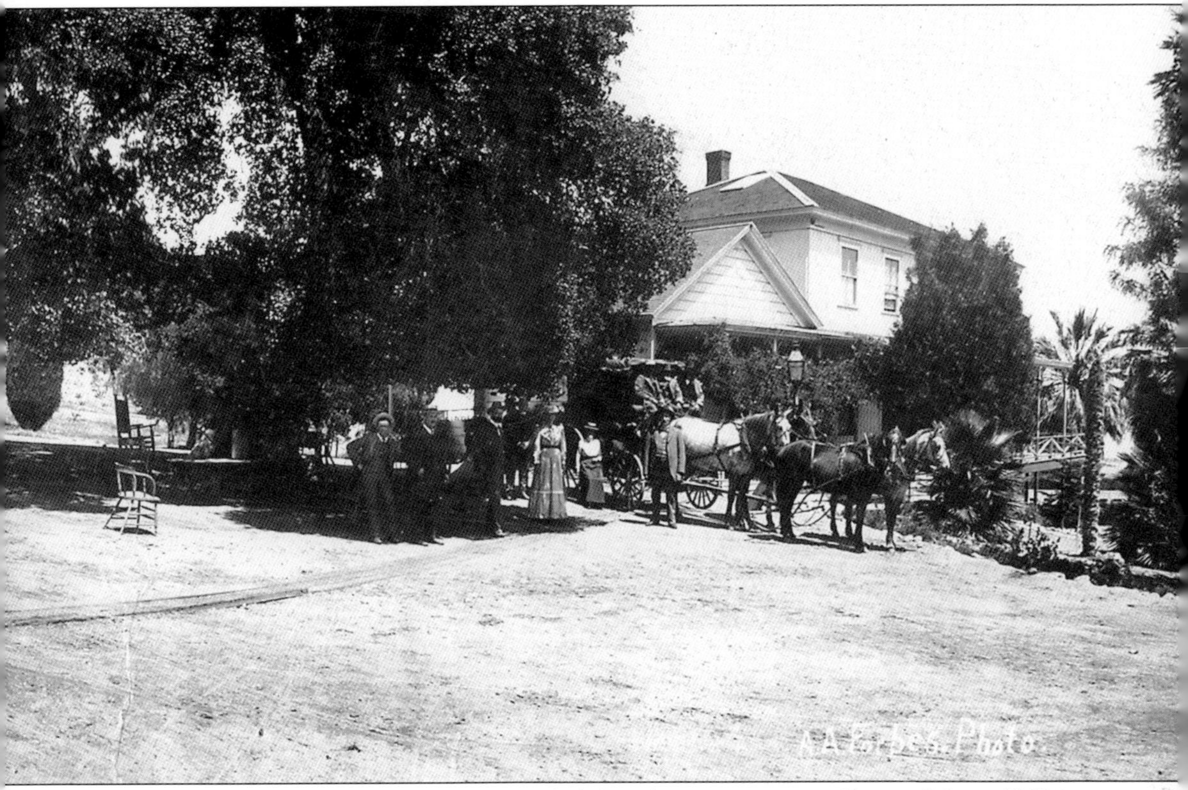

profusion. Stage meets afternoon train at Soledad and carries you over famous Salinas Valley good roads, a distance of only eight miles." (Courtesy of Edward Whalen.)

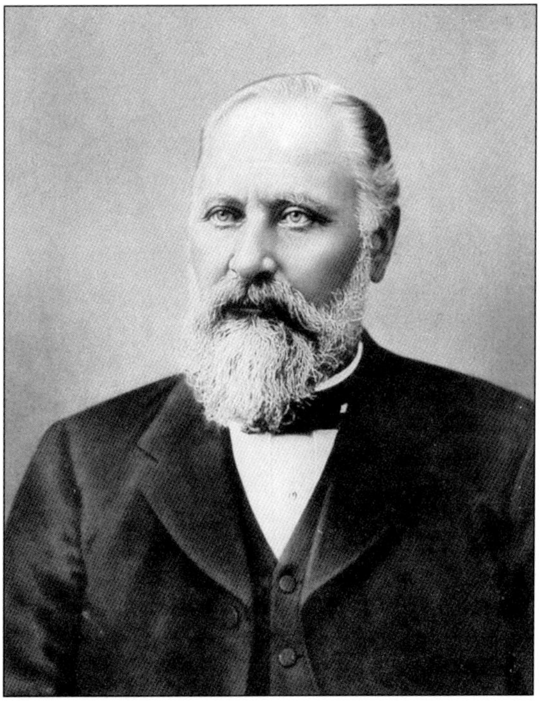

Sugar-king Claus Spreckels maintained his own cottage at Paraiso Springs. Like many others, Spreckels was attracted to the therapeutic spring waters, hunting and fishing, picnics, and other social activities at the popular resort.

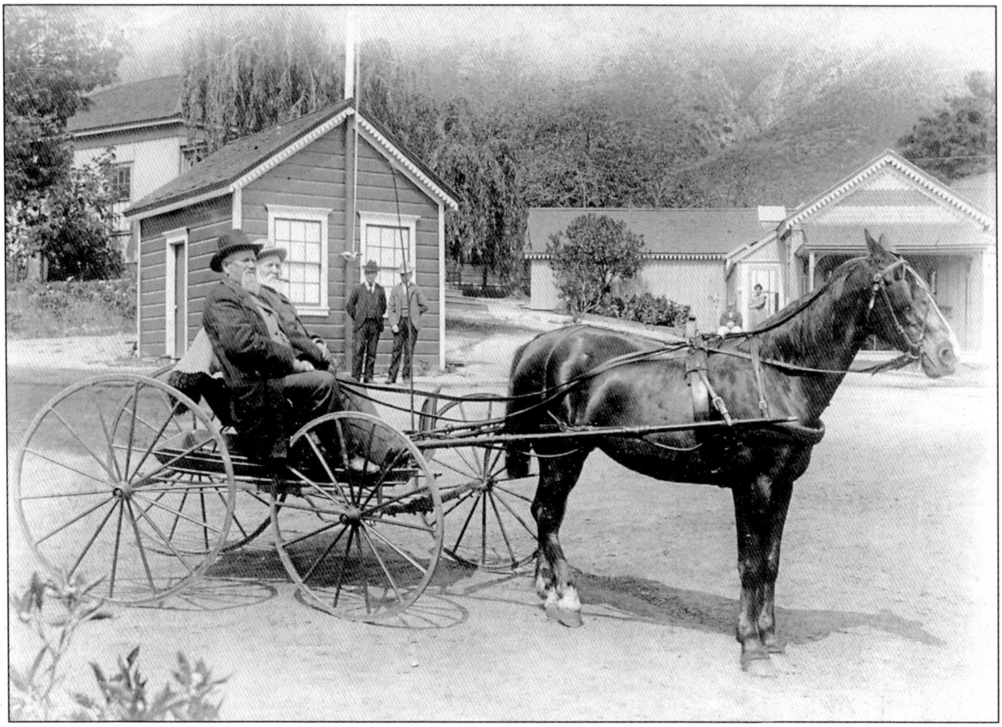

Claus Spreckels (holding reins) and Charles Romie are pictured on an outing at Paraiso Springs. Romie had extensive property holdings outside of Soledad, including Paraiso Springs. Spreckels and Romie collaborated on the establishment of Fort Romie, Romie leasing land to the Salvation Army and Spreckels promising to buy the sugarbeets they raised. Romie was popular throughout Monterey County, being described as "a royal entertainer and the prince of good fellows." (Courtesy of the Monterey County Historical Society.)

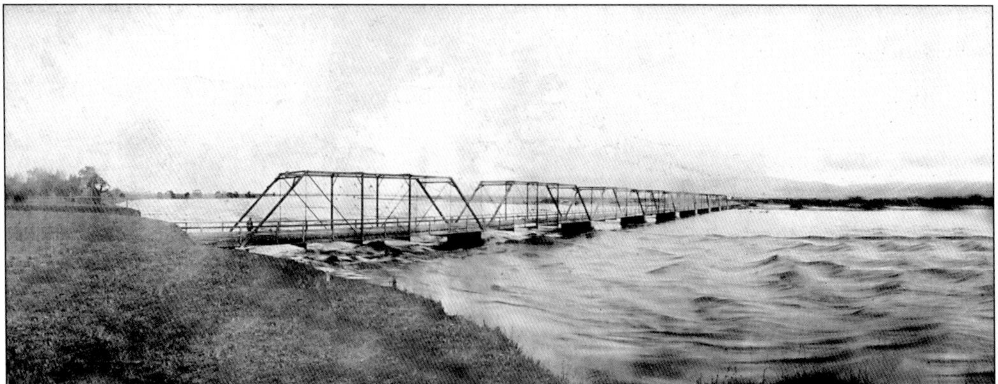

Rising floodwater threatened the Soledad Bridge in the winter of 1914. The *King City Rustler* reported, "The Salinas River swelled to great depths and widths by storms of the past two weeks, has washed out bridges in both Soledad and King City, leaving Greenfield stranded . . . Bridge after bridge gave way up and down the valley. The Soledad wagon bridge, with concrete piers, tipped over and sunk from view in quicksand. The bridge at King City was likewise washed away . . . the river was 20 feet deep and half a mile wide. Houses, barns and farmlands have also been washed away by the rampaging Salinas, the roar of which could be heard for miles."

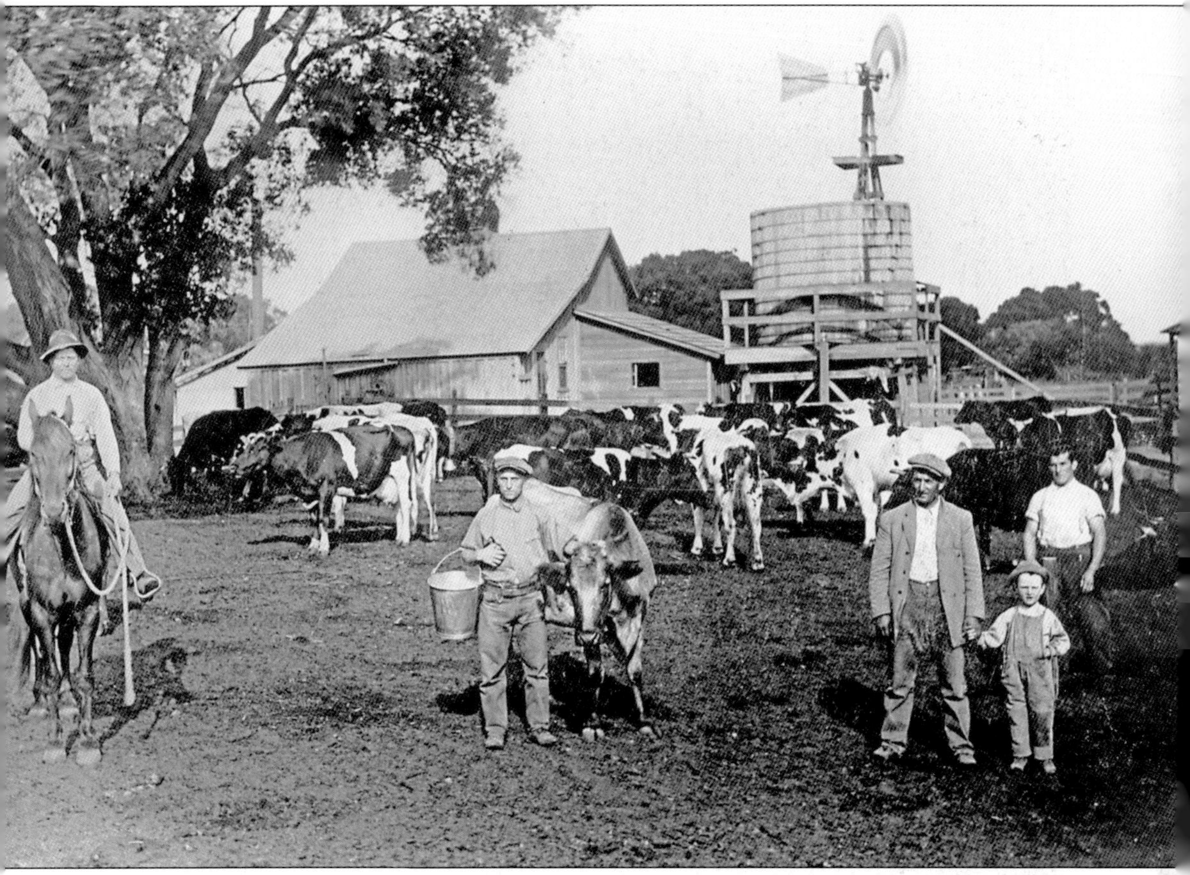

The Celestino Pelucca diary was located on the west side of Highway 101 near Soledad. In 1914, Pelucca, along with Mr. Codoni, won first prize for the best cheese at the state fair. The *King City Rustler* wrote that they "raised the good alfalfa that fed the good cows from whose milk they made the good cheese that took the first prize."

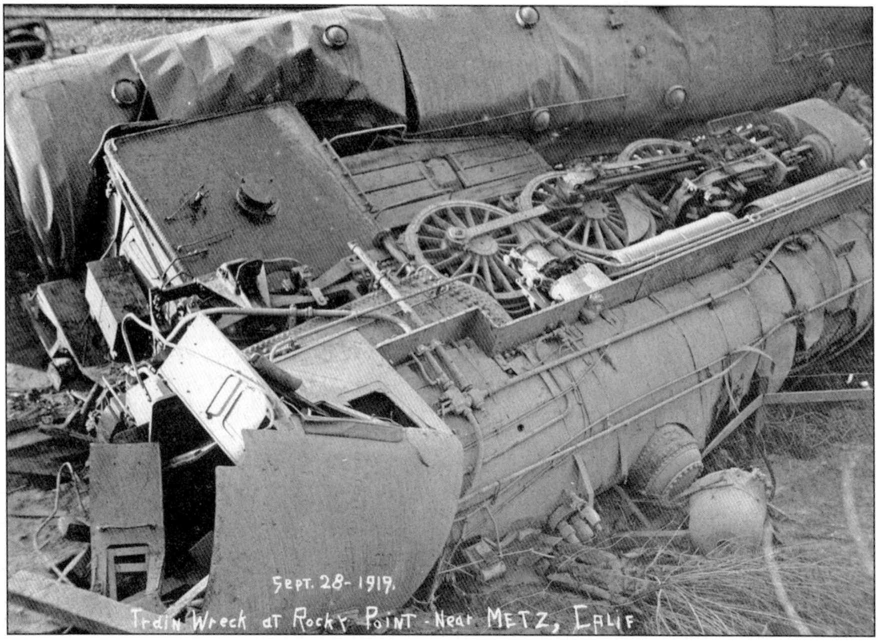

On September 28, 1919, a passenger train was wrecked at Rocky Point near Metz while rounding a dangerous curve. Engineer Walter Patrick and fireman E. Reinhart were killed. A special train carried 40 injured passengers up to the Southern Pacific hospital in San Francisco. Another wreck occurred in the same location nine years earlier. Southern Pacific was convinced that the curve was too dangerous, so in 1928, a tunnel was built to straighten out the route.

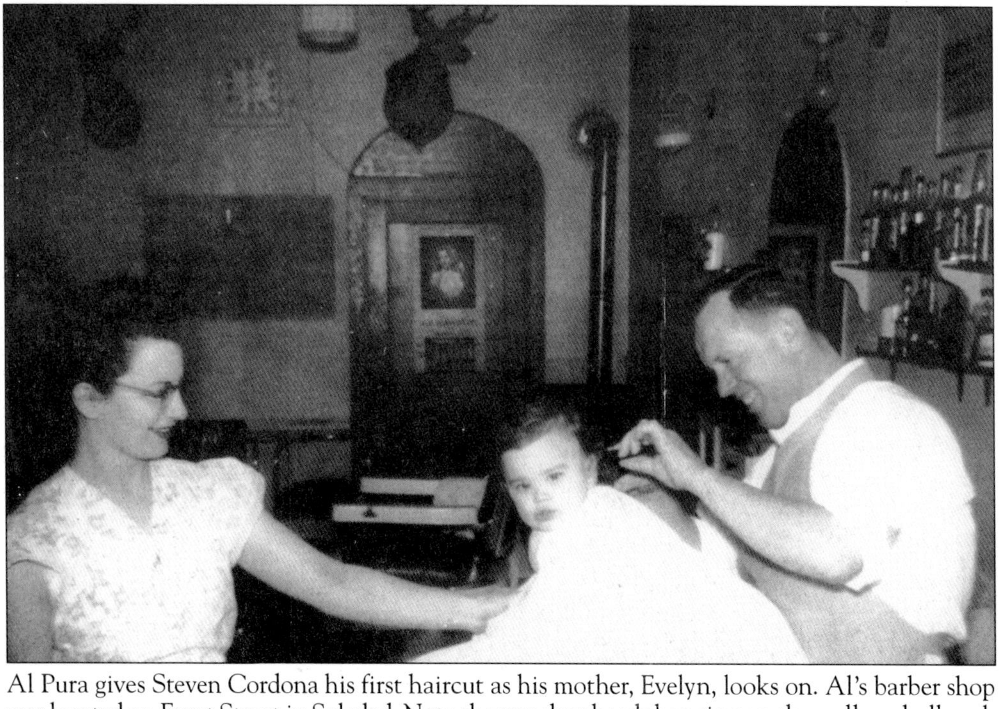

Al Pura gives Steven Cordona his first haircut as his mother, Evelyn, looks on. Al's barber shop was located on Front Street in Soledad. Note the two deer heads hanging on the wall—a hallmark of the shop. (Courtesy of the Soledad Historical Society.)

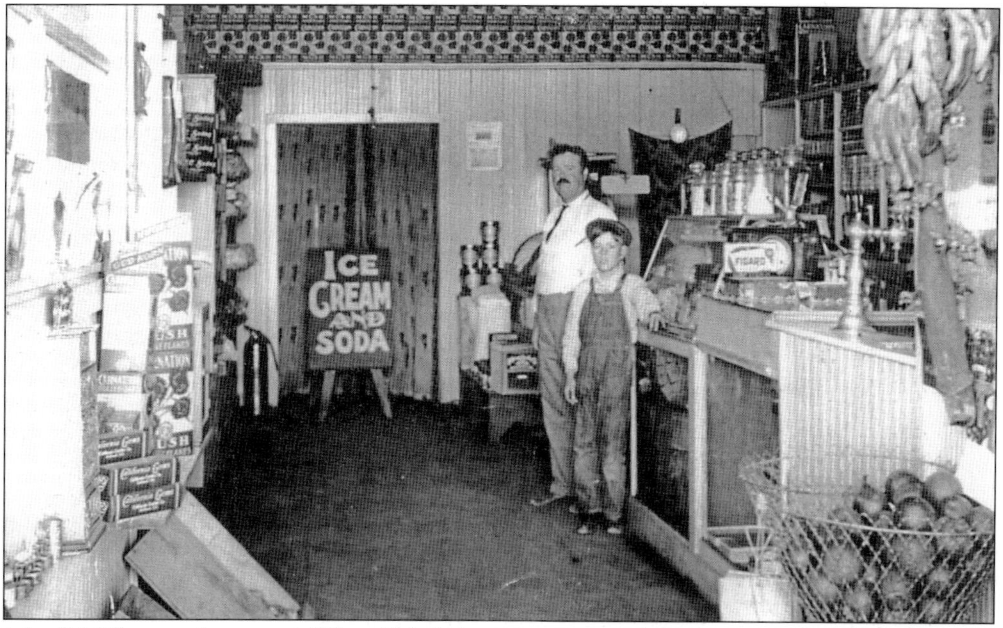

John P. Mills was a busy man. When Soledad was incorporated, he was named city judge, serving from 1915 to 1923. By trade, he was a barber but also ran a fruit and candy store. He built an adobe house in 1905, where he lived with his wife, Dora, and 10 children. He is pictured here in the store with his son John Mills Jr. (Courtesy of the Soledad Historical Society.)

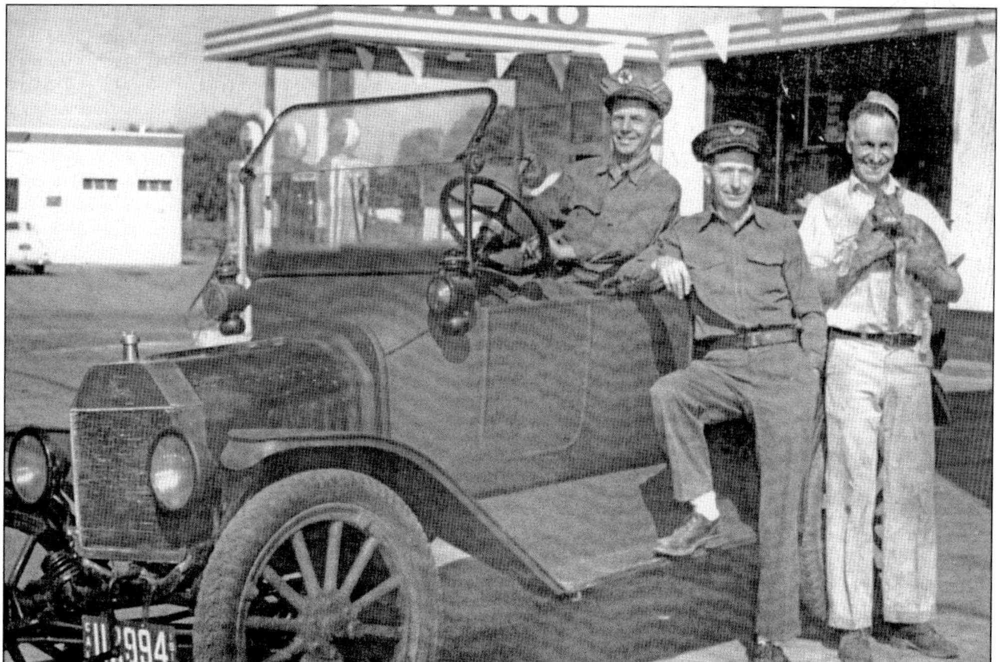

Al Anderson, Huey Mayer, and George Teves pose in front of Soledad's Texaco station.

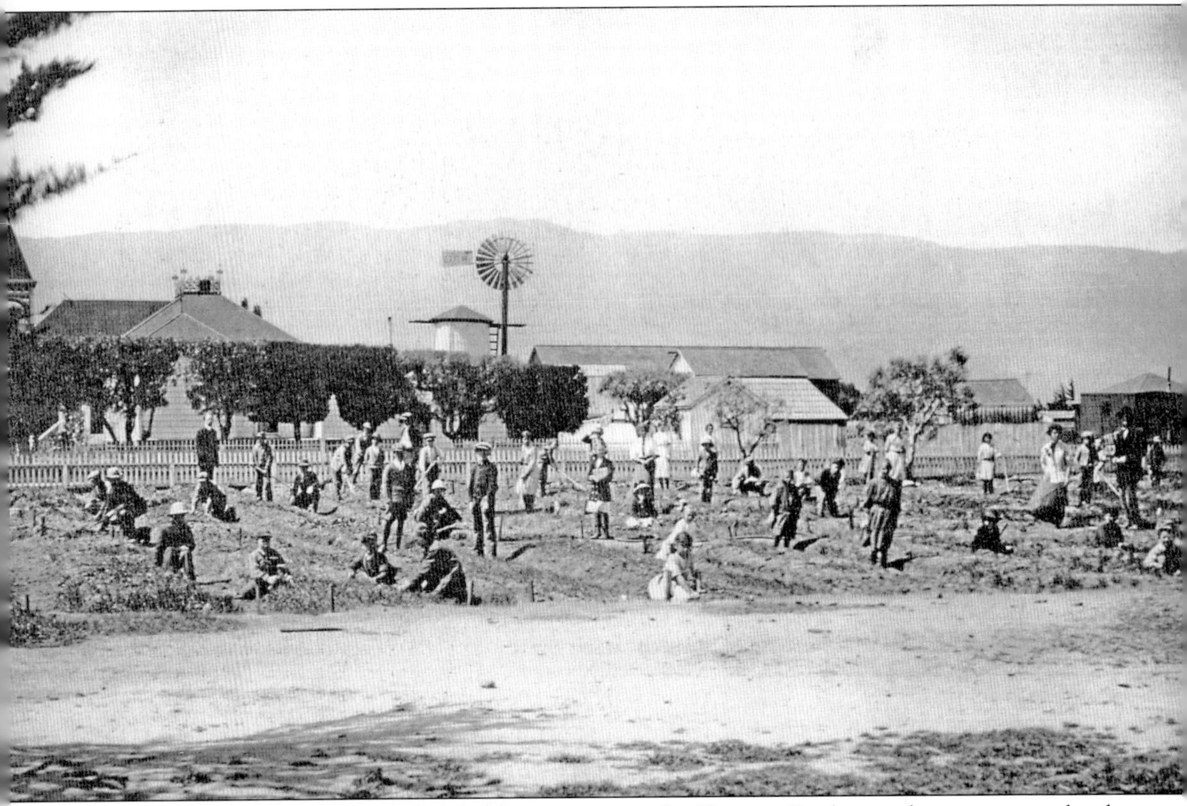

During World War II, Soledad children maintained a Victory Garden at the grammar school located on Main and Market Streets. The National War Garden Commission encouraged all citizens to raise and preserve food so more resources could be made available to the military. The Commission distributed patriotic booklets with gardening advice and canning instructions. (Courtesy of the Soledad Historical Society.)

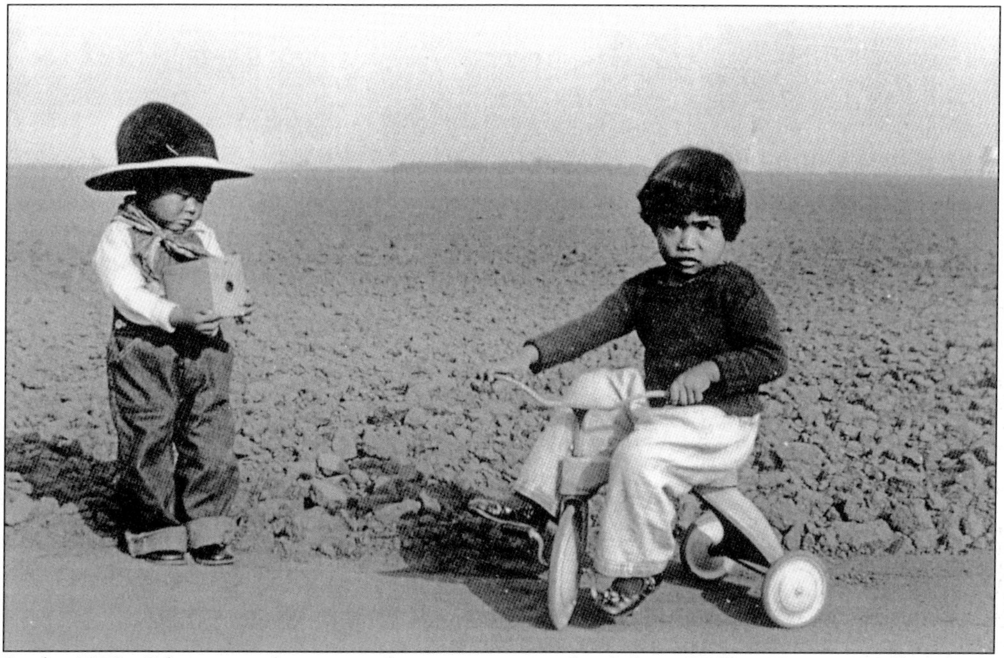

In the 1920s, Filipino workers started immigrating to the Salinas Valley. Honorio Della Sr. was among them. He lived with his wife, Rufina, and son Honorio Della Jr. at Garin Camp, which was located across from the Soledad prison. Few children lived at the camp and little Honorio became a favorite with his "uncles." He is pictured photographing a playmate with his brownie camera. (Courtesy of the Soledad Historical Society.)

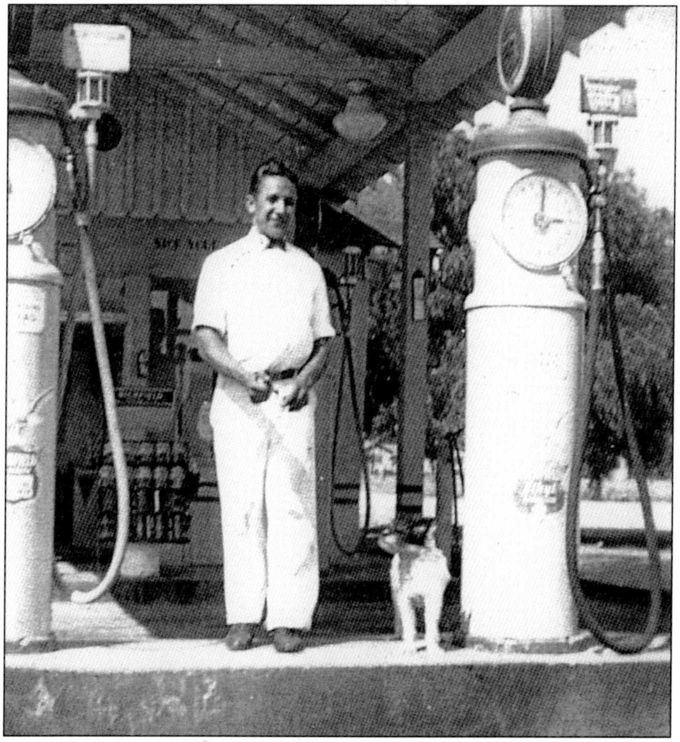

John Mill Sr. owned this Richfield Service Station on the corner of Oak and Front Streets in Soledad. Pictured is attendant Rob Baumann. (Courtesy of Soledad Historical Society.)

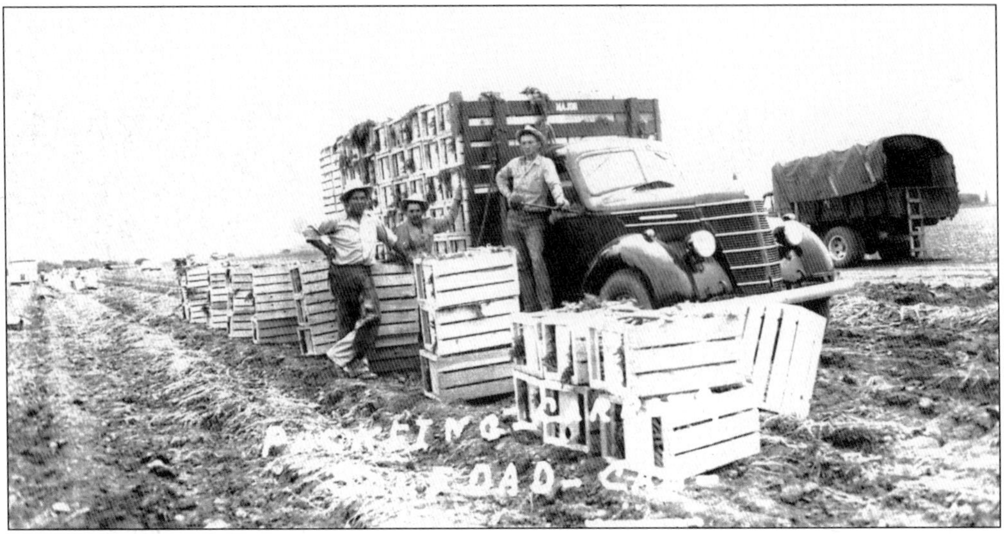

Jesse Gallardo and his family were migrant workers until they settled in Soledad in the 1930s. They worked for Major Farms and lived at Major's Camp, south of Soledad. Jesse continued working for the same company for over 55 years. His intense interest in baseball led to his deep involvement with the community. He helped build two baseball parks in town, plus he coached, managed, and umpired for teams for more than two decades. In July 1994, the baseball park across from the community center was named for him. Jesse is standing next to the truck. (Courtesy of the Soledad Historical Society.)

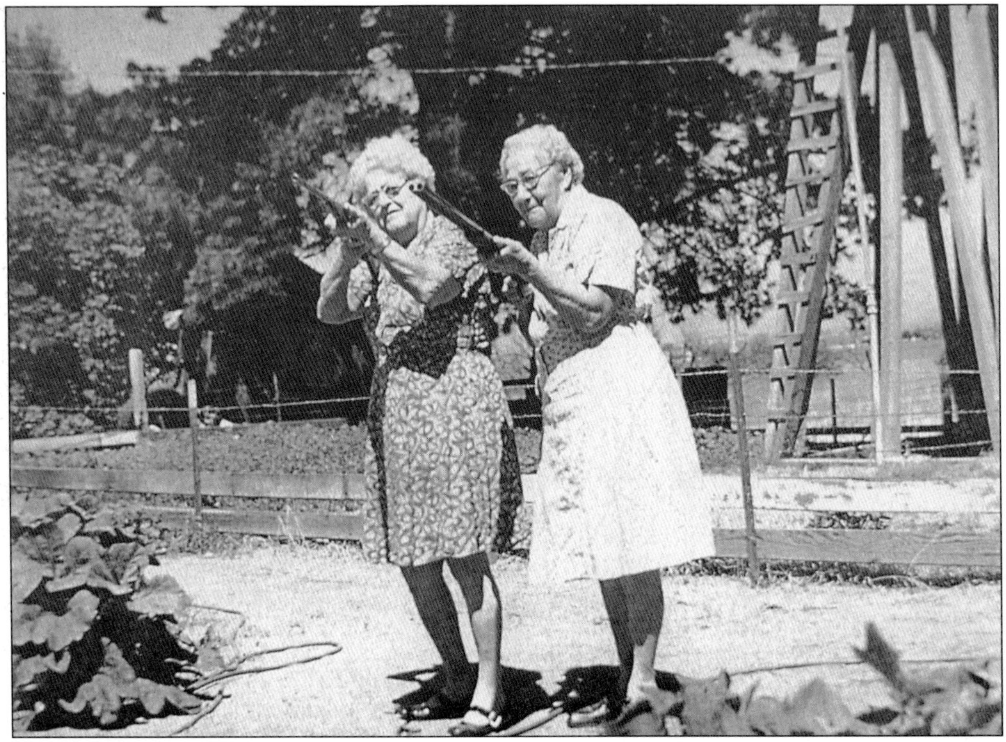

Sisters Isabel Bianchi Tonini and Tillie Bianchi Binsacca take aim at chicken-hunting hawks with their double-barrel shotguns. (Courtesy of the Soledad Historical Society.)

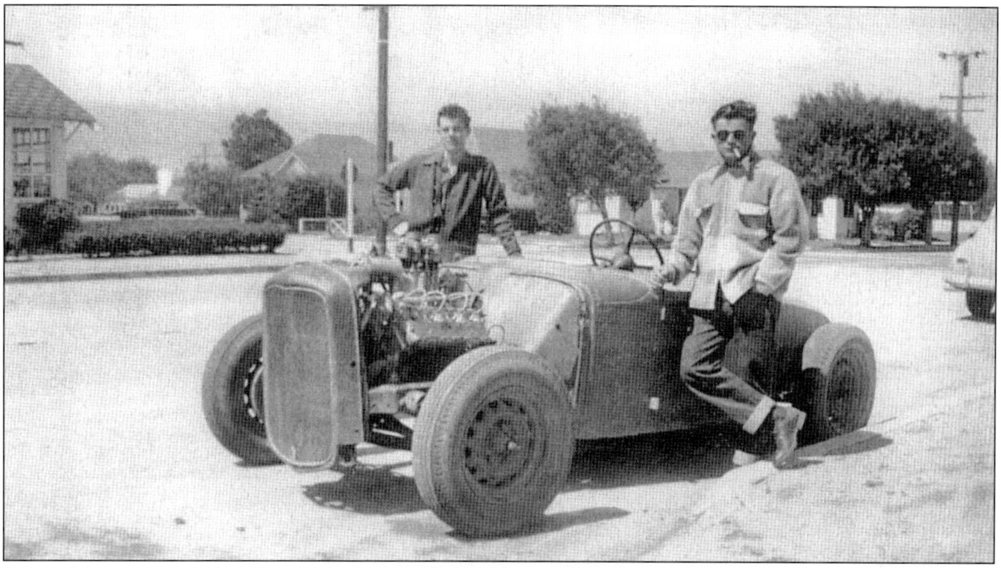

Lester Zanetta and Art Bigiogni show off their hot rod on a Soledad street. Art enjoyed racing cars, and today is known as the "Carrot King" of B and P Packing. (Courtesy of the Soledad Historical Society.)

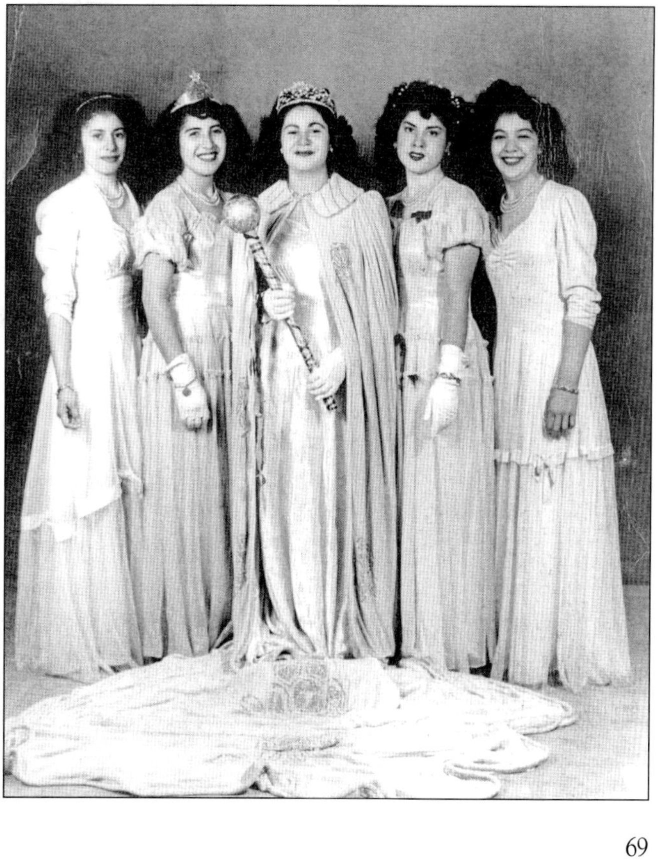

Fiestas Patrias queen Lucy Saavedra poses with her court on September 16, 1946. Pictured, from left to right, are Ramona Robledo, Esperanza Garcia, Lucy Saavedra, Eva Mena, and unidentified. (Courtesy of the Soledad Historical Society.)

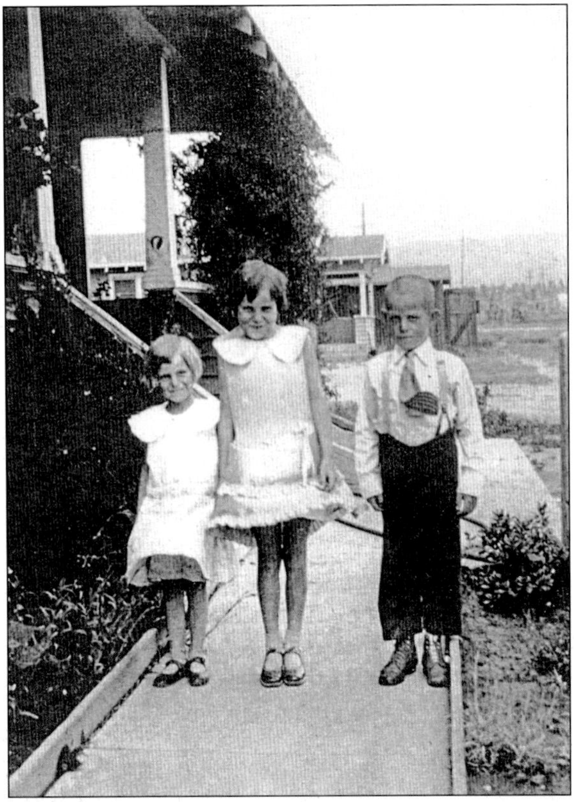

The famous Salinas Valley wind ruffles the hems of the Peverini girls and lifts the tie of their brother. Frank C. Livingston recalled that "The wind made the Salinas Valley . . . it has always blown and I guess it always will. It was no problem for kids, but it was very hard on the mothers and fathers . . . Some families sold out and left." Pictured, from left to right, are Irene, Thelma, and Emil. (Courtesy of the Soledad Historical Society.)

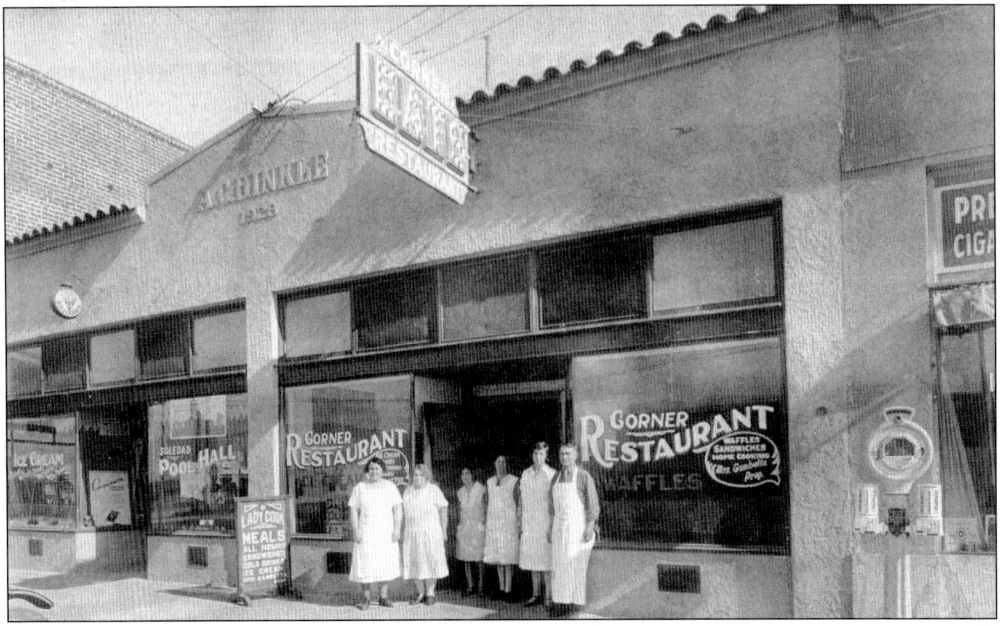

Employees of Katie Daly's Corner Restaurant, located on Front Street, line up for a photograph in the 1930s. The restaurant was included in Ripley's Believe It or Not column as the "Corner Restaurant in the middle of the block." Pictured, from left to right, are Katie Gambetta Daly, Vivian Hansen, and Lorena Schlesinger. (Courtesy of the Soledad Historical Society.)

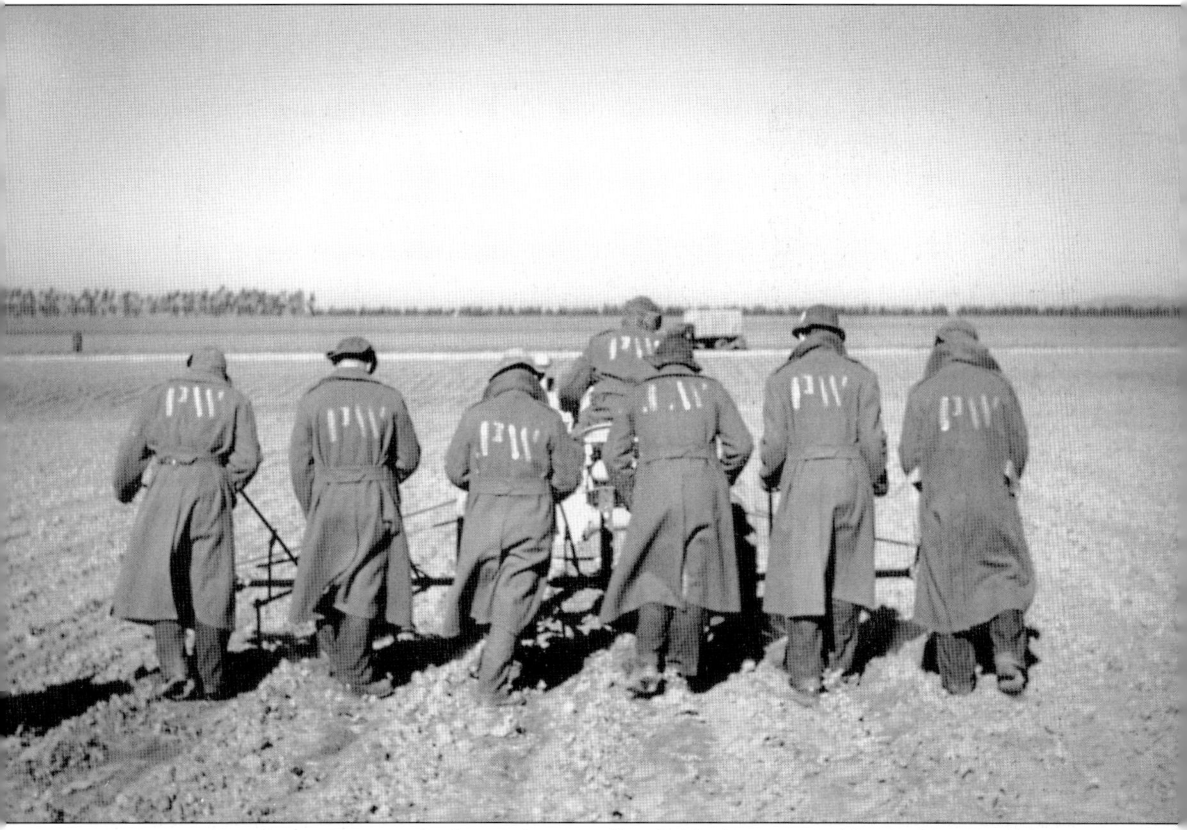

German and Italian POWs worked in Salinas Valley fields during World War II. In 1944, 500 Italians harvested guayule and were housed at Camp McCollum. A German POW camp was located behind the Main Street School in Soledad. Prisoners, wearing blue caps, worked in the sugar beet and lettuce fields. Although well-guarded, there was one incident where three escaped. They were found three days later in the Jamesburg area. Here prisoners tend young guayule plants.

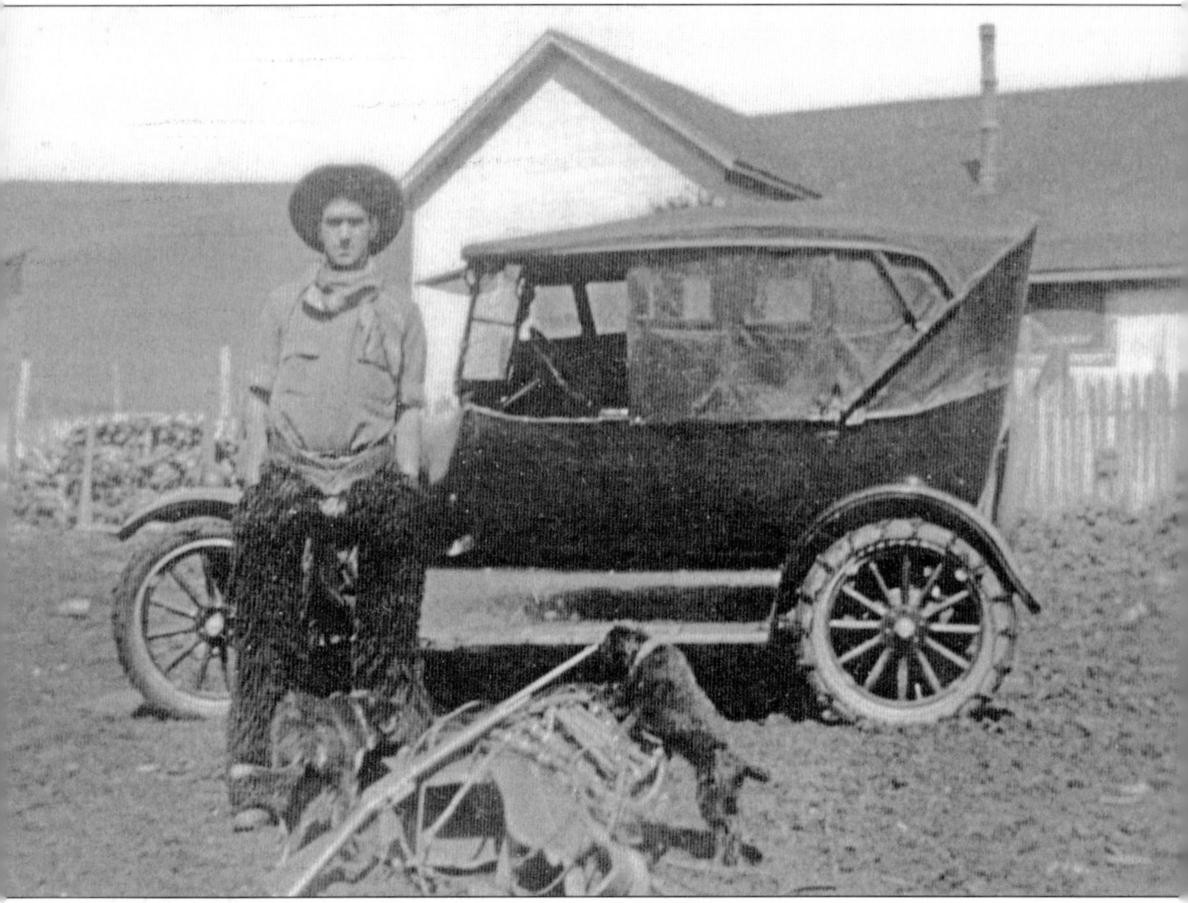

Peg Fratis is pictured on the Gularte Ranch near Soledad. Lee Gularte remembers that she invited him to dinner and he stayed on as a ranch hand for the rest of his life. As a boy in San Luis Obispo, he delivered milk. Later he discovered that some of the milk bottles were laced with "hooch." (Courtesy of the Soledad Historical Society.)

Five

GREENFIELD

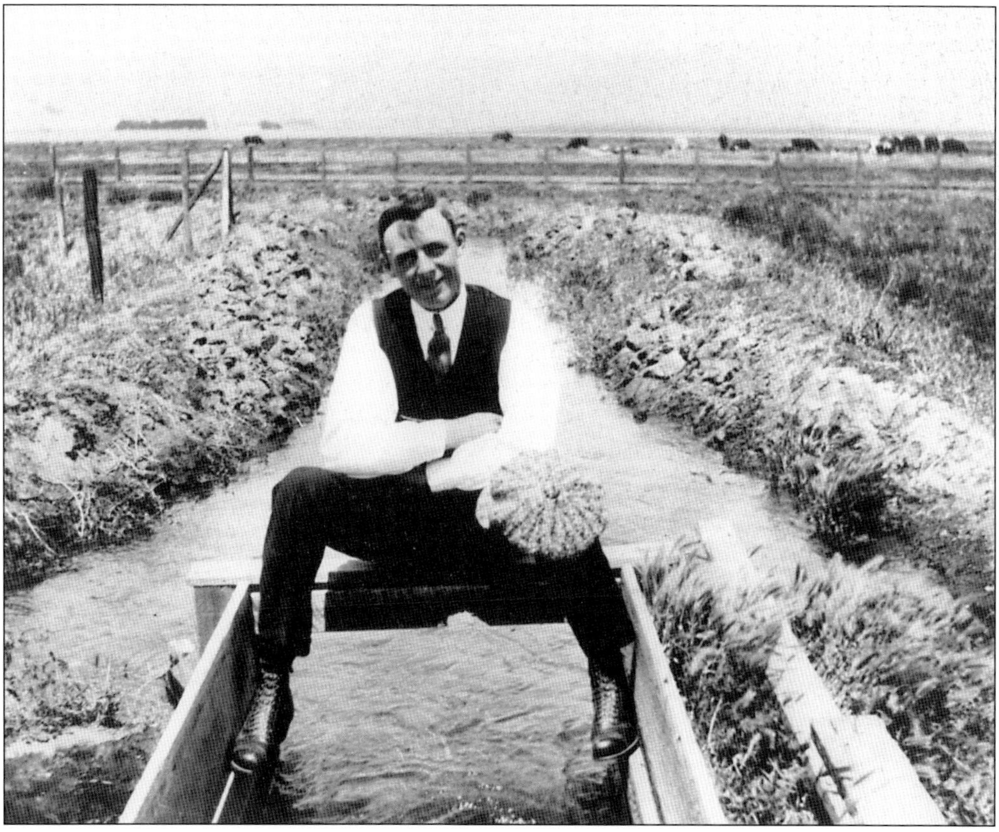

In 1904, the Arroyo Seco Improvement Company bought 7,000 acres of the Arroyo Seco Rancho. They secured water rights and began constructing canals. The following year, they sold out to the California Home Extension Association, who laid out Clark Colony, now Greenfield. Land was sold for $37.50 per acre, including water. Pictured is Morris Lorentzen irrigating his farm near Cherry Avenue. (Courtesy of Helen McDonald.)

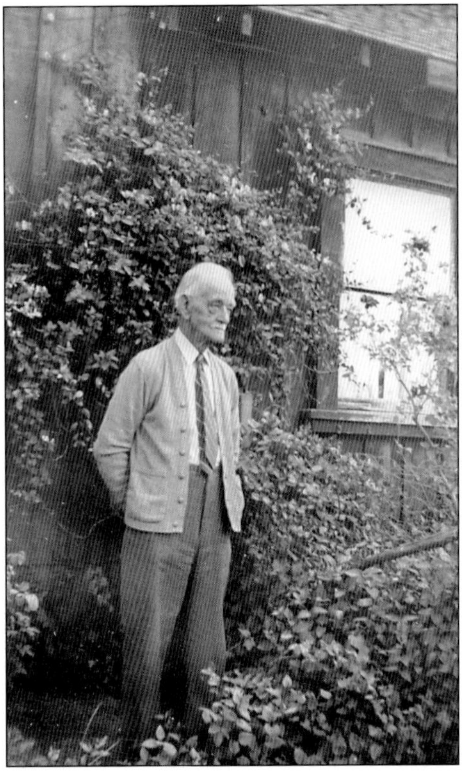

William Harvey Livingston, prominent Greenfield pioneer, moved from Illinois to the Salinas Valley in 1905. He bought 10 acres and set up a tent made of posts and canvas. This was home to the family for two years, until a house was finally built. Mrs. Livingston was Greenfield's first teacher, driving a horse and buggy seven miles to the Arroyo Seco School. The famous valley wind blew so hard that the reins would form an arc from her hands to the horse's mouth. "When she'd get home she'd be so covered with layers of dust that we couldn't find mother." (Courtesy of Frances Johansen.)

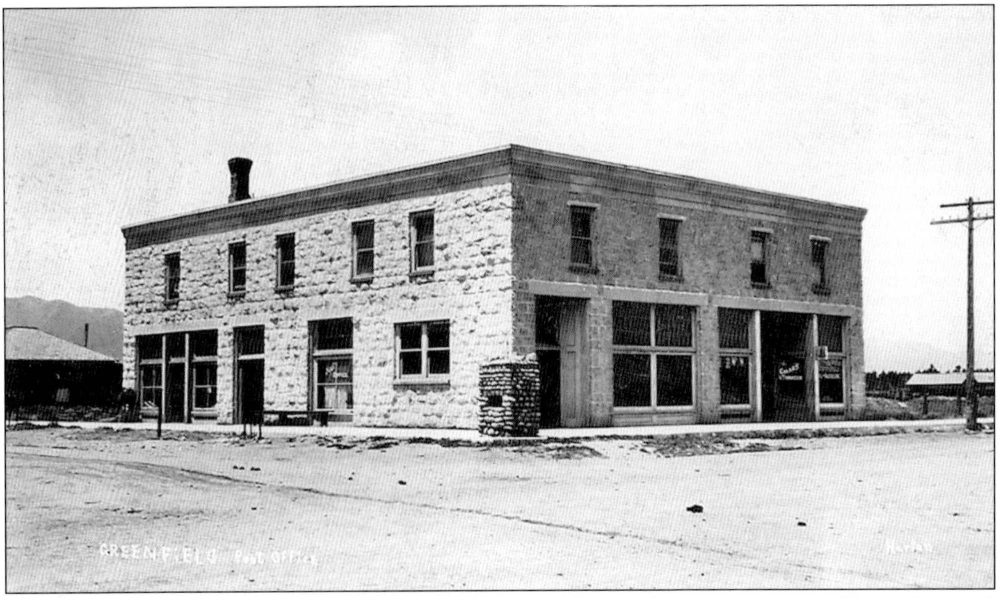

One of the first buildings to be constructed in Greenfield was this stone business block. Located on the north corner of Oak and Highway 101, it was built at a cost of $3,500. The structure housed the post office with Mildred Pickering as postmistress. A grocery store and hardware store occupied the ground floor while upstairs was a hall for community functions. During the 1930s, the stores were operated by the Rianda brothers, Buck, Beans, and Eddie. (Courtesy of Helen McDonald.)

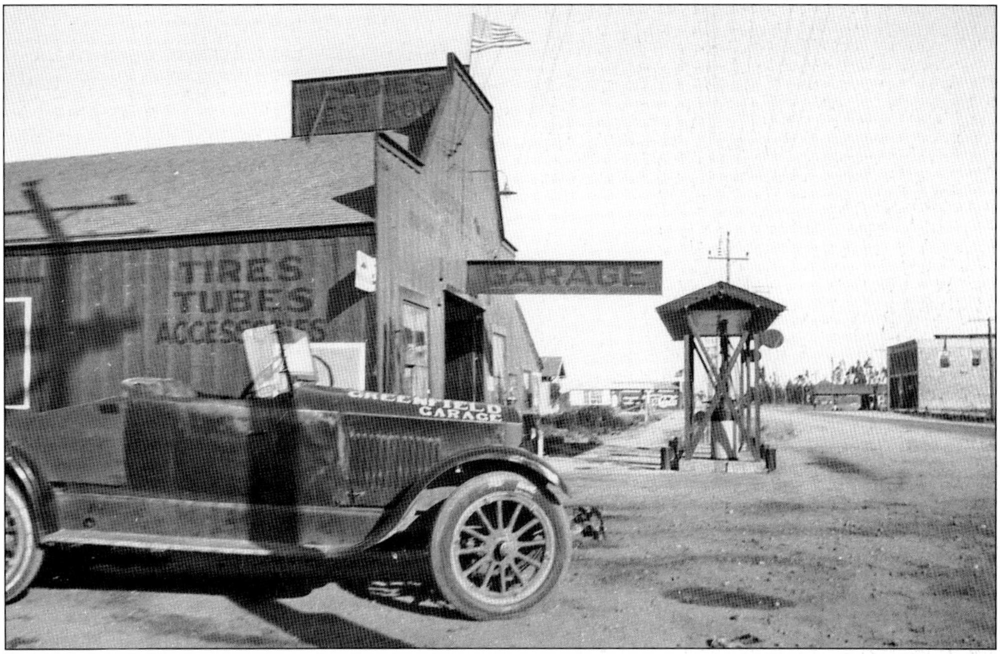

The Greenfield Garage was located on the south side of Palm Street. During the 1930s, it was owned by the Walker family. Helen McDonald remembers the handsome Walker boys, who owned an Austin car. As a prank, some kids silently carried it into the entry way of the Methodist church, forcing Sunday worshippers to exit out the back door. The garage was later owned by the Martin family and then Kenneth Benson. (Courtesy of Helen McDonald.)

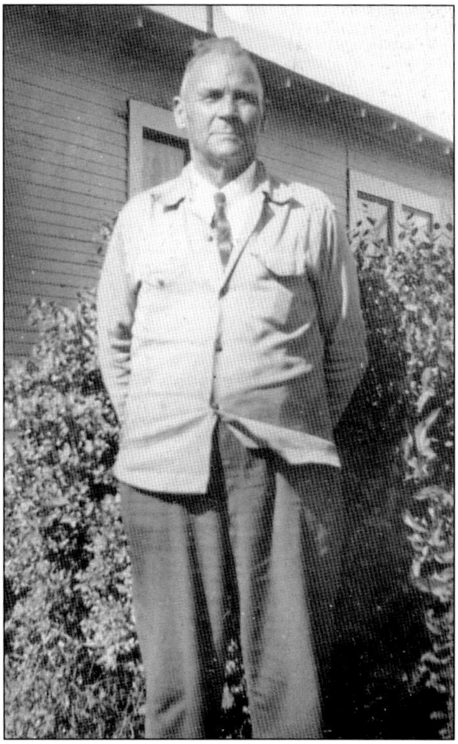

Greenfield's first mayor was Tom Rogers, known as a poet, philosopher, and community volunteer. Rogers moved his wife and six daughters to Greenfield in 1905. They came down the valley in a six-horse wagon. When the driver pulled up at a lone, run-down building, Tom asked why they were stopping. The driver answered, "This is Greenfield." Tom's daughter Frances Johansen still lives in King City. (Courtesy of Frances Johansen.)

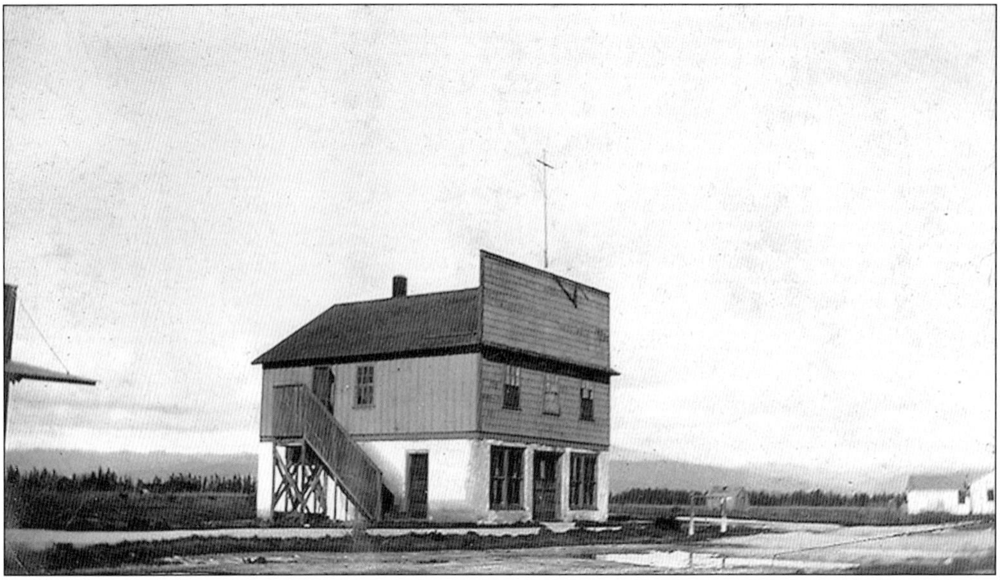

J. G. Yeoman and J. A. Brock from San Dimas built the Pettitt building for $3,000, one of Greenfield's first businesses. Mr. Yeoman operated a hardware store and lumberyard. Later the building served as a grocery. In 1916, Mr. and Mrs. William Page purchased the building and opened the Page Hotel. William Page was considered an excellent chef, and he offered delicious meals at the hotel. For several years, the Greenfield branch of the county library occupied a corner of the hotel's parlor. In 1944, Elmer Padgett bought the business, changing the name to Hotel Greenfield. (Courtesy of Helen McDonald.)

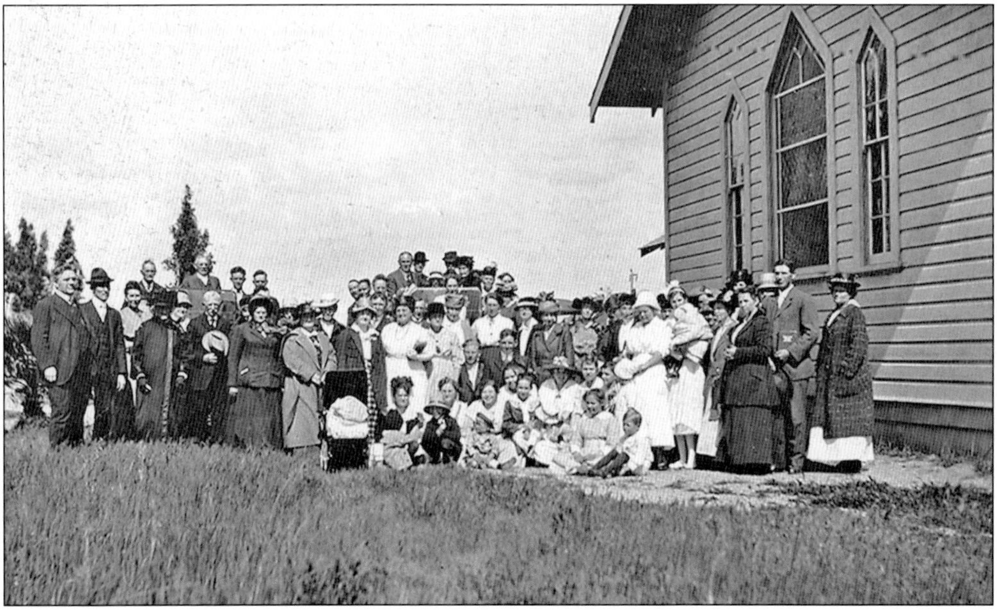

The congregation of the Greenfield United Methodist Church gathered for a trip to Monterey. Greenfield residents held church services in an old granary until they bought a closed church in Gonzales for a dollar. The building was dismantled board by board, loaded into buckboards, and hauled 20 miles south to Greenfield where it was reconstructed at Ninth and Palm Streets. (Courtesy of Helen McDonald.)

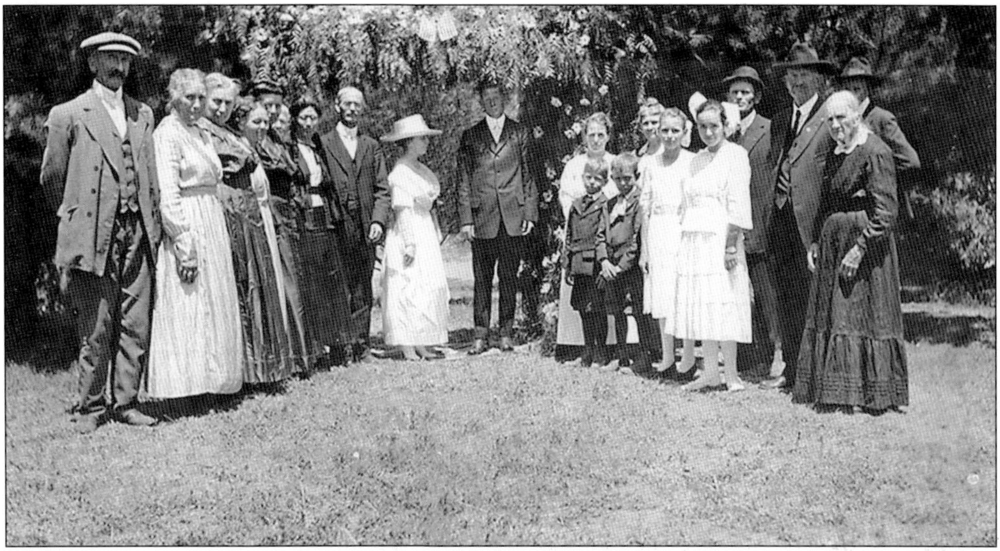

Elmer Courtney and Lena Eckert married in his family's garden in Greenfield. Elmer helped his father on their farm and later went on to raise hogs, manage the water company, and work at the prison. Helen McDonald has preserved Lena's elegant voile dress. (Courtesy of Helen McDonald.)

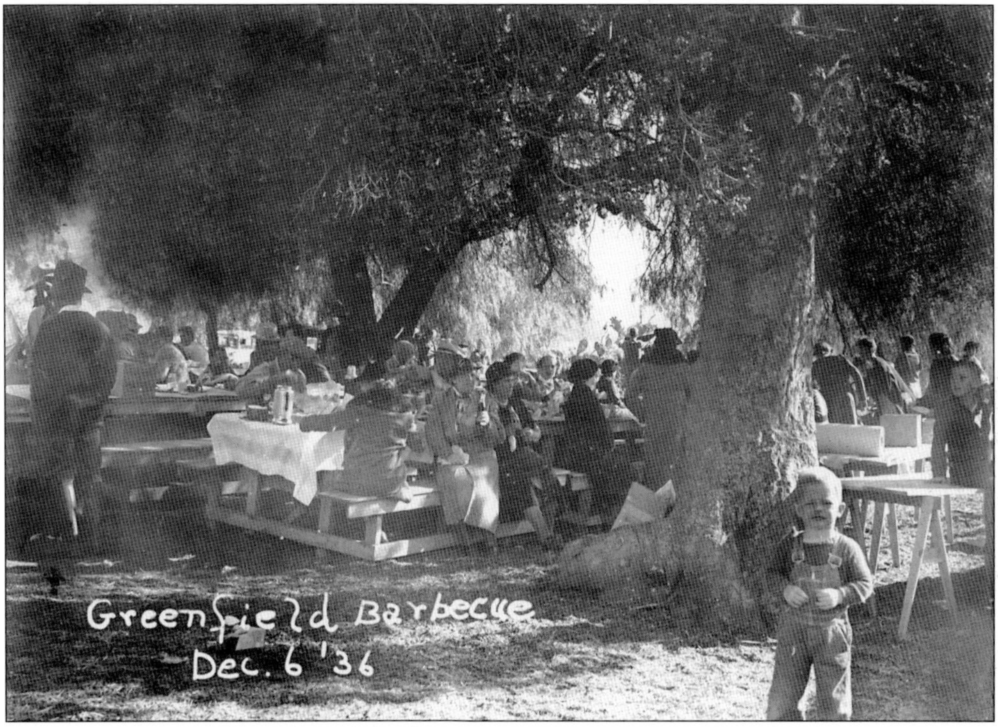

Residents of Greenfield celebrated the discovery of oil in Reliz Canyon with a festive picnic. The canyon was a favorite spot for picnics. In 1887, the *Salinas Weekly Index* described the canyon as a "Monterey Beauty Spot," writing "among the many little sheltered valleys and nooks that open into the Salinas, few present more attractions to the seeker after nature in her quiet moods than Reliz Canyon." (Courtesy of Frances Johansen.)

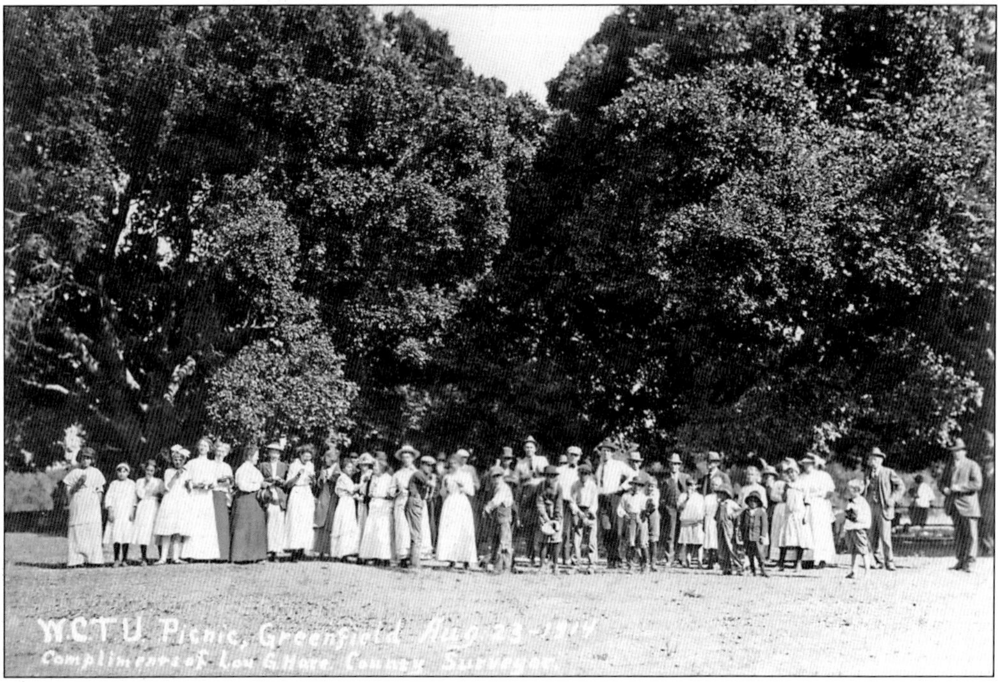

Greenfield's Oak Park has been a gathering place for local families and groups for many years. Here the Women's Christian Temperance Union gathered on August 23, 1914, for a picnic and baseball game. Land for the park was set aside in 1905 when Clark Colony was subdivided. It was maintained for many years by the water company. (Courtesy of Edward Whalen.)

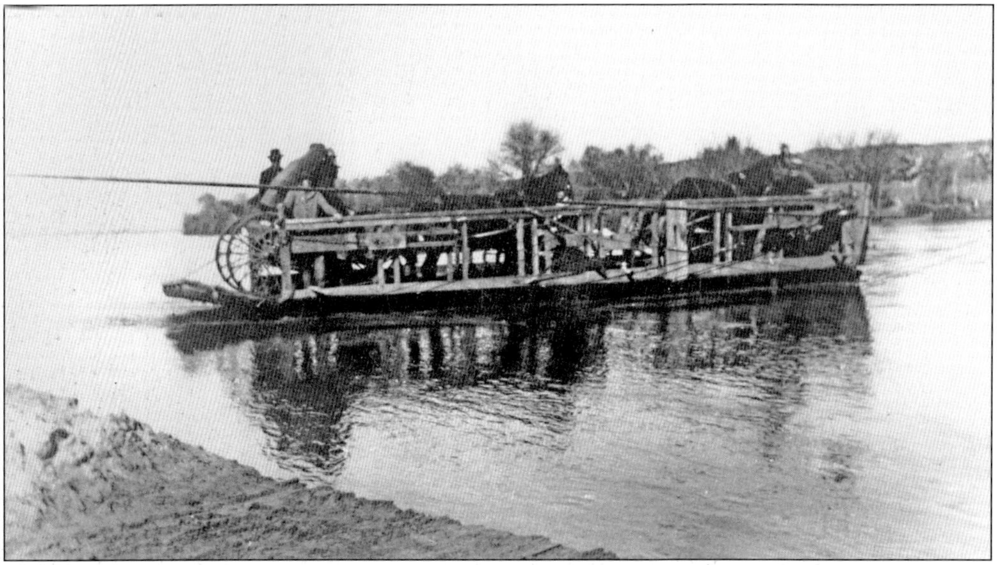

Joe Thorp and his brother-in-law Ben Inman were hired by the Monterey County Board of Supervisors to build and operate this ferry after flooding washed away the Salinas River Bridge near Greenfield. This photograph was taken on January 2, 1914, by Leslie Carson Sr. He and his wife, Myrtle, were using the ferry service to float box springs, a stove, a table, and dishes across the river to furnish their new home on the northeast corner of Third and Apple Streets in Clark Colony, today known as Greenfield.

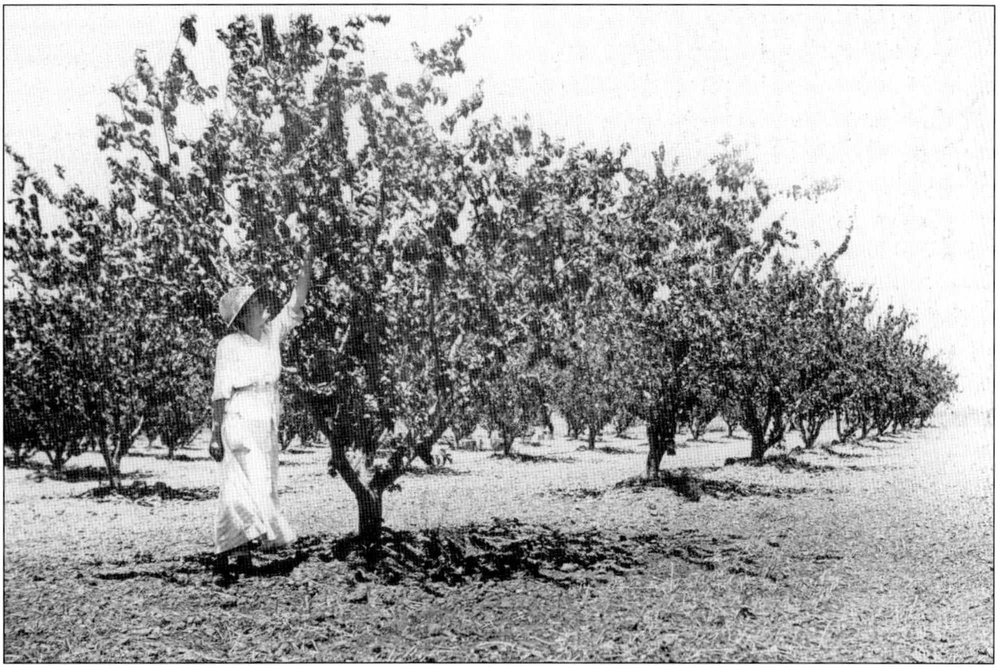

Beginning in the 1920s, many Greenfield farmers began planting fruit and nut trees. To shield their orchards from strong Salinas Valley winds, they planted wind breaks of eucalyptus trees at intervals of 800 feet. Many of these wind breaks can still be seen today. Apricots, almonds, and walnuts did particularly well. Here a young lady reaches for an apricot in the Whitney orchard near Greenfield.

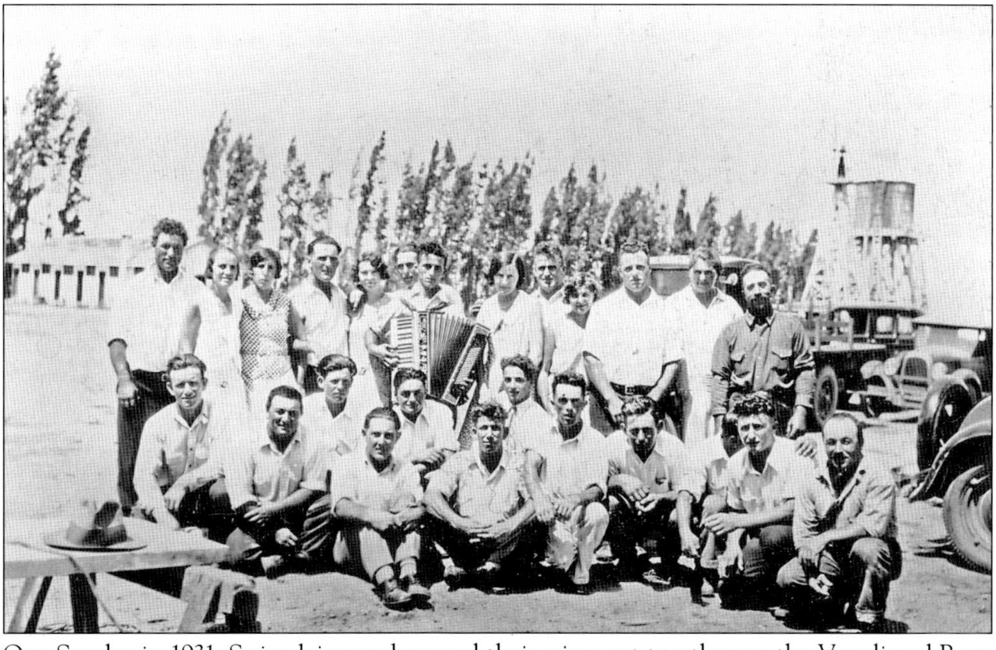

One Sunday in 1931, Swiss dairy workers and their wives got together on the Vanoli and Rava Dairy in Greenfield to enjoy good food and accordion music. Pictured, in the second row to the right, are Mr. and Mrs. Jim Vanoli and Mr. and Mrs. Dasanti.

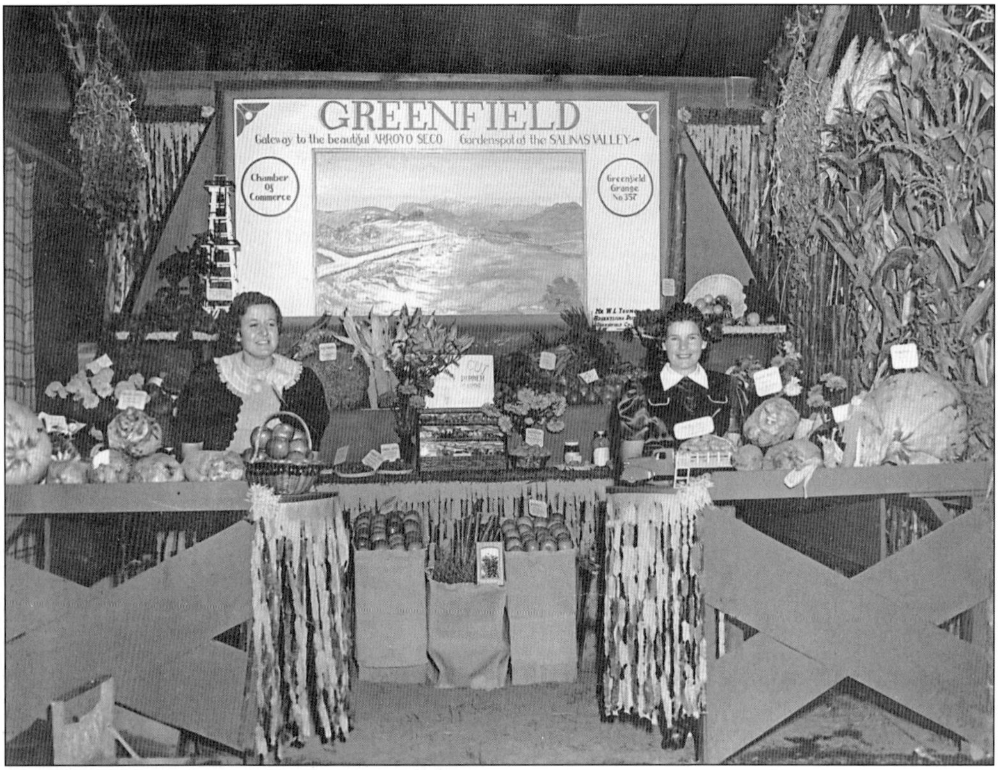

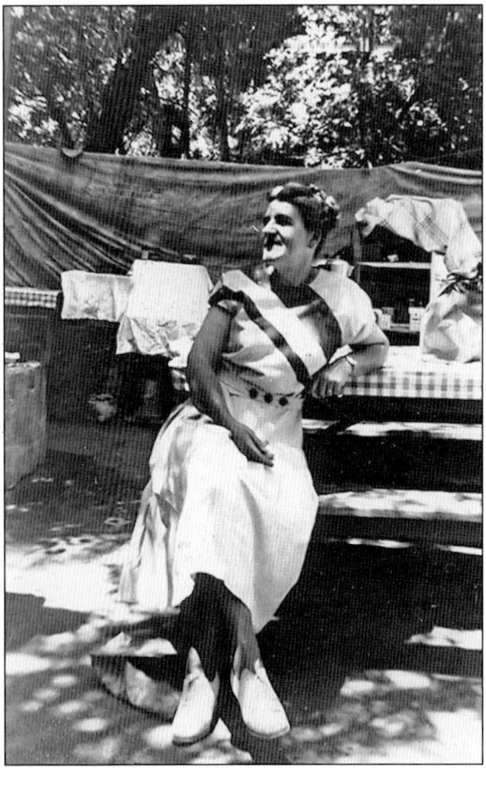

Greenfield's bountiful harvest is exhibited by the Greenfield Grange and Chamber of Commerce. The 1915 *King City Rustler* boasted that the community had "hundreds of acres of alfalfa with dairies and cheese factories, orchards loaded with delicious fruits, groves and alignments of stately gums, fragrant acacias and flower gardens on every hand; wind-mills in all directions spreading their white sails to the wind." Tom Roger's daughter Bernadine is seated on the right. (Courtesy of Frances Johansen.)

Six-year-old Ethel Page arrived in Greenfield in 1905 with her parents, William and Lillian Page. They traveled to the former Clark City in a wagon pulled by a horse named Midget. Ethel later married Cecil Page and set up housekeeping in a home on Peach Avenue. Helen McDonald remembers, "Ethel's soft speaking voice, her politeness, her happy attitude spilled out onto others . . . her braided dark thick hair, piled over the top of her head in a head band fashion." (Courtesy of Helen McDonald.)

Six

King City

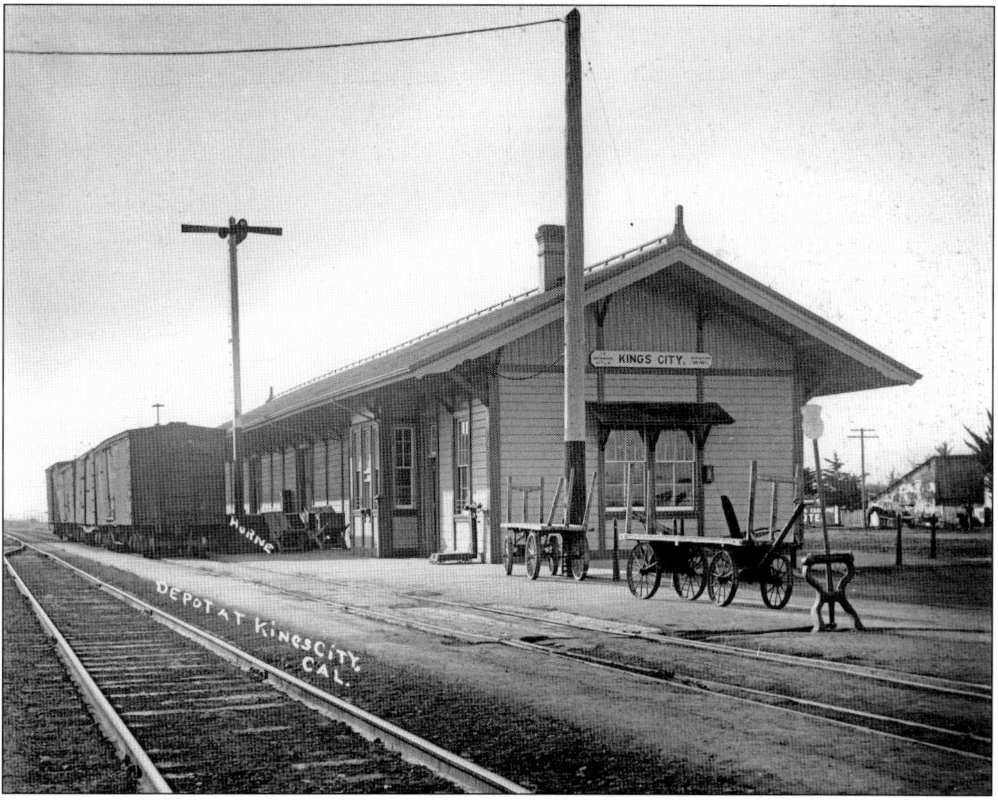

Soledad was the southernmost terminus of the Southern Pacific Railroad until 1872. Charles King's successful wheat crop attracted the attention of his old friend, railroad magnate Collis P. Huntington. Before long, 1,500 Chinese laborers started to lay track toward the King Ranch. King allowed the Southern Pacific to cut straight across his ranch with only one condition, "protect my cattle." Today the line runs eight straight miles over the old King ranch lands. On Saturday, July 3, 1886, the first locomotive rolled past King's ranch buildings, and King's Station was born. Soon after, this depot was constructed.

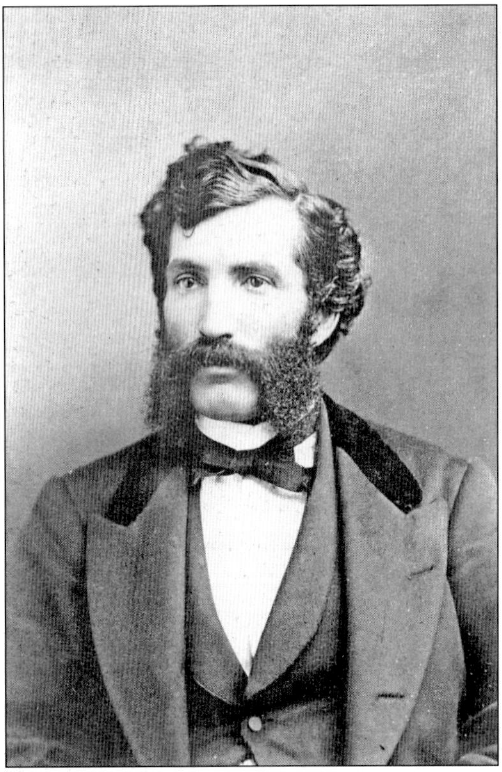

Charles H. King came west to California in the 1850s. After trying different occupations, including teaching, he became involved in the lumber business. By 1880, financial success enabled him to move to Oakland. In 1884, King purchased 13,000 acres of the Rancho San Lorenzo for $50,000 and began to cultivate wheat. Two years later, the Southern Pacific Railroad crossed his land and King's Station was born. This photograph was taken in Eureka in 1872 when King was buying and selling parcels of redwood timber.

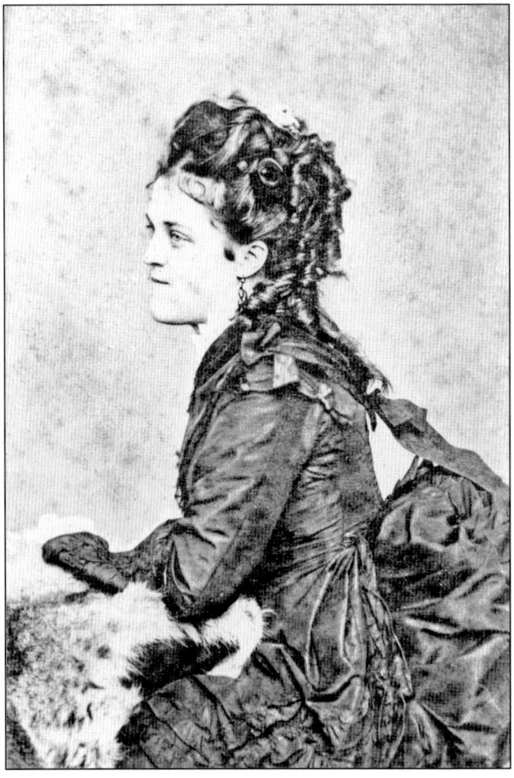

Charles King, founder of King City, married Katherine Brown in San Francisco on September 16, 1875. This photograph of Katherine was taken in 1873 when she worked as a teacher in a school, then called a seminary, operated by her family in Yreka. Her niece Pearl also taught at the school and later became King City's first teacher.

Charles H. King and Ling, the cook, stuff a turkey for Thanksgiving.

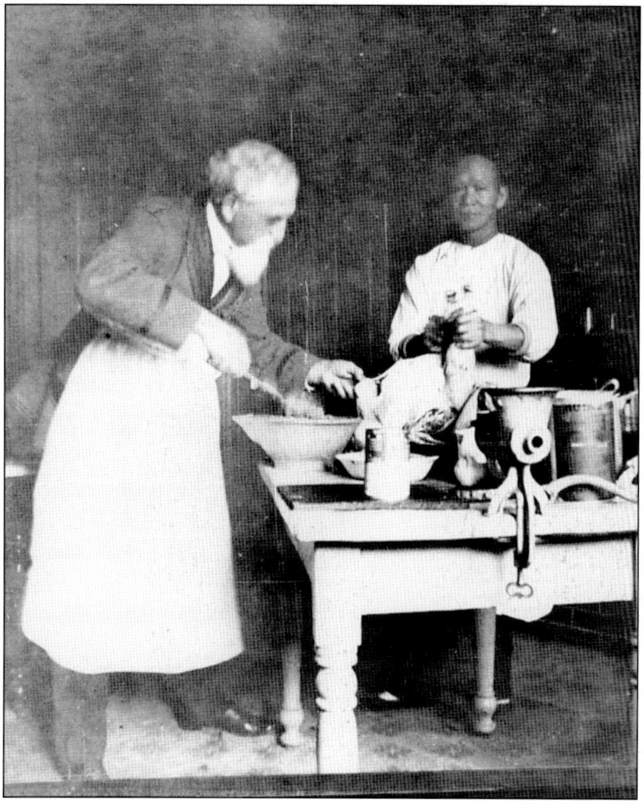

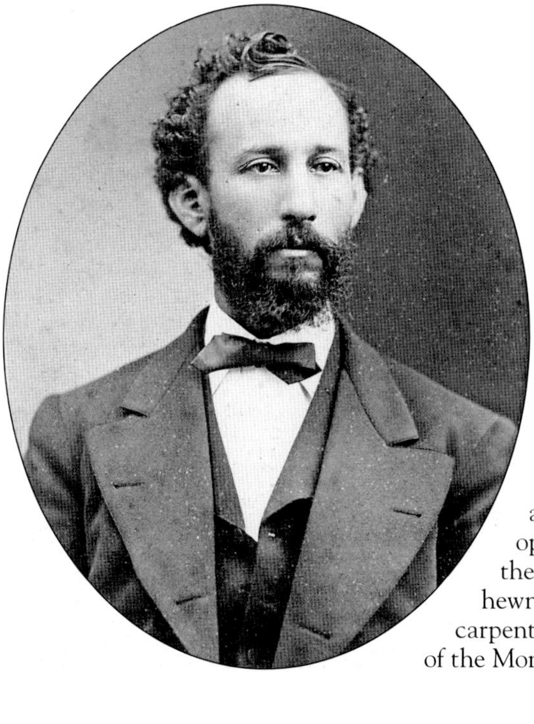

King City was barely surveyed when William Vanderhurst arrived in town with seven railroad cars of lumber to build the town's first store on Third and Broadway. Vanderhurst, a partner of the successful Vanderhurst, Sanborn, and Porter mercantile firm, never let an opportunity pass by. He also opened one of the first stores in Salinas in 1868. A rough-hewn hotel, the Buster was erected to house carpenters building the new store. (Courtesy of the Monterey County Historical Society.)

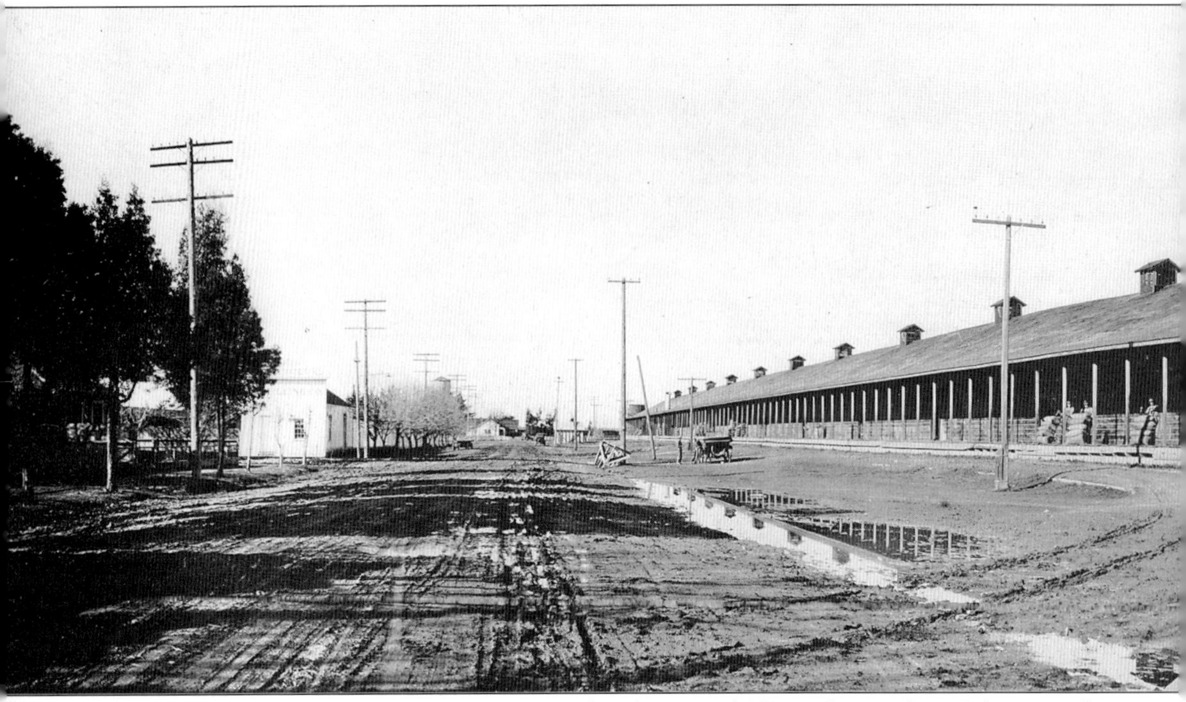

The Southern Pacific Milling Company owned and operated 25 warehouses from Salinas south to Santa Paula. In King City, J. Ernst Steinbeck, John Steinbeck's father and one of King City's first residents, served as agent and bookkeeper for many years. Local farmers brought their grain

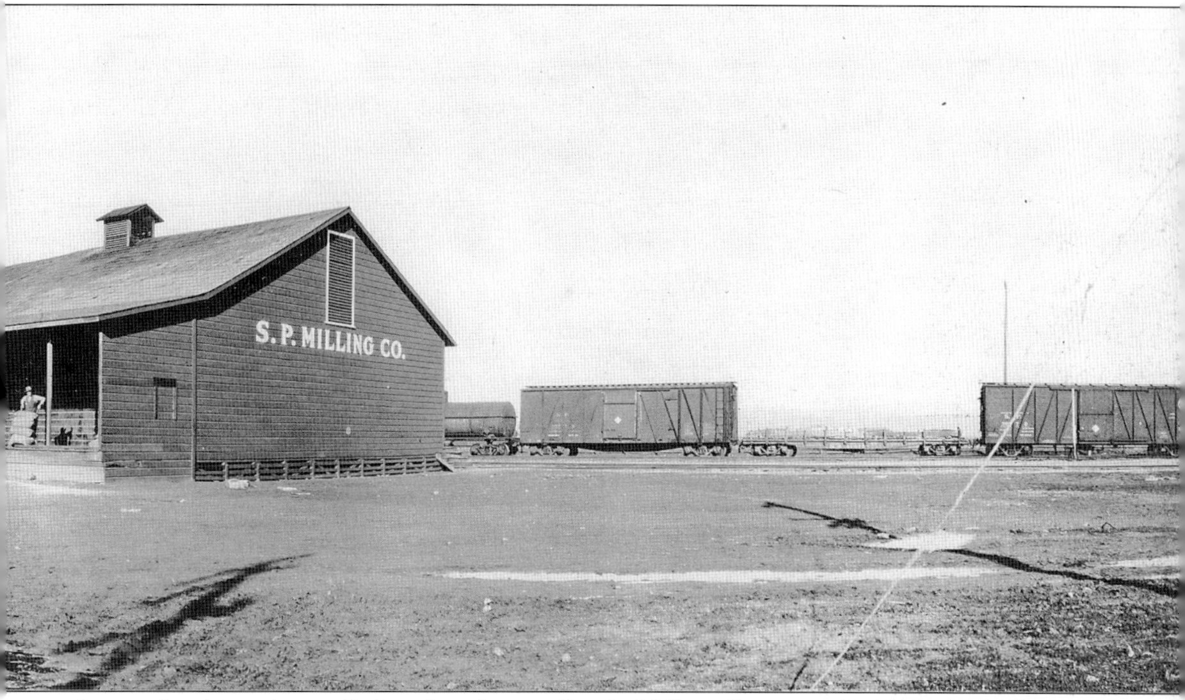

here to be shipped or milled at the adjacent Pacific Milling Company. By 1888, the Mill was producing 150 barrels of flour a day. By 1915, King City shipped 1,500 tons of wheat and 6,000 tons of barley annually.

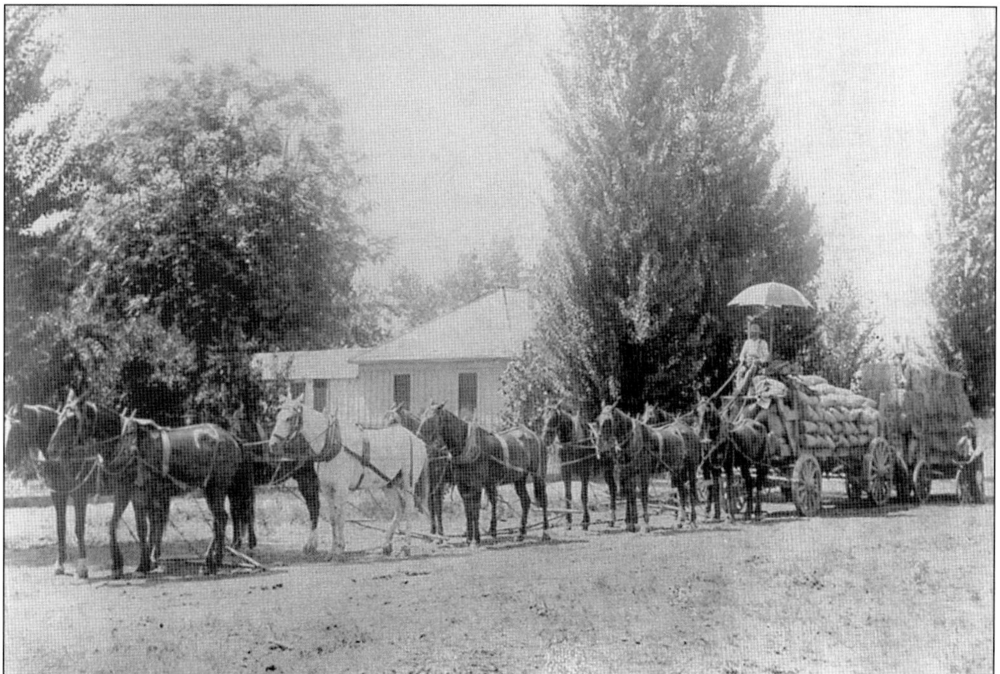

A 10-horse team sets out for the long, hot drive to the Southern Pacific Milling Station. The driver is well prepared with a shade umbrella. (Courtesy of Pat Hathaway, California Views.)

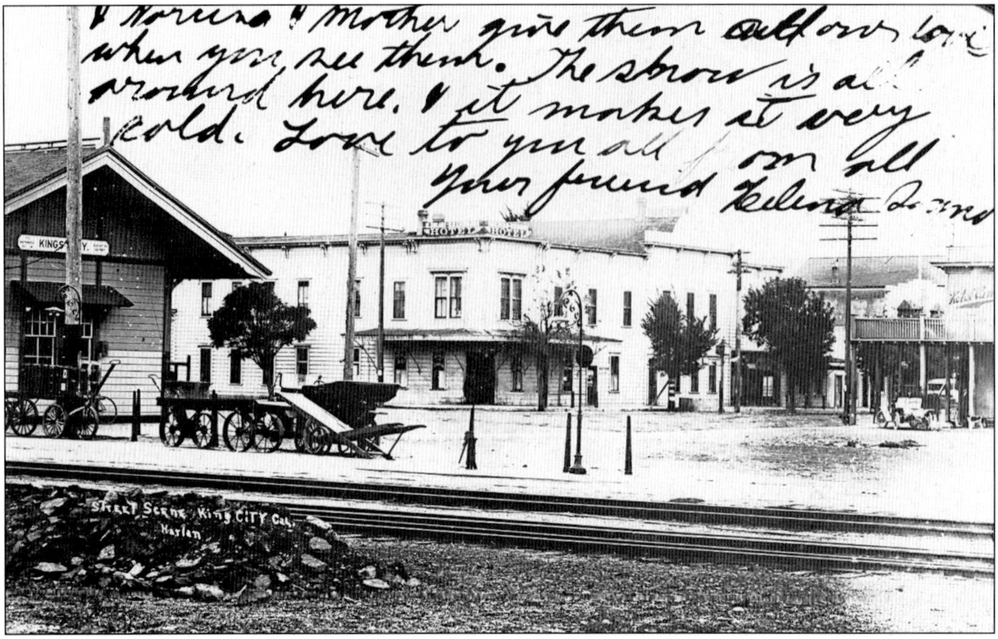

King City's Railroad Exchange Hotel (in the center of the photograph) was built in 1888 by W. F. Schroeder. It was advertised as "strictly first class and its table is not to be excelled and its terms are most liberal." They advertised French-, German-, and American-style cooking, a billiard hall, and sample rooms for commercial travelers. Across the street was the Hotel Camino Real, known for its popular bar and restaurant. (Courtesy of Monterey County Historical Society.)

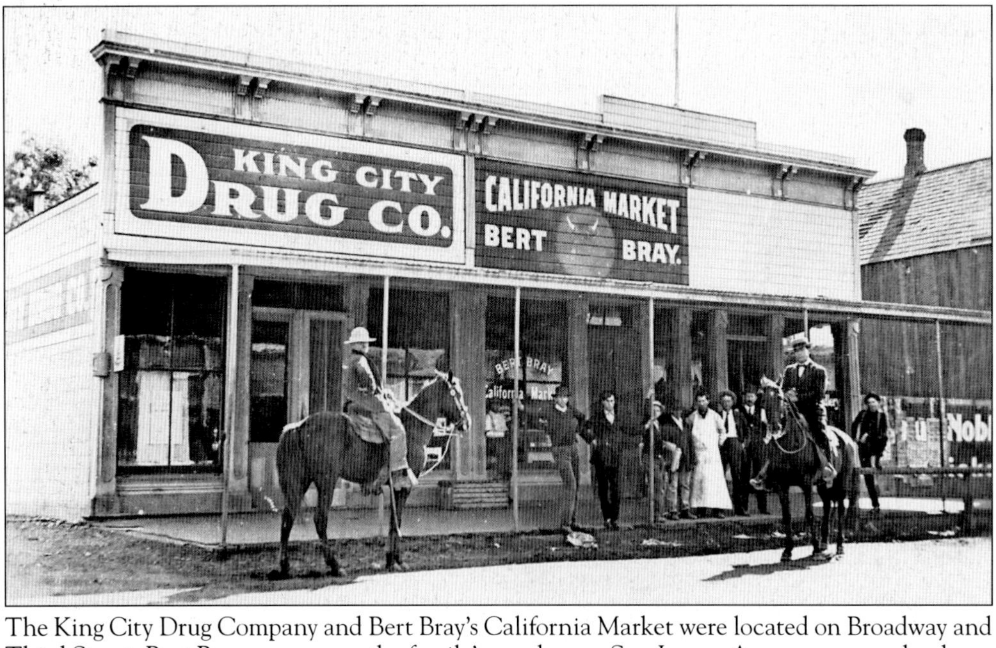

The King City Drug Company and Bert Bray's California Market were located on Broadway and Third Street. Bert Bray grew up on the family's ranch near San Lucas. As a young man he drove a team for the Spreckels Sugar Company. He later bought the California Market, a butcher shop. (Courtesy of the Monterey County Historical Society.)

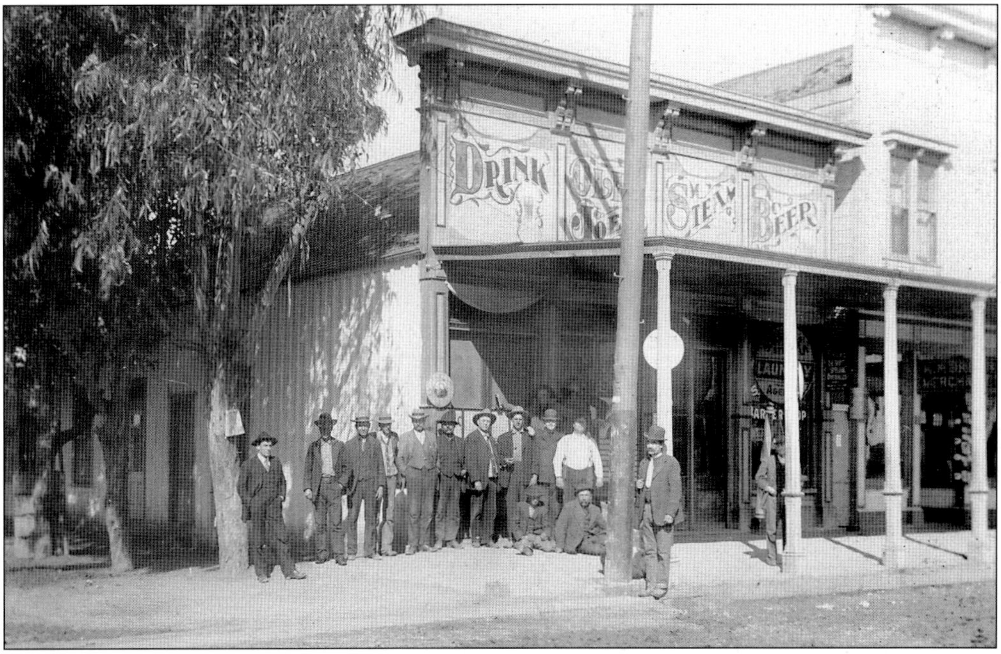

In 1909, patrons of one of King City's 14 saloons pose for a photograph. King City's population had grown to 500 people by 1909. Most businesses lined Broadway, described by the *King City Rustler* newspaper as "a mud-hole in the rainy season and from which arose a stifling cloud of dust in the summertime."

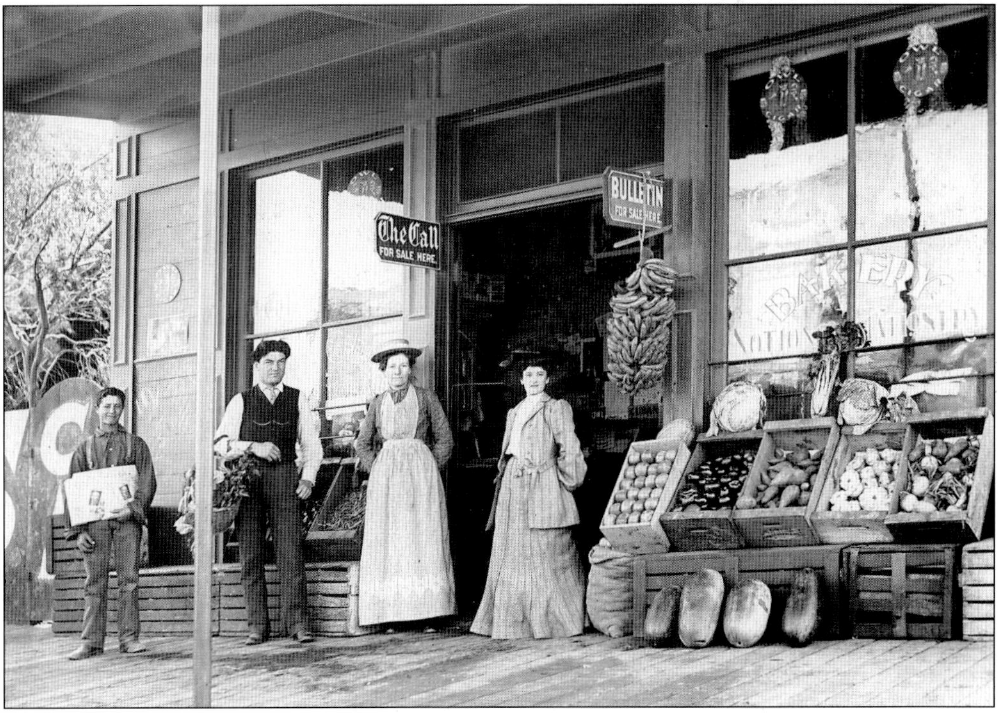

Kiko Brunetti (holding the basket) stands in front of his general store with his sister (wearing an apron), a well-dressed customer, and a paperboy. Locally grown produce is featured for sale.

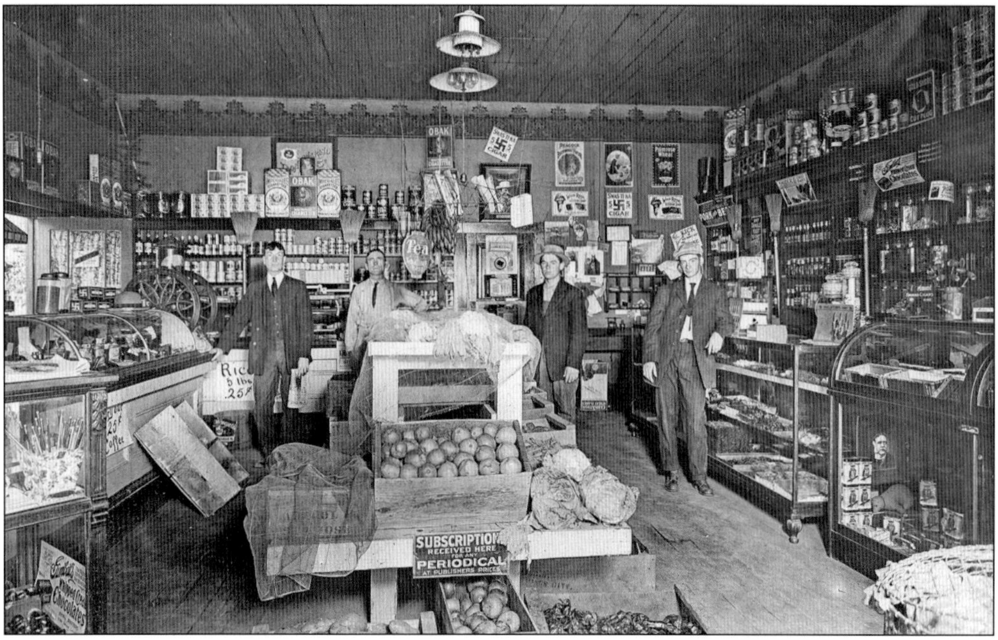

Like all general stores, the Brunetti store in King City was everything to all people. Its stock accommodated the special needs of the town, from a spool of thread to a keg of nails. The store was a gathering place to exchange gossip, catch up on political news, and arrange social gatherings

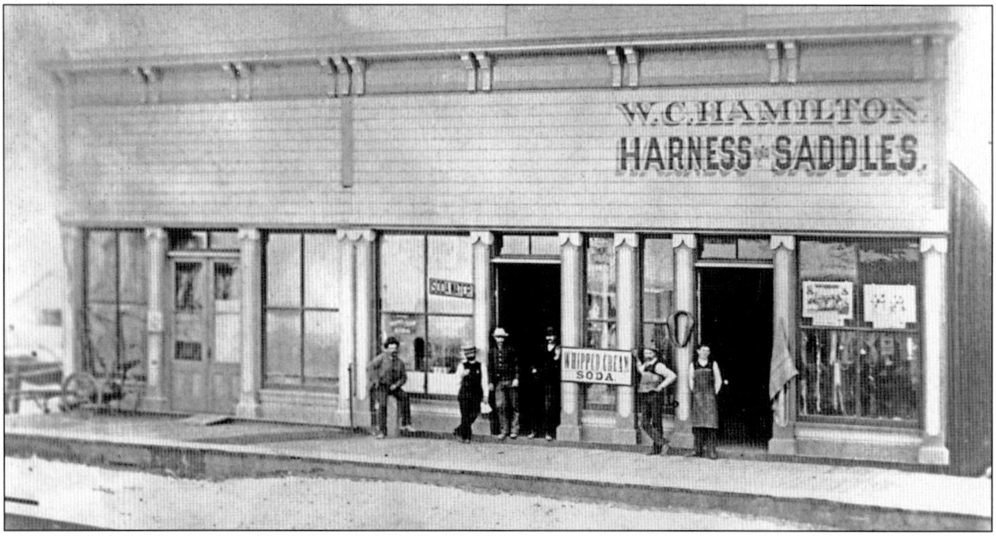

William C. Hamilton, John Steinbeck's uncle and a prominent figure in the book *East of Eden*, arrived in King City from Iowa in 1886. His harness and saddle shop was one of the first businesses opened in town. He also served as a judge, city trustee, and justice of the peace. On March 6, 1889, Hamilton married Birdie King, niece of town founder Charles H. King. Their marriage is said to be the first in King City.

Located just one block from the train depot, on the corner of Second Street and Broadway, the French Hotel and Restaurant started to cater to King City visitors in the 1890s. Manager Fannie Brunetti advertised good clean rooms, reasonable prices, and home cooking.

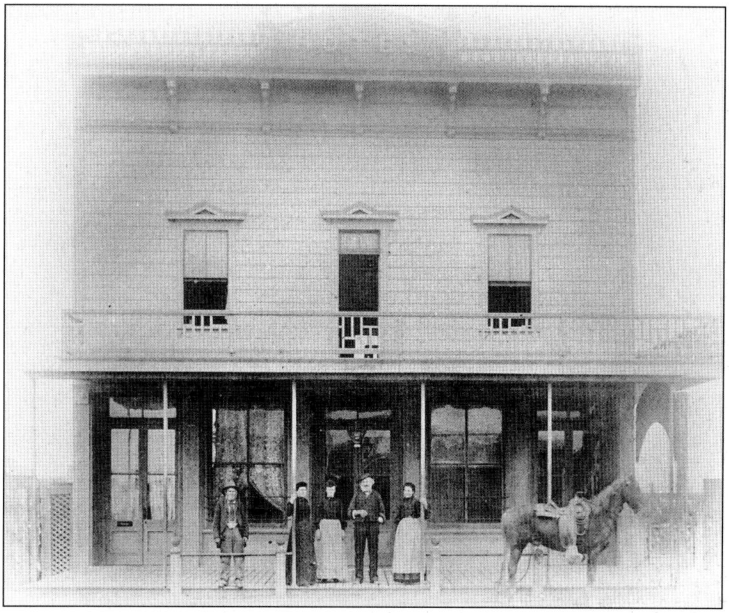

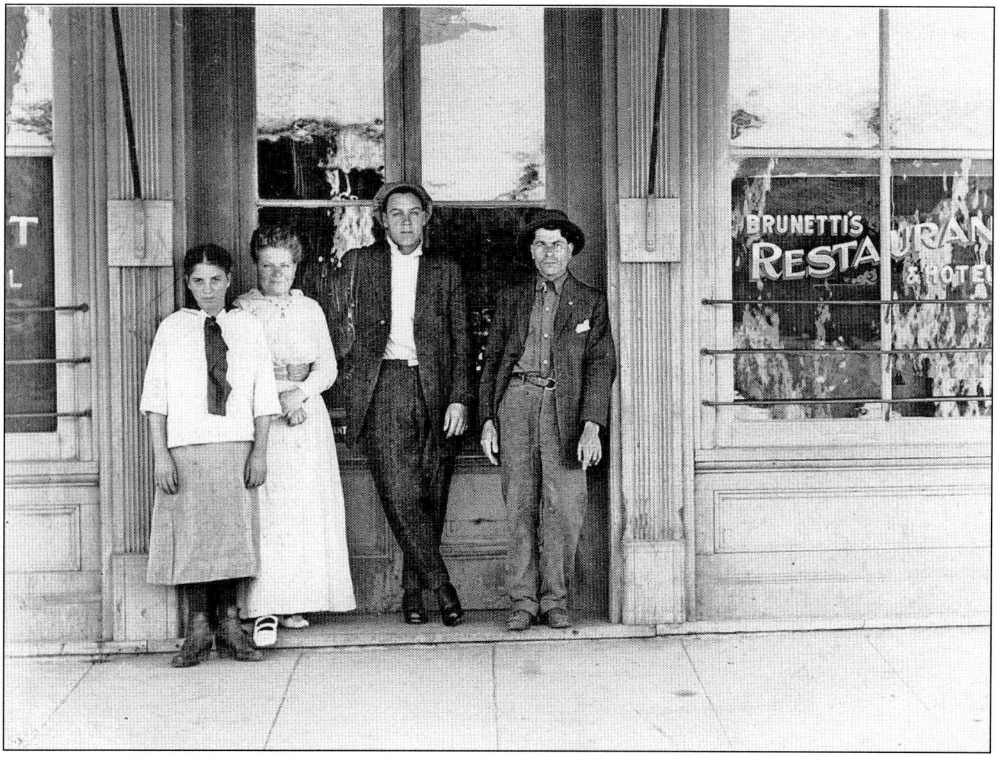

From left to right, Agafita Ortiz, Fannie Brunetti, Antonio Nunez, and Mateo Anduga stand in front of the Brunetti hotel and restaurant in 1915. Known as the French Hotel and Restaurant, the hostelry was one of two businesses operated by the enterprising Brunetti family, early King City settlers.

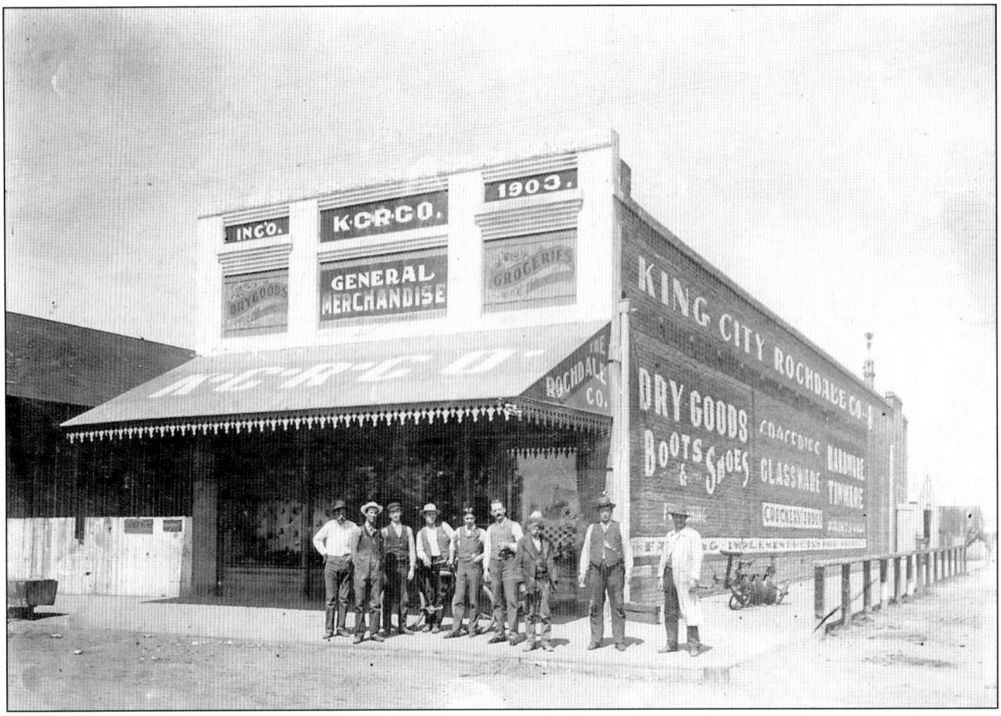

The King City Rochdale Company was constructed for Meacham, Cooper, Ubrey, and Company in 1889. Pictured in 1903, the store was located at Second Street and Broadway.

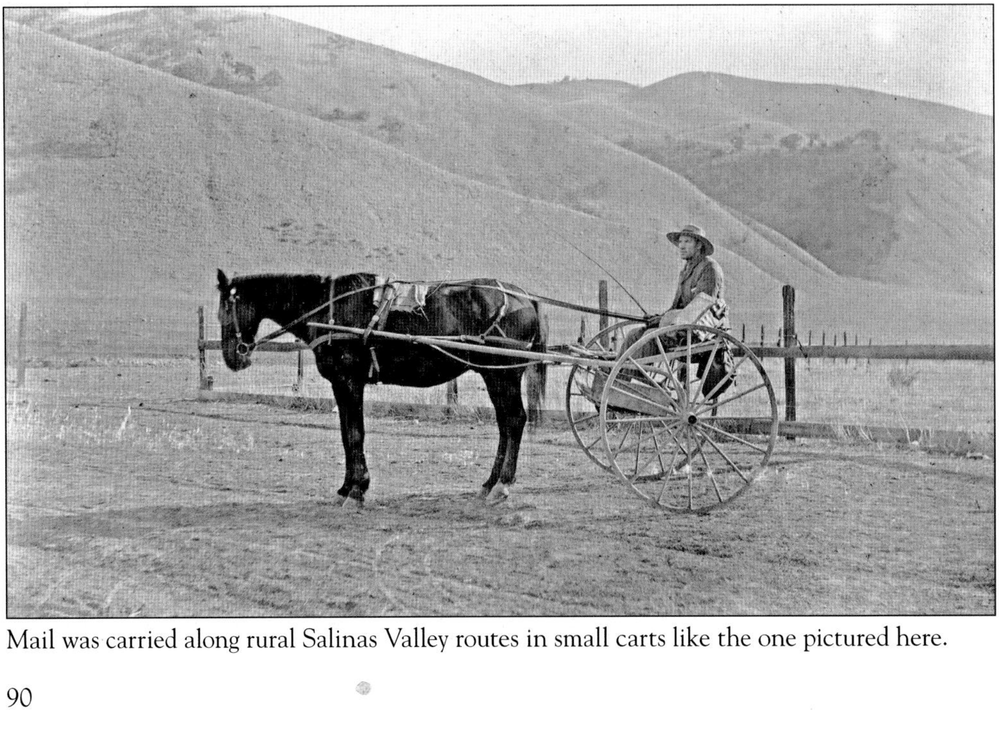
Mail was carried along rural Salinas Valley routes in small carts like the one pictured here.

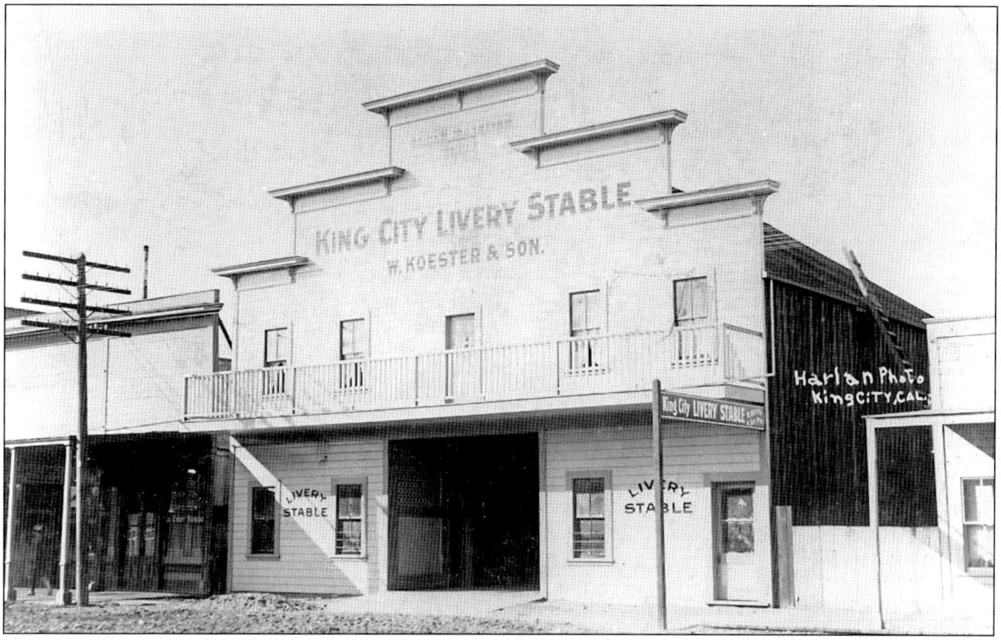

The King City Livery Stable, owned by William Koester, is pictured about 1910. The Koesters also operated a wine, liquor, and cigar store.

J. W. Bennett operated this barbershop on the north side of Broadway in King City in 1901. Two earlier barber shops were owned by Gus Burchard and T. J. Himmah. To increase business, one doubled as a saloon while the other sold produce on the side. By 1915, King City had grown, engendering praise from the *Salinas Daily Journal* that wrote, "The first impression one gets of King City is most favorable. Here are broad streets lined with substantial buildings and a spirit of progress pervades the little town, which has more than doubled its population within three years."

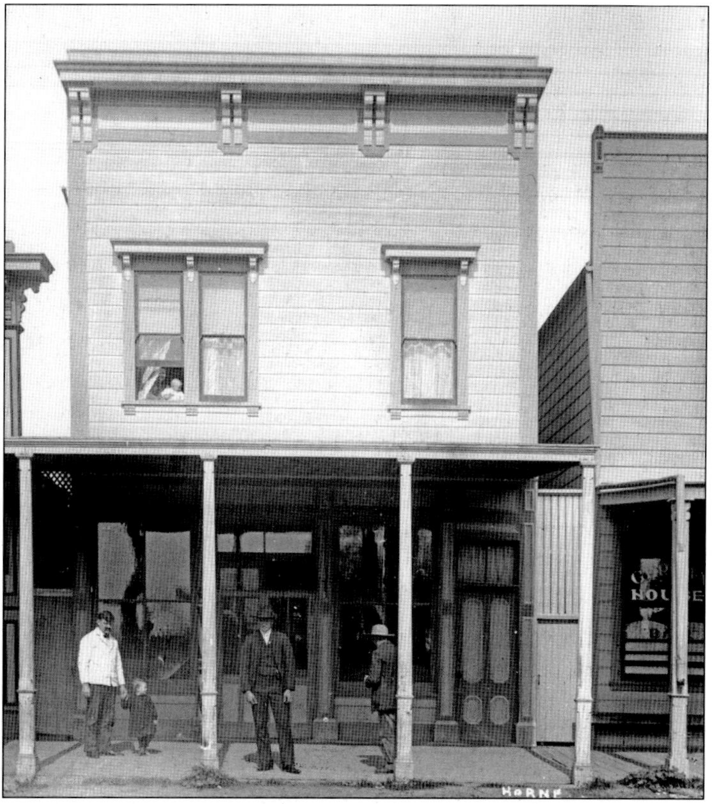

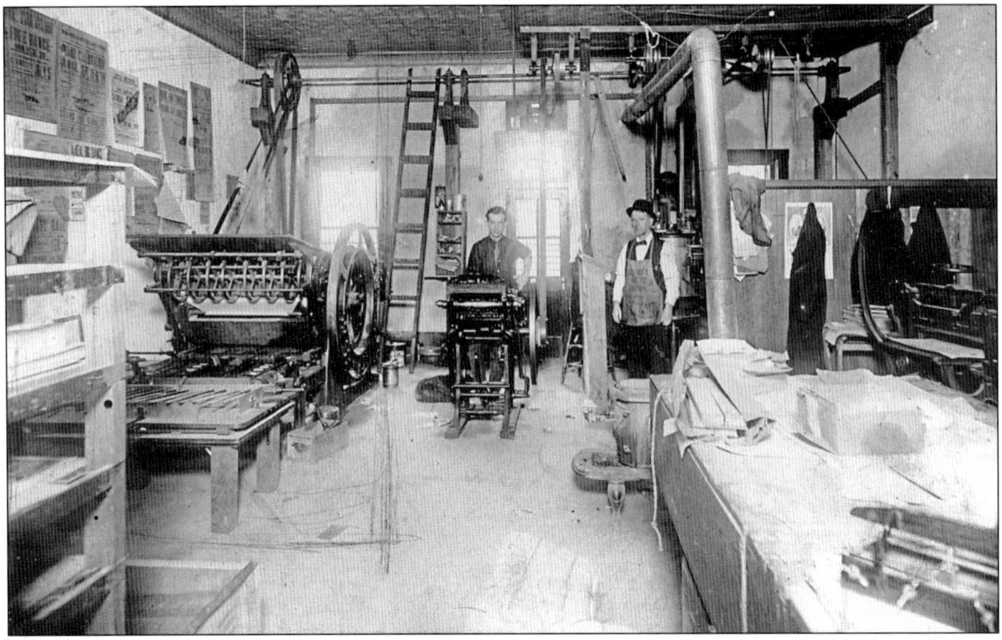

Frederick Godfrey Vivian (with derby hat) and Joe Bastido are pictured in the shop of the *King City Rustler* newspaper. At the turn of the 19th century, Vivian rode his bicycle down the length of the Salinas Valley, searching for a promising community to start his newspaper. In 1901, he settled on King City, opening his printing business on the southeast corner of Second and Lynn Streets.

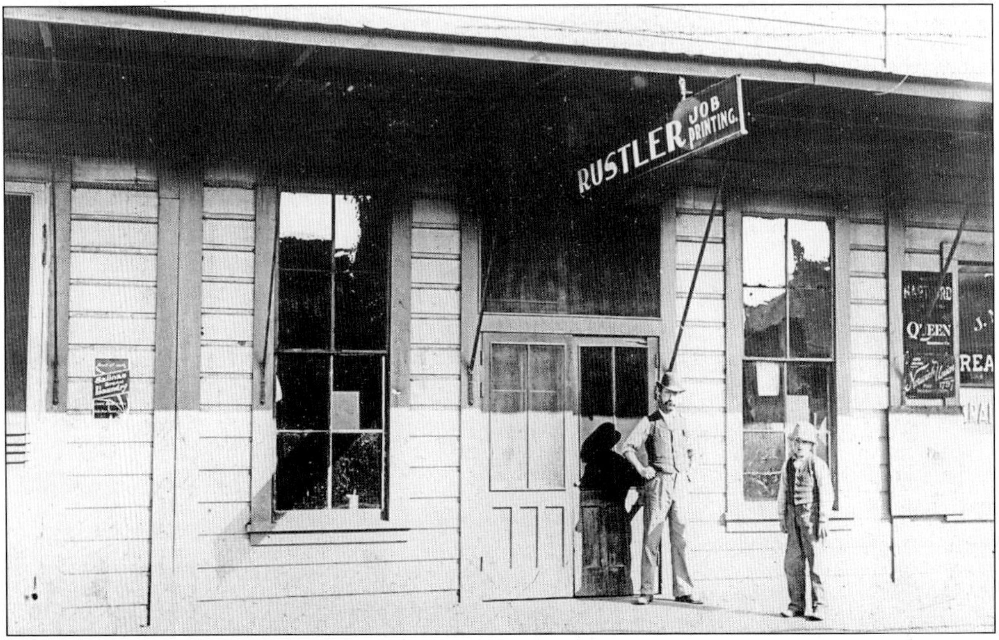

When Frederick Vivian started the *King City Rustler*, his assets were limited to one silver dollar and $450 worth of old printing equipment. The *Salinas Index* sneered at "the optimism of a young fellow named Vivian in starting a paper in King City—a hamlet of 150 half-starved souls." Vivian is pictured in front of his printing office.

Fred Vivian founded the *King City Rustler* at the turn of the 19th century and the newspaper is still in production today. Here in the early 1950s, printers in the back shop work on the "stone," making up the page forms in the "chases." The type was hot metal, moveable with some handset letters, but most was machine cast on the linotype. Phil Garcia, then an apprentice, is pictured in the foreground. He continued to work as a pressman for 40 years.

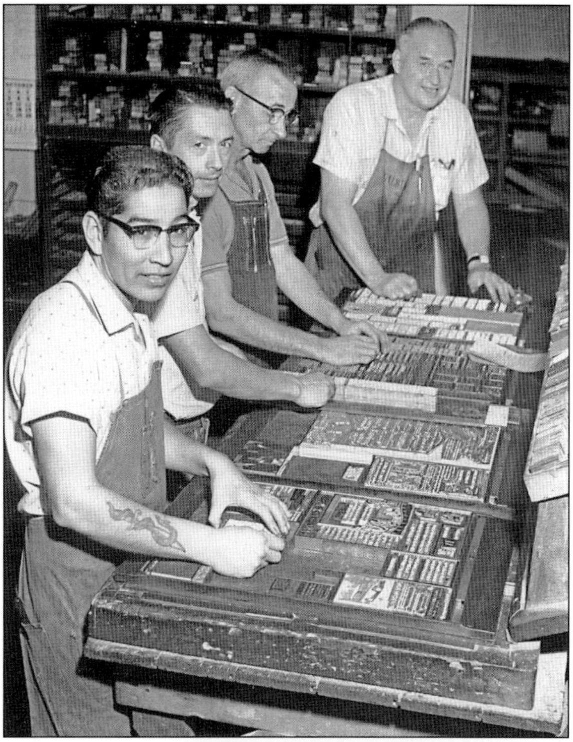

King City High School welcomed the first freshman class in 1914. Only six years later it boasted a well-developed sports program, including football, baseball, and the girls basketball team pictured here.

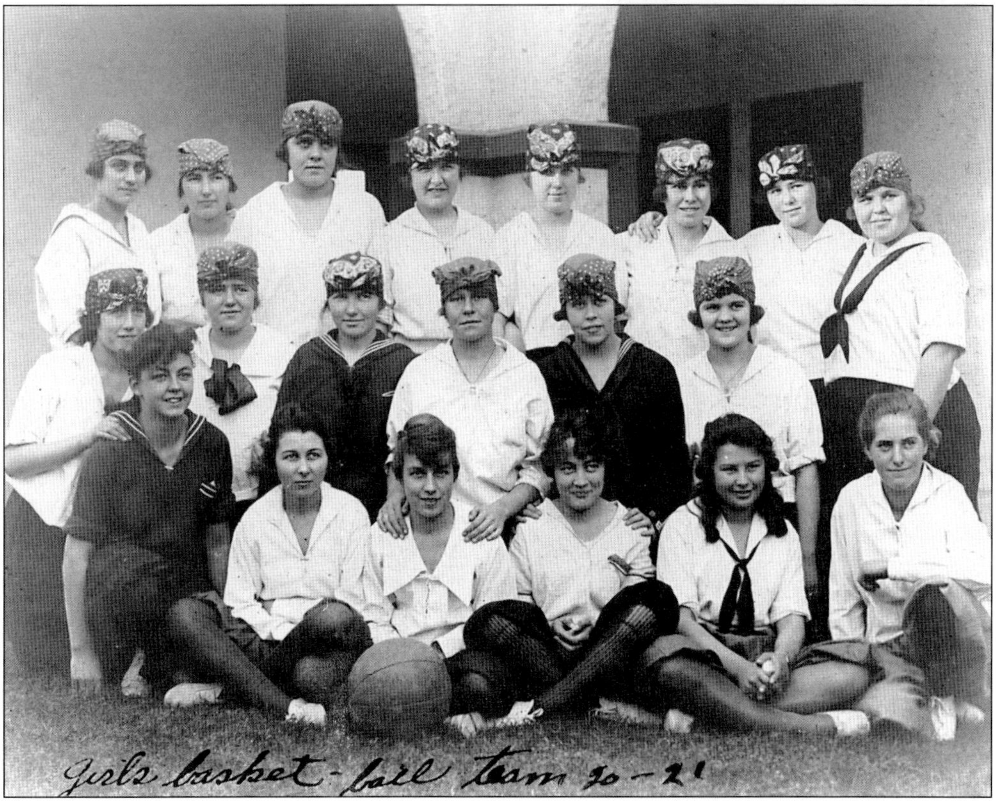

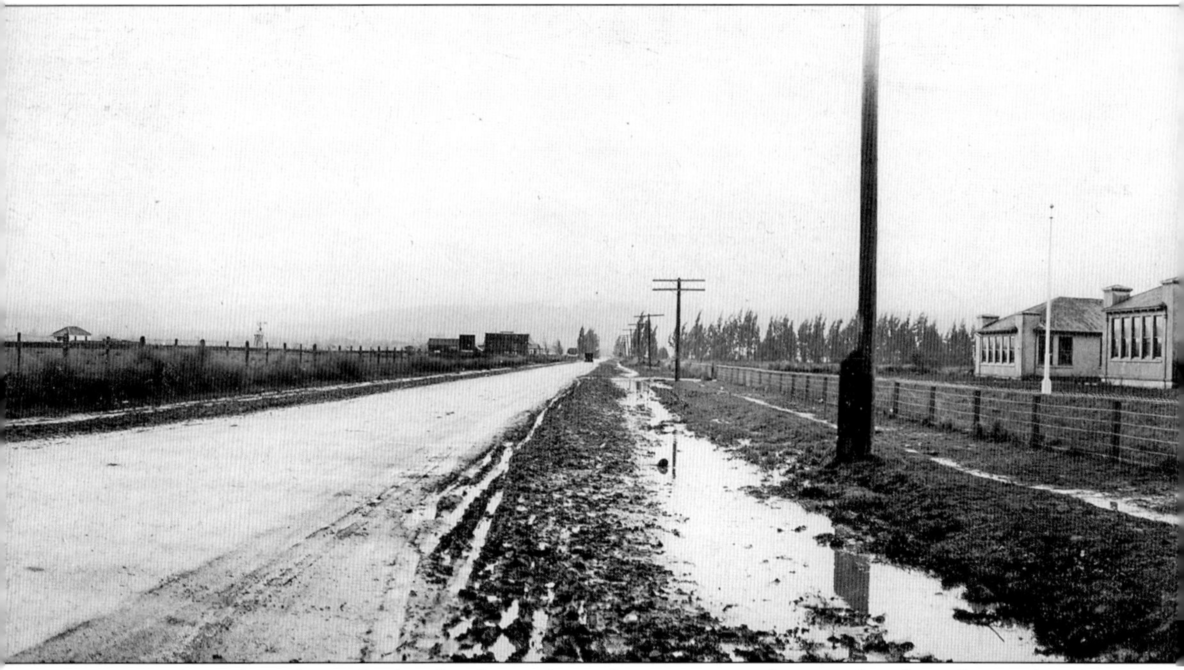

King City's brand-new high school stands ready to open its doors to local students. A 1920 chamber of commerce brochure described the school as having an "unusually broad curriculum, artistically landscaped campus and good athletic facilities. The school operates free buses, thus

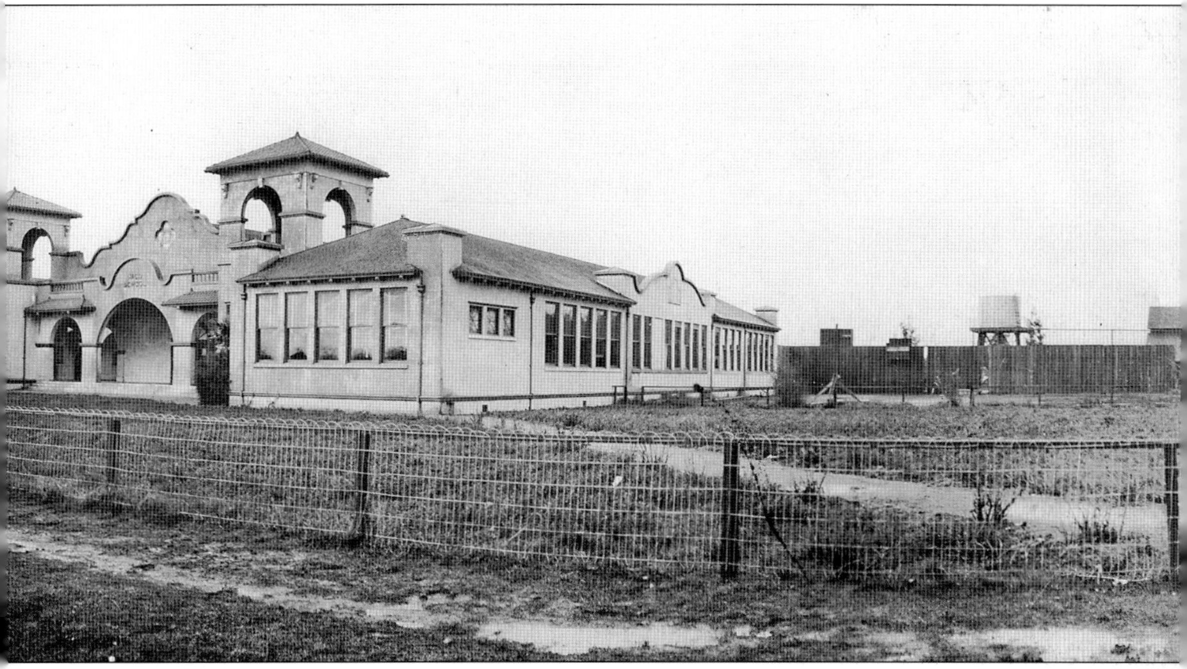

giving farm boys and girls equal privileges with town pupils in all the advantages of education that King City offers, both in training for vocation or for college entrance."

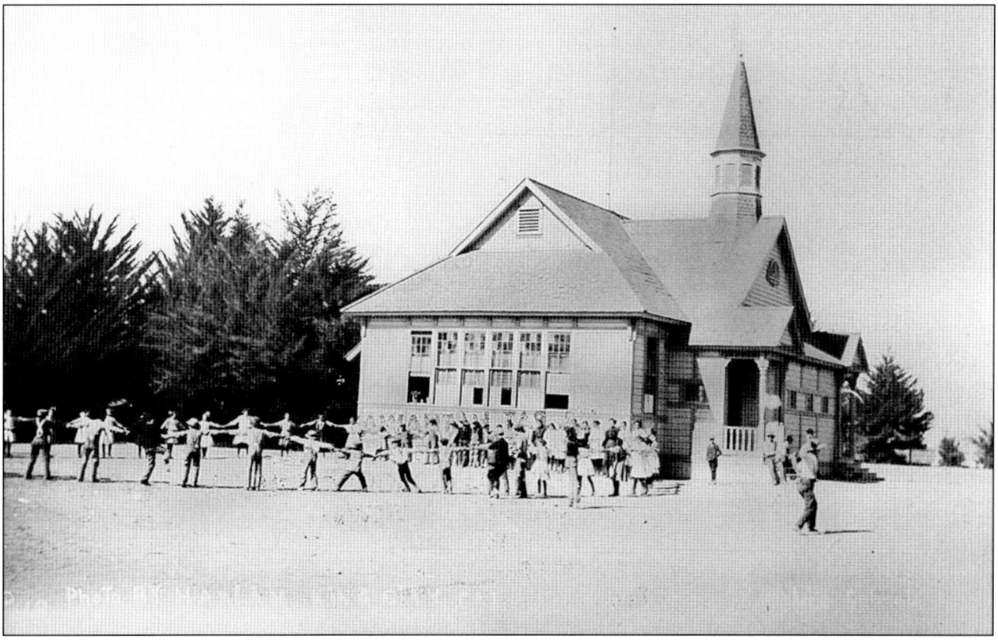

King City's first grammar school is pictured in 1890. Built in 1888, the *Salinas Index* reported that "public enterprise can be used to no better advantage than in providing suitable buildings for the education of the young. The building when complete and furnished will cost over $2500." This building was later used as city hall, then for Boy Scout meetings, and was finally demolished. (Courtesy of Pat Hathaway, California Views.)

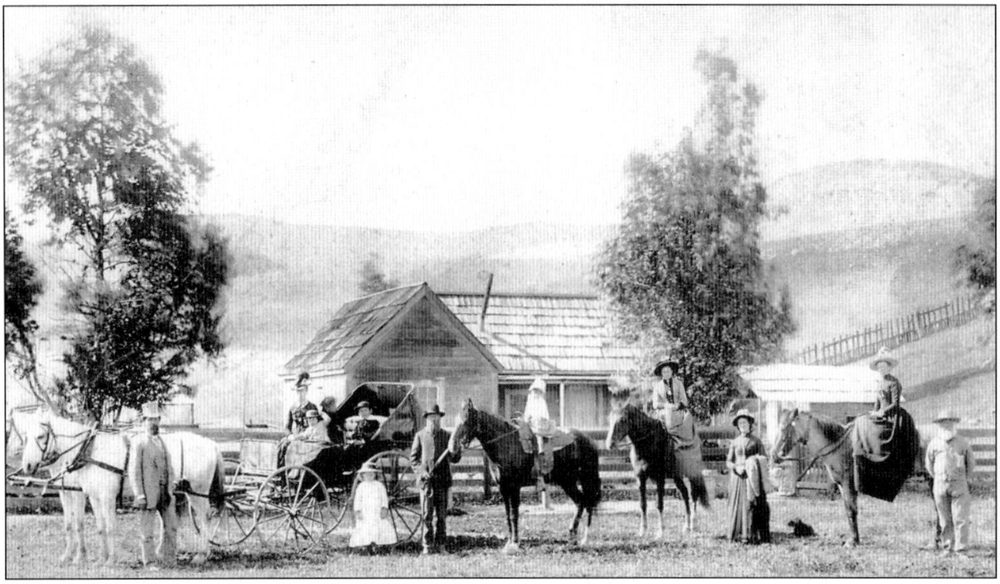

In the 1860s, the Rogers and Margetts families settled on 3,000 acres outside of King City and raised sheep. The families had a dispute over the children driving a buggy into King City to see the circus, and their partnership was dissolved. Pictured in happier times are both families standing in front of the ranch house on Lonoak Road near San Lorenzo Creek. From left to right are Charles Usher Margetts, Eleanor Hawksley Jennings Margetts (in the buggy) with children Frances, Percy, and Ethel. Amy is standing. Robert Rogers holds the horse, with Ann Gwendolyn Rogers in the saddle. Margaret Esther Rogers is seated on the next horse, and Elizabeth Ann Margetts Rogers stands nearby. Evelyn Mary Rogers is seated on the last horse, with hired hand Adolphus Bandlitz on the far right. (Courtesy of Bob Oates.)

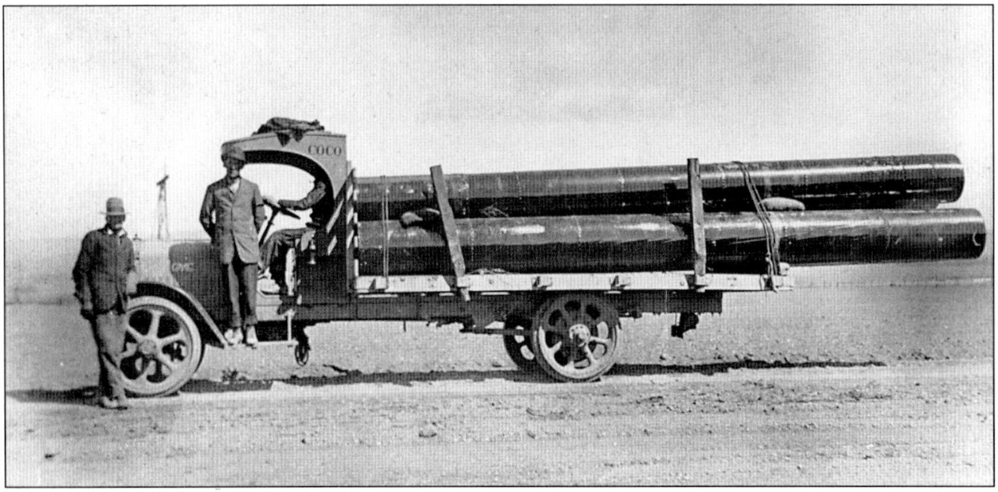

A truckload of irrigation pipe is shown here in 1920, ready for delivery to Salinas Valley farmers. Farmers did not pursue irrigation methods until the end of the 19th century, when a 10-year dry spell brought water concerns to the forefront. By 1920, over 47,000 acres in Monterey County were irrigated and more than two-thirds of this had been brought under irrigation within the previous decade. By 1924, the Spreckels Company was pumping over 130,000,000 gallons per day—more water than the city of San Francisco used.

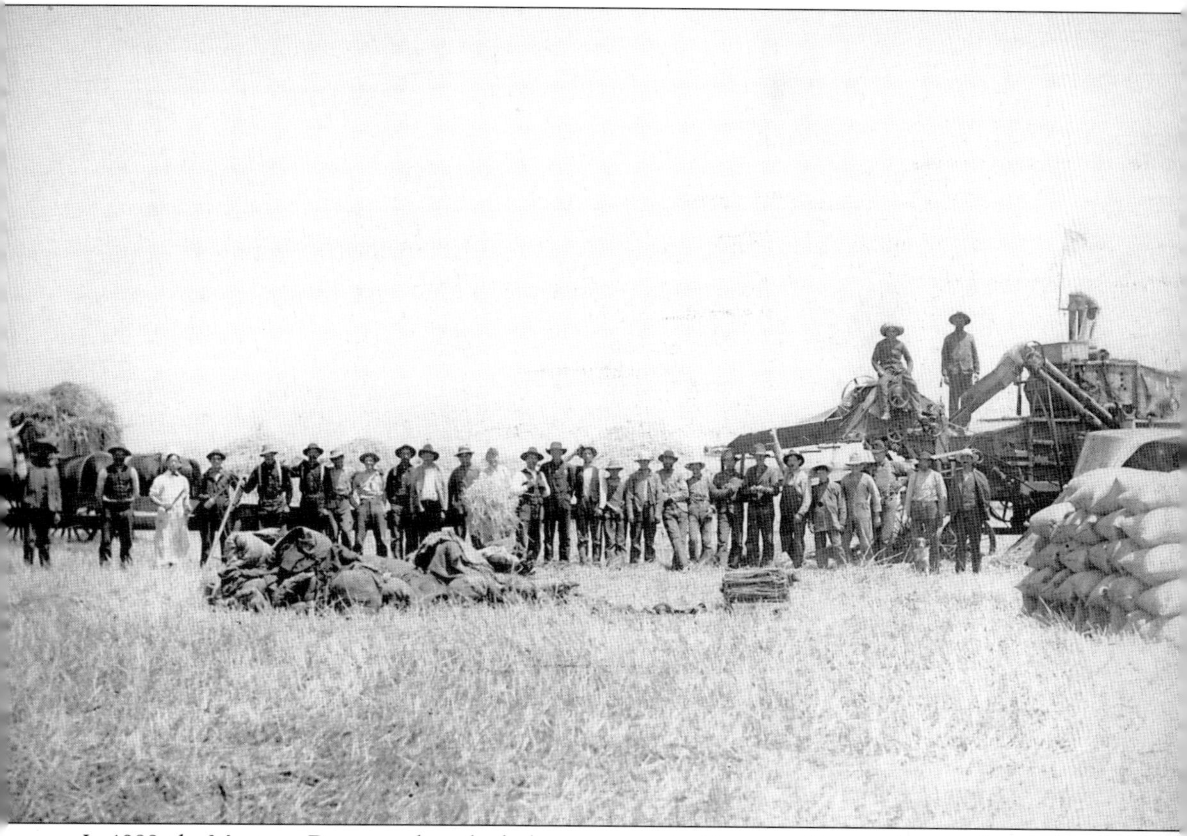

In 1888, the *Monterey Democrat* described a harvest scene in Monterey County, "A spacc has been cleared by the headers in the center of a mighty field of yellow, waving grain; a field so vast that its area may be more rapidly computed in square miles than square acres. To this spot has been drawn what appears at first to be an old-fashioned locomotive, but which is in reality a steam boiler on wheels . . . there were in the Salinas Valley last season twenty such threshing outfits . . . and they threshed about 1,200 tons of grain per day."

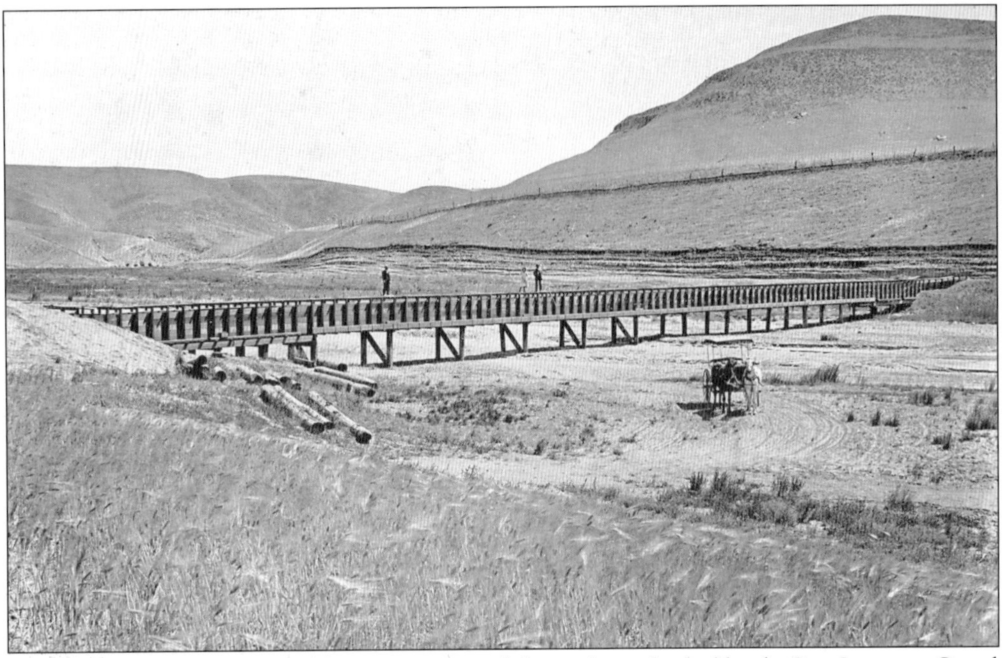

Built in 1896, this irrigation flume was part of the eight-and-a-half-mile San Lorenzo Canal system. During the winter months, floodwaters were diverted from San Lorenzo Creek and used to water close to 800 acres of land near King City.

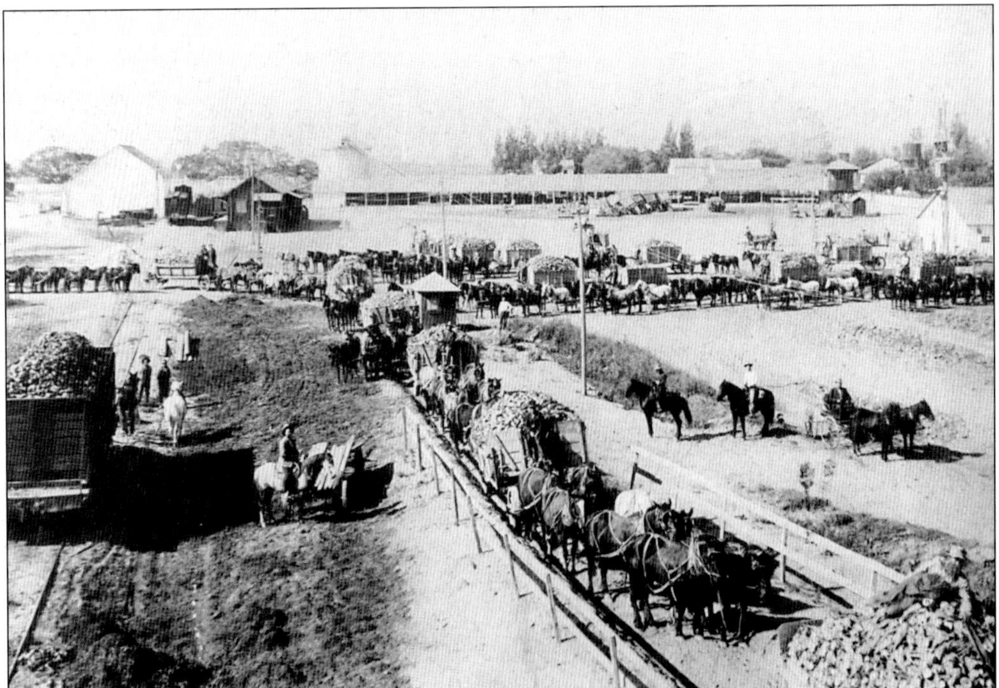

Wagonloads of sugar beets pulled by eight-horse teams lined up at the King City depot in 1913. The beets were reloaded into waiting gondolas for shipment to the Spreckels Sugar factory in Salinas. Salinas Valley farmers harvested 140,216 tons of beets that year, averaging 8.84 tons per acre.

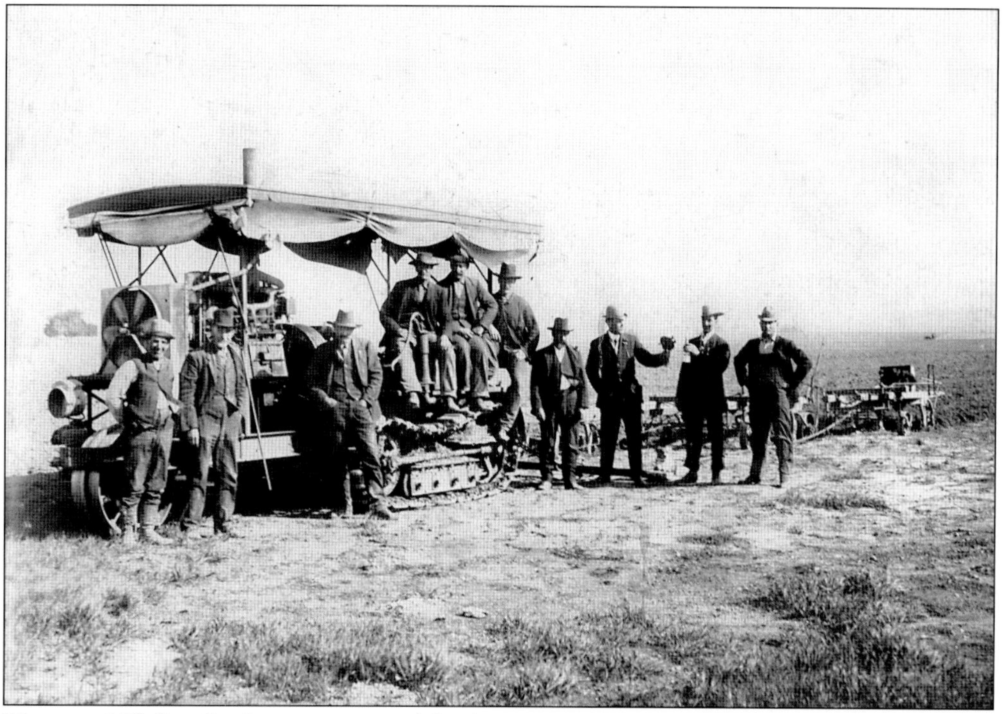

The proud Walker Brothers toast one of the first tractors to come to King City.

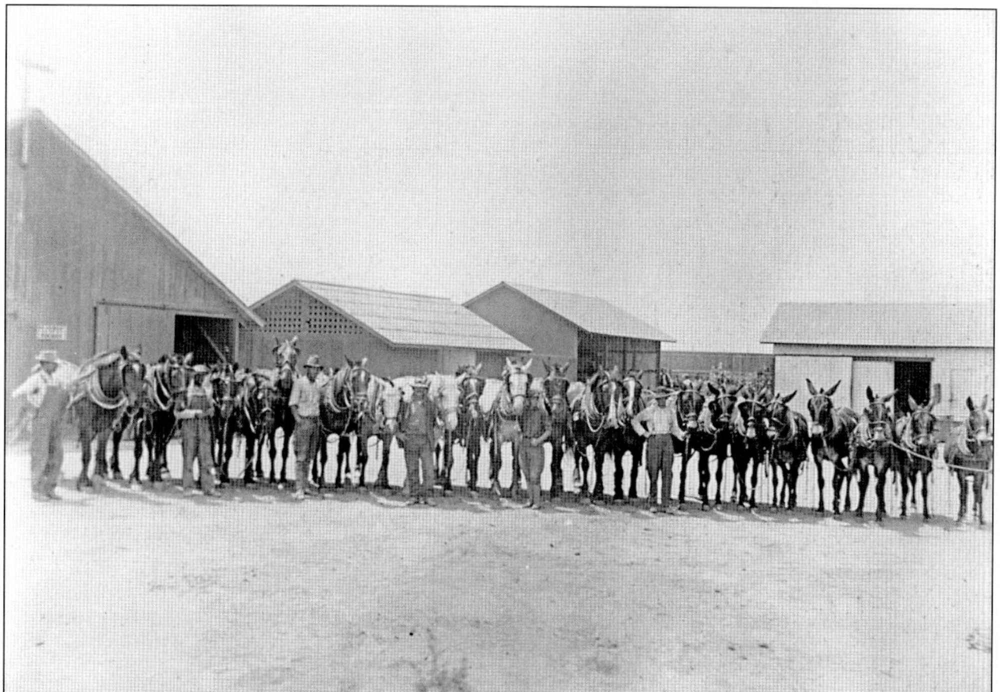

In this 1921 photograph, California Orchard Company employees gather horses and mules for a day's work in the fields. With cheap hay and grain, horses and mules were a less expensive power source than tractors, due to the high prices of machinery, mechanics, gas, and oil.

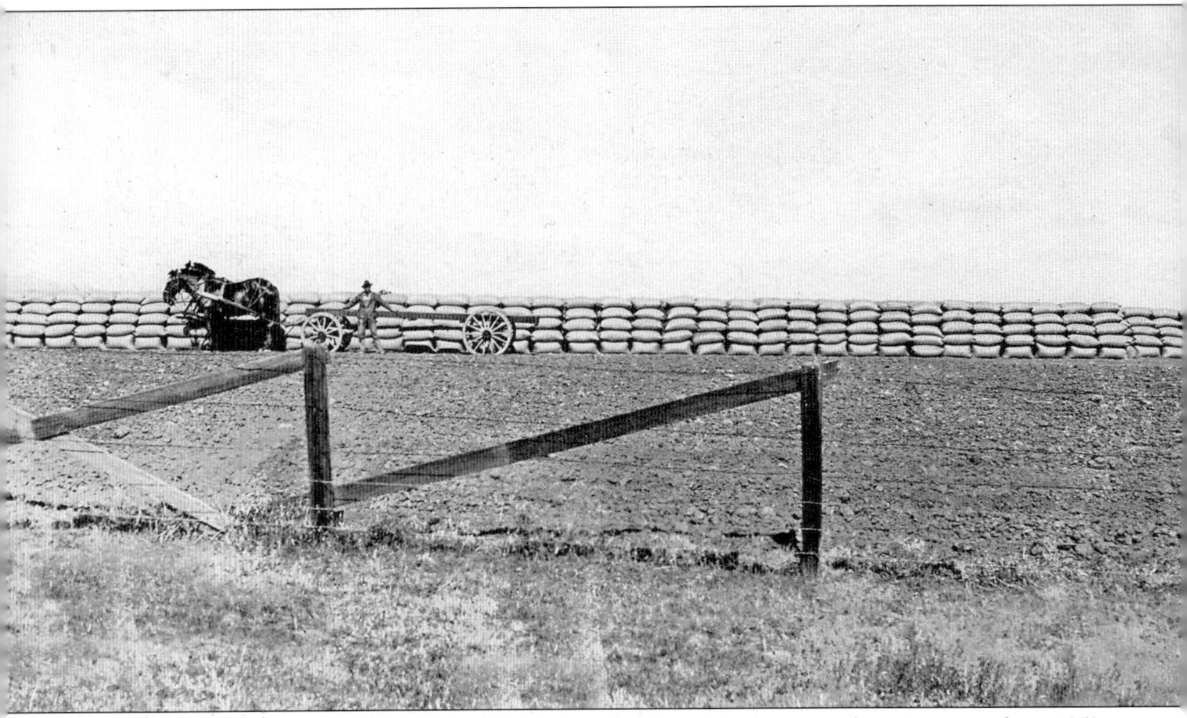

Dry farming dominated Salinas Valley agriculture during the 1870s and 1880s. As early as 1852, James Bryant Hill introduced barley to a 95-acre tract on the "Salinas Plains." Shipping terminals at Monterey and Moss Landing, as well as the railroad's extension south, encouraged farmers to increase productive acreage. Huge threshing machines harvested the valley's crop, at times producing 2,100 sacks per day. The average crew employed two sack sewers who earned $3 a day. Here hundreds of sacks of barley await shipment. Each sack weighed 145 pounds.

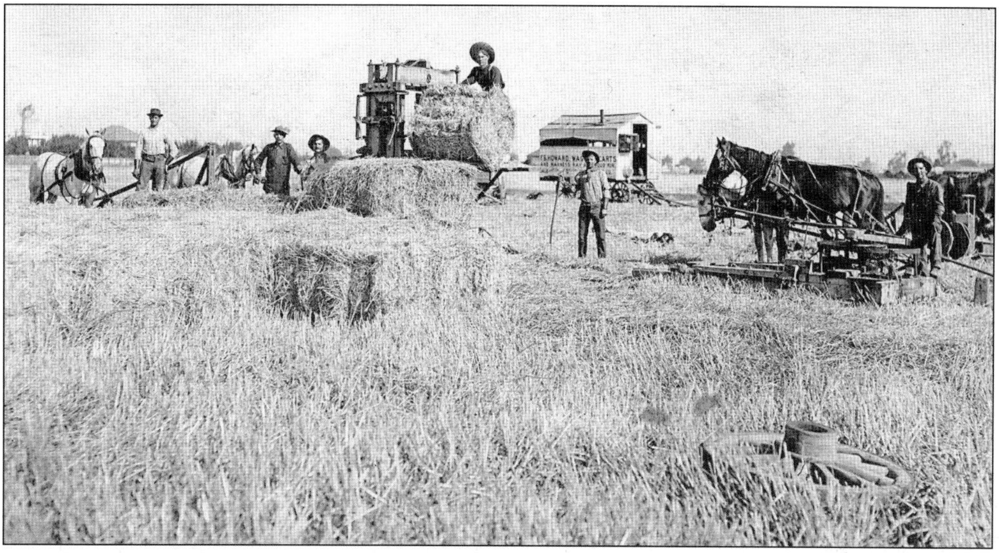

After hay was cut and stacked, farmers hired a crew to press the hay into bales that weighed over 300 pounds. This photograph was taken on the Paul Talbott ranch near King City. (Courtesy of the Monterey County Historical Society.)

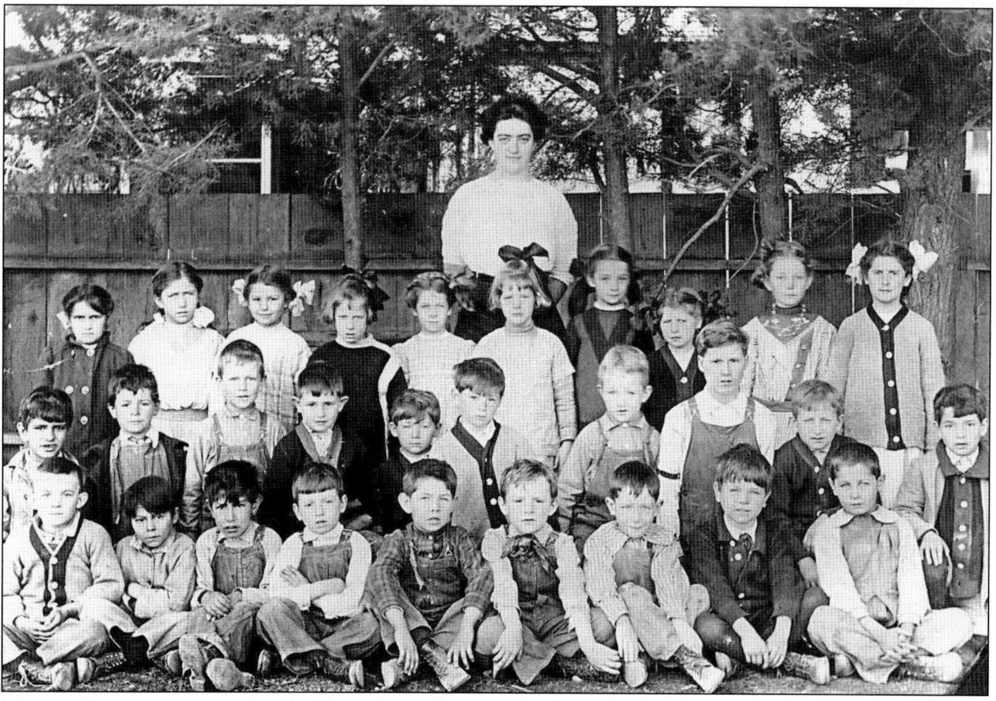

Mamie Casey is pictured with King City's first grade class of 1911–1912. From left to right are the following: (first row) Johnnie Garcia, Paul Carol, Chauncy Brunetti, Sam Rutherford, Walter Lundy, Jimmy McCoy, Wayne Harwood, and Ralph Small; (second row) Willie Bonita, George Cavalli, Hubert Garner, Edward McLaren, Rollo Mansfield, Kenneth Mansfield, Earl Garner, Chester Copley, Carson Lund, and Freddie Delamore; (third row) Lucy Joseph, Marie Mahler, Velma Campbell, Dorothy Walker, Helen Hamilton, Jean Matthews, Elva Small, Gertrude Barney, Ethelda Bruce, and Nellie Barney.

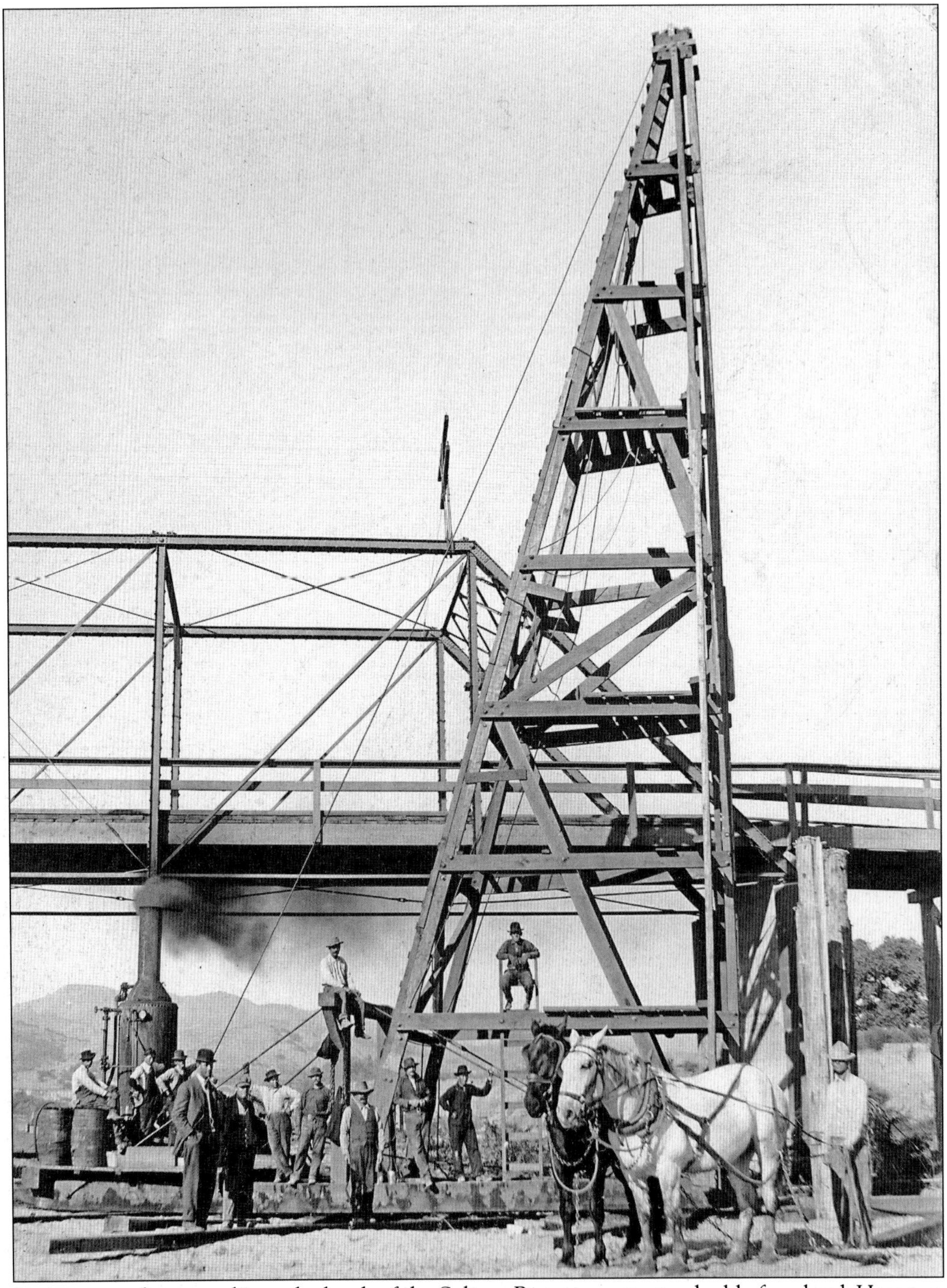

Jetties were often nosed into the bank of the Salinas River to protect valuable farmland. Here two crews and pile drivers were competing to see who could drive the most pilings. This photograph, taken under the King City Bridge in 1911, shows the winning crew. (Courtesy of the Monterey County Historical Society.)

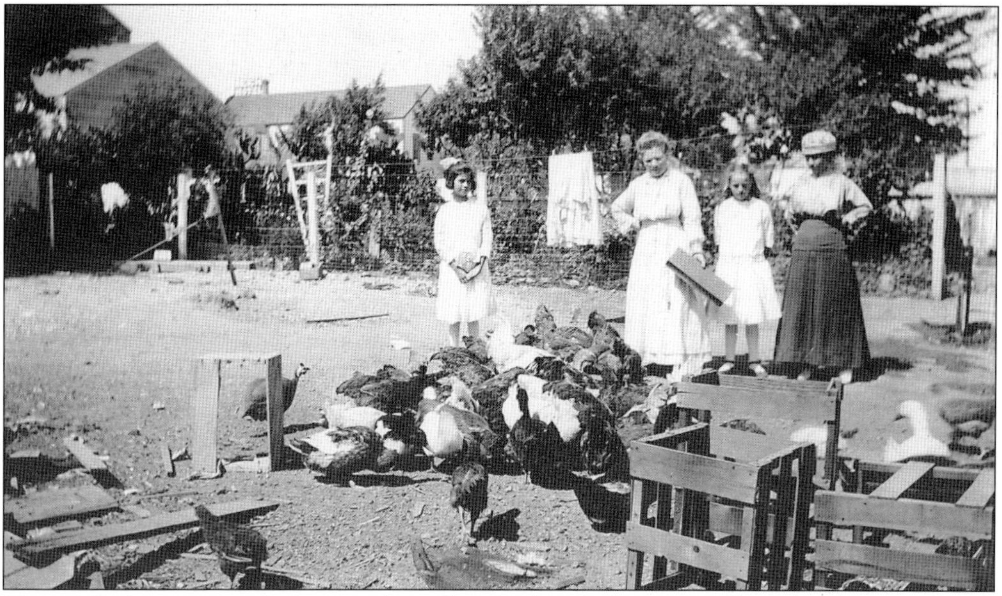

Town folks kept various farm animals in their backyards for eggs, milk, and pulling the buggy. Here Gussie Brunetti (holding pan) feeds chickens and ducks in her King City backyard.

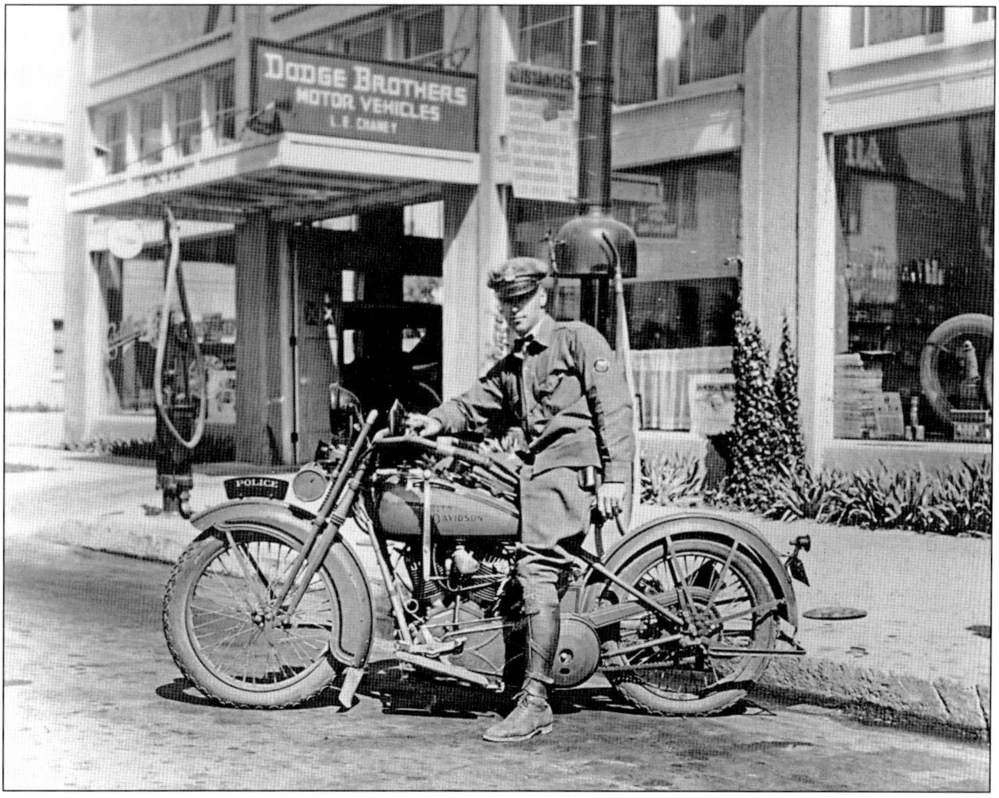

Clarence Dodge, one of King City's first traffic officers, poses in front of Los Osistos Garage, owned by L. E. "Doc" Chaney. Dodge was killed while chasing a speeder in 1926.

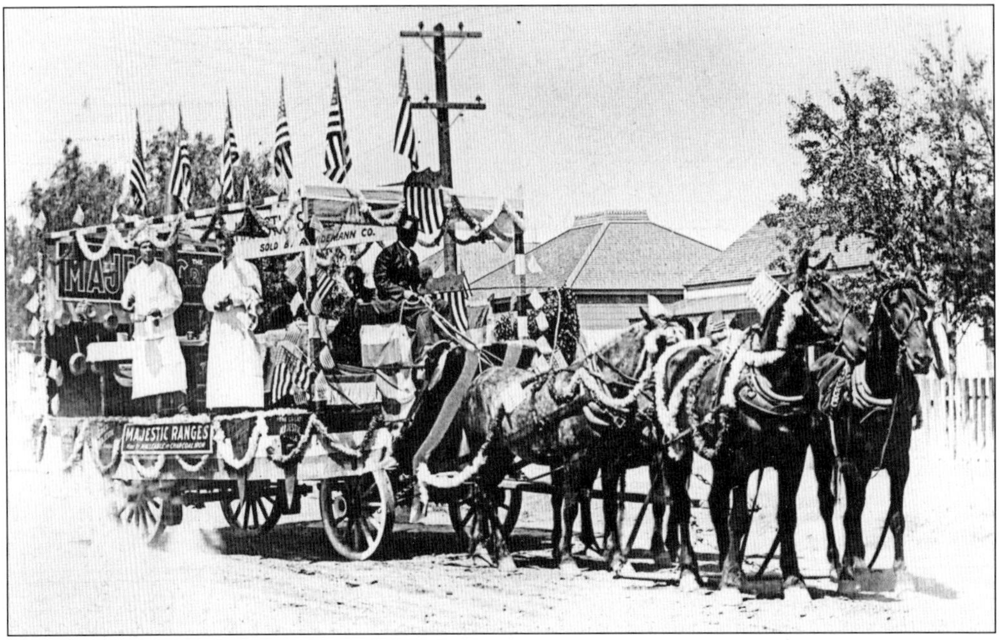

For almost 100 years, Broadway in King City has been the site of a Fourth of July parade. Here the Widemann Company, a successful mercantile firm in the Salinas Valley, uses its parade float as an opportunity to advertise their line of Majestic ranges.

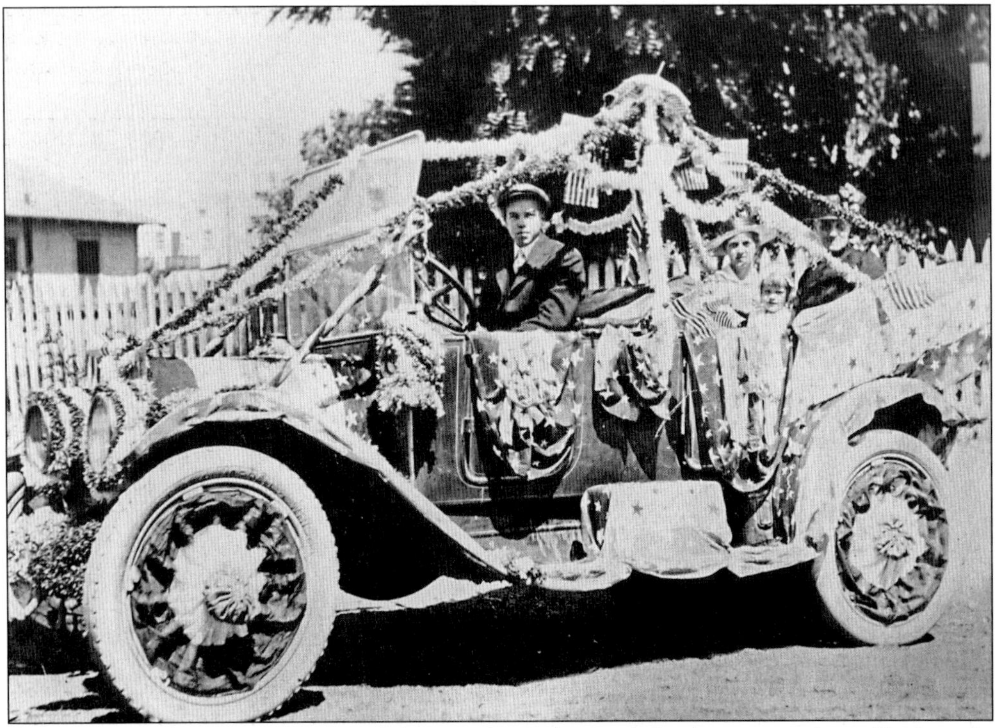

A King City family joined the fun of the Fourth of July parade by decorating their old jalopy for a drive down Broadway. Plenty of garlands, star spangled bunting, and fluttering flags certainly made this parade entry stand out.

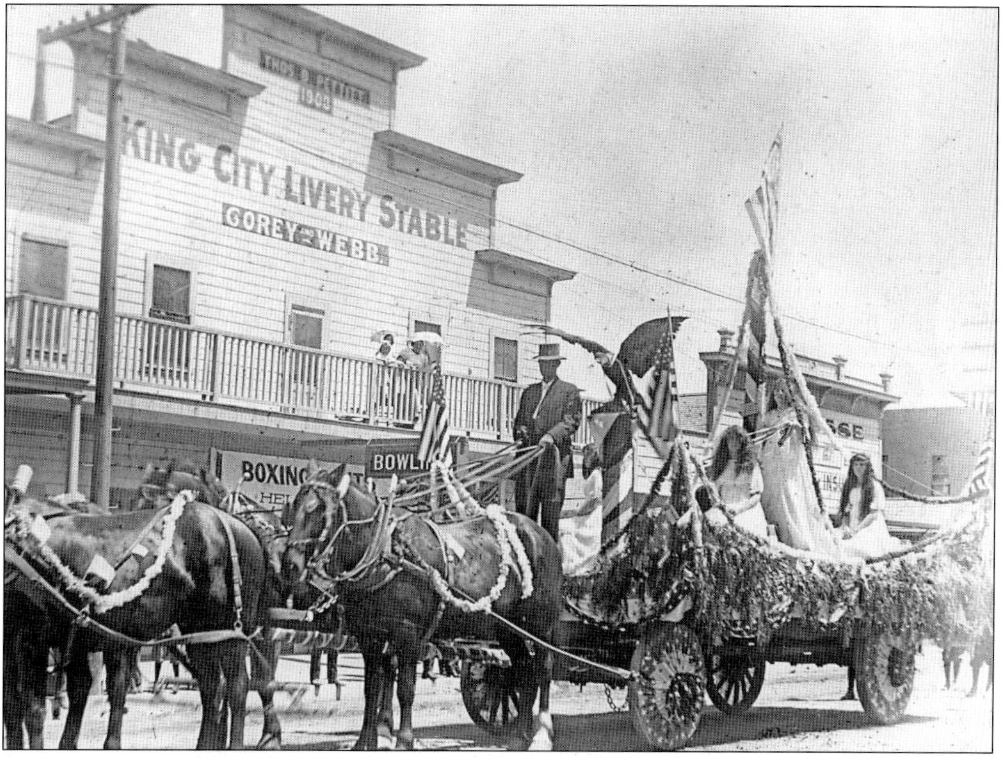

King City celebrated Fourth of July with a grand parade down Broadway. This tradition is still alive today and is sponsored by the Monterey County Agricultural and Rural Life Museum. Pictured here is one of the elaborate "floats" occupied by four King City beauties.

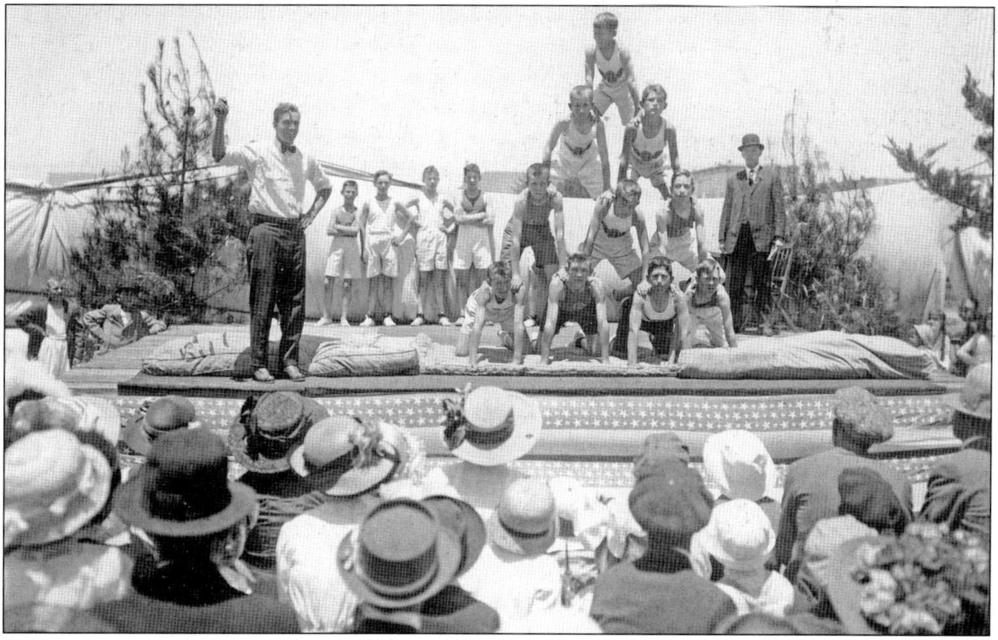

Bill Steglich shows off the skill of his gymnastic class during King City's Fourth of July celebration in 1916. Mayor Al Carlson is pictured on stage wearing a derby hat.

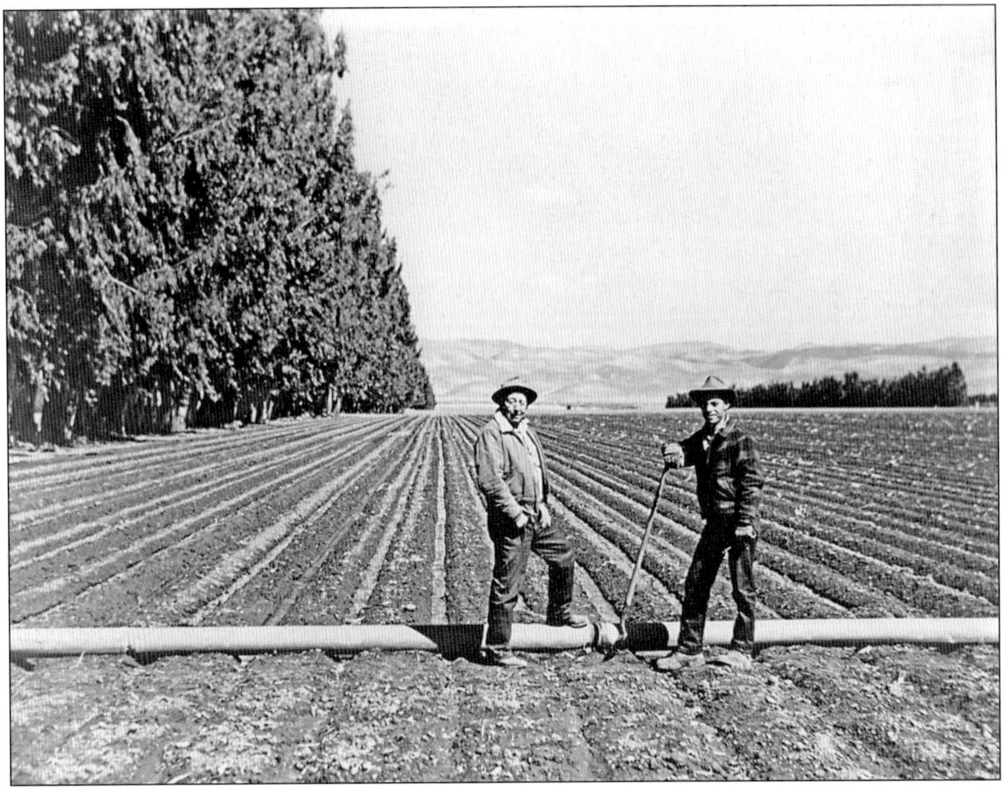

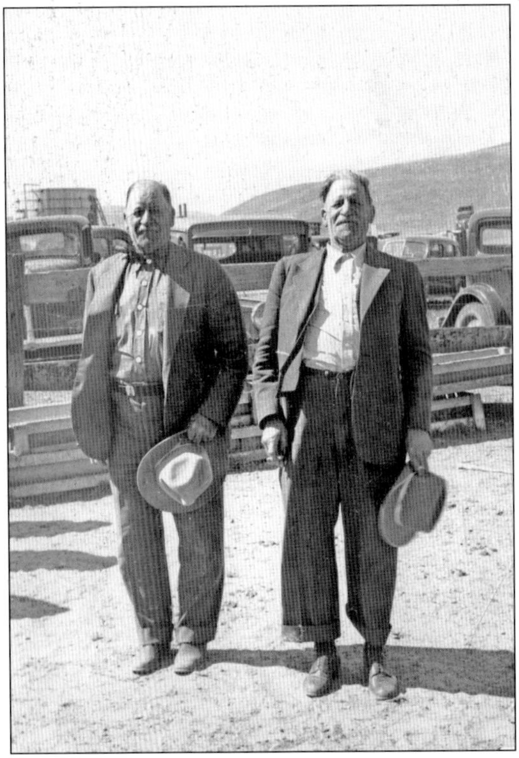

The Salinas Land and California Orchard Company leased land to farmers on a sharecropping basis, usually at 300 acres each. Pictured here are tenants Les Smart and Larry Silva. Early crops were dominated by the King City pink bean, but by the late 1930s and 1940s, sugar beets, tomatoes, peppers, spinach, and onions could be seen in valley fields.

Twins Jess and Warren Cornwall opened their ranch in Hog Canyon, three miles east of King City, for the King City Stampede. The Stampede, first held in 1936, originated as a celebration of King City's 50th anniversary.

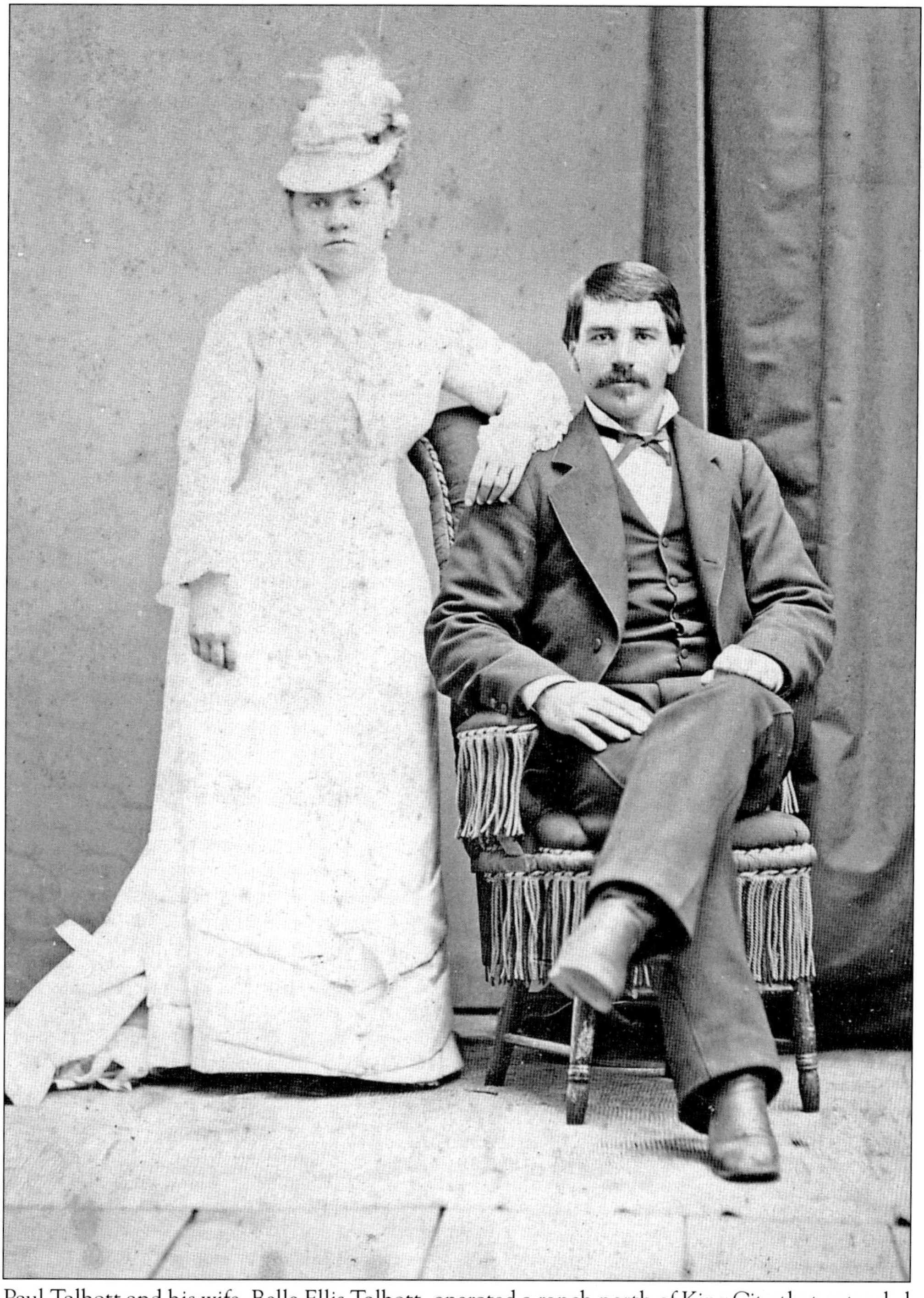

Paul Talbott and his wife, Belle Ellis Talbott, operated a ranch north of King City that extended for several miles along the Salinas River. Cattle and grain were their most important products. He served as the third district supervisor for 32 years, taking particular interest in King City's schools and campaigning for the extension of the state highway through his district. (Courtesy of the Monterey County Historical Society.)

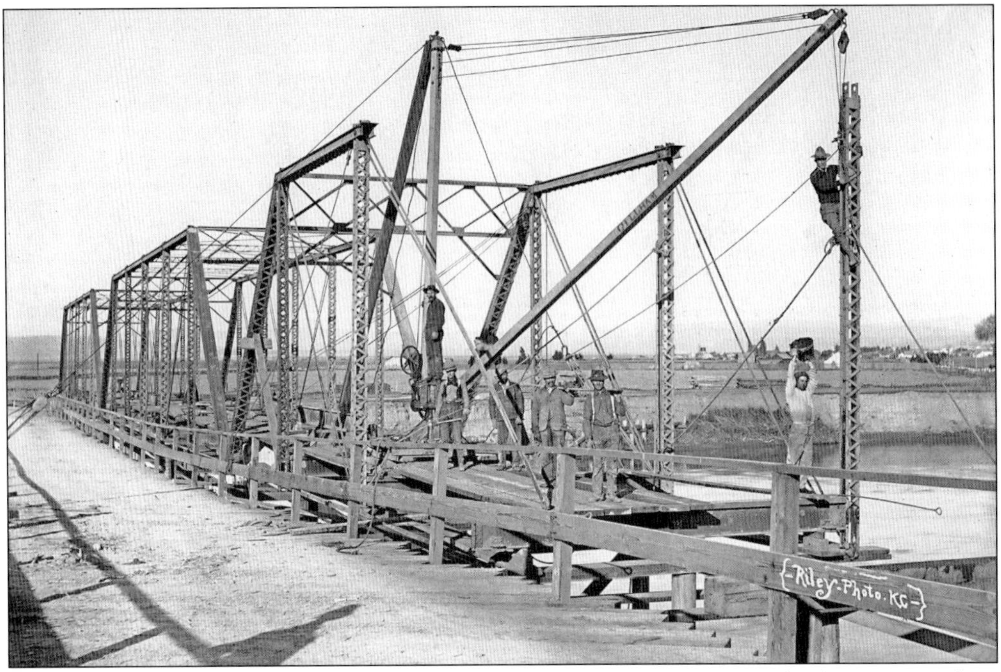

In February 1914, the Salinas River washed away 340 feet of the King City bridge. Here workers construct a new 2,800-foot-long span.

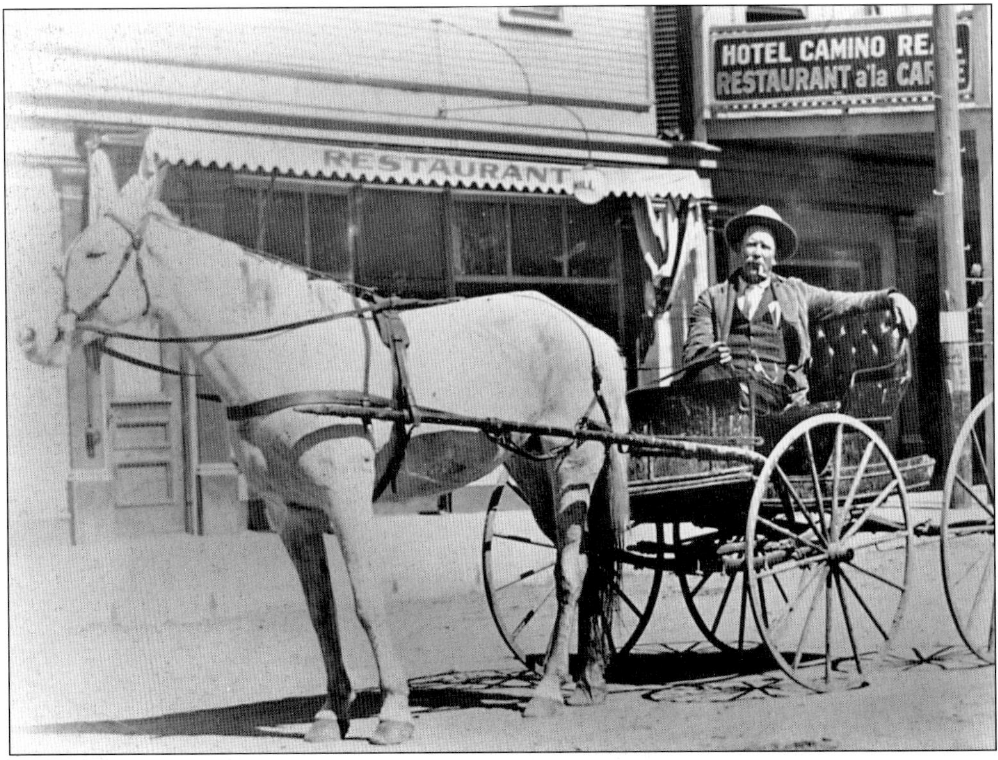

By 1911, 699 people lived in King City and the community voted to incorporate. W. G. Curran, pictured here in his buggy, became King City's first marshal, serving until 1918.

Seven

San Lucas

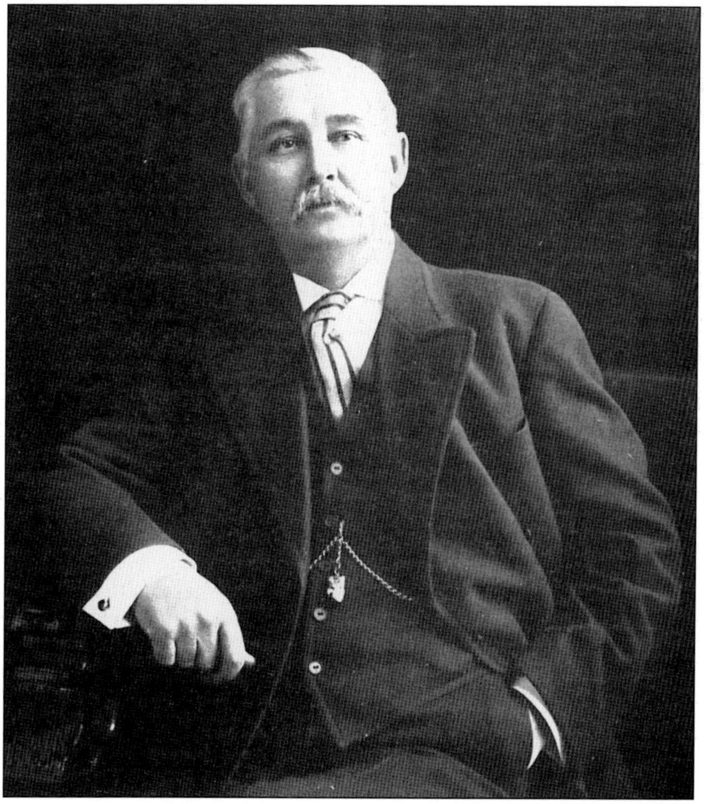

Julius Trescony, son of prominent pioneer Alberto Trescony, took over the management of his father's Rancho San Lucas in 1876. Ten years later, when the Southern Pacific Railroad pushed south to the county line, Julius laid out the town of San Lucas. Lots were 120 feet deep and sold for $150 each. Trescony built a grain warehouse, reputed to be the largest in southern Monterey County. By 1888, over 11,000 acres of grain were cultivated around San Lucas, with 8,000 additional acres in nearby valleys. (Courtesy of the Monterey County Historical Society.)

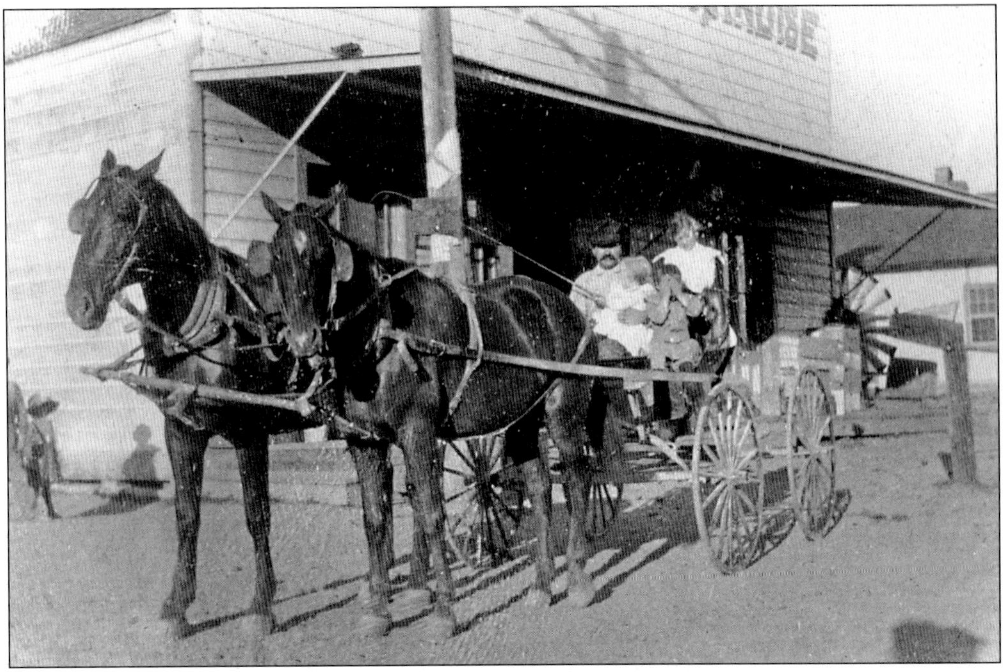

The first store in San Lucas was opened in 1886 by the Goldwater family, ancestors of Arizona senator Barry Goldwater. Sam (Bampa) Bunte bought the store in 1897. Sam's brother Dick ran a blacksmith shop at the back of the store and upstairs was a dance hall. Pictured are Mr. and Mrs. Sam Bunte, their daughter Carol, and niece Muriel Bunte.

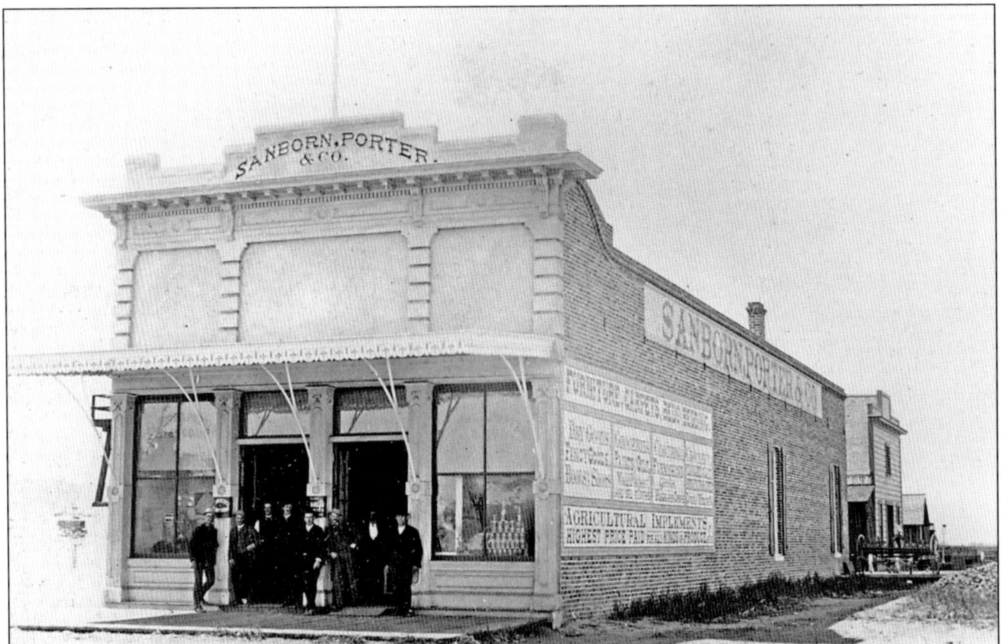

The Sanborn, Porter, and Company store in San Lucas was one of "two good stores, which do a large cash and credit business and supply the main trade for a radius of many miles toward Lockwood, Jolon, Pine Valley, and the Long Valley, Peachtree and Oasis sections."

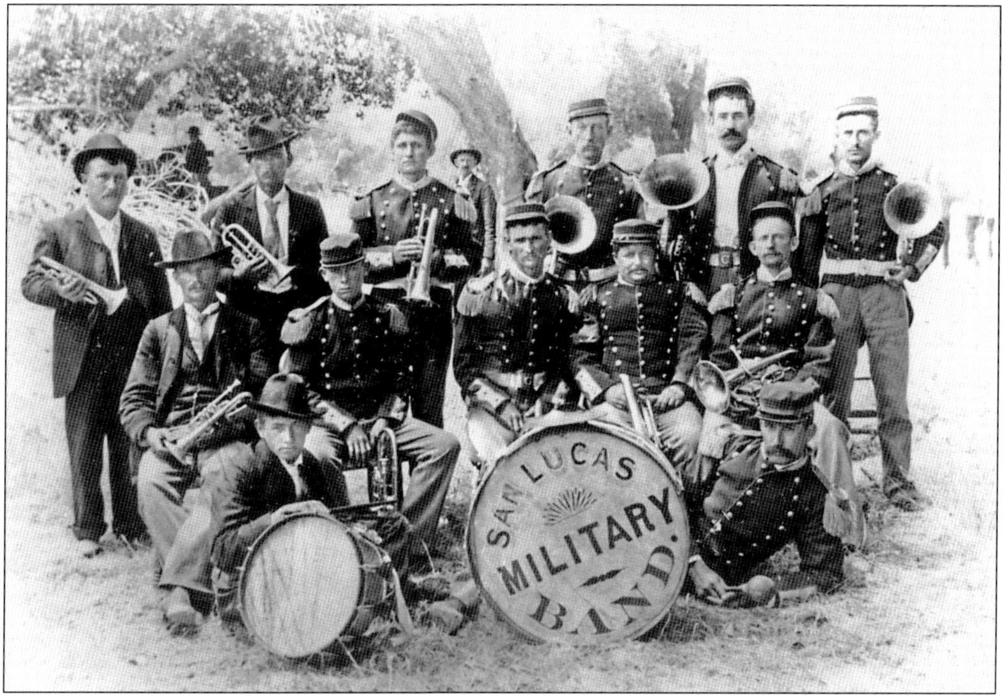

The popular San Lucas Band was composed of members of the Knights of Pythias, Beatrice Lodge No. 154. Once a week, wearing their uniforms, they treated the community to a concert.

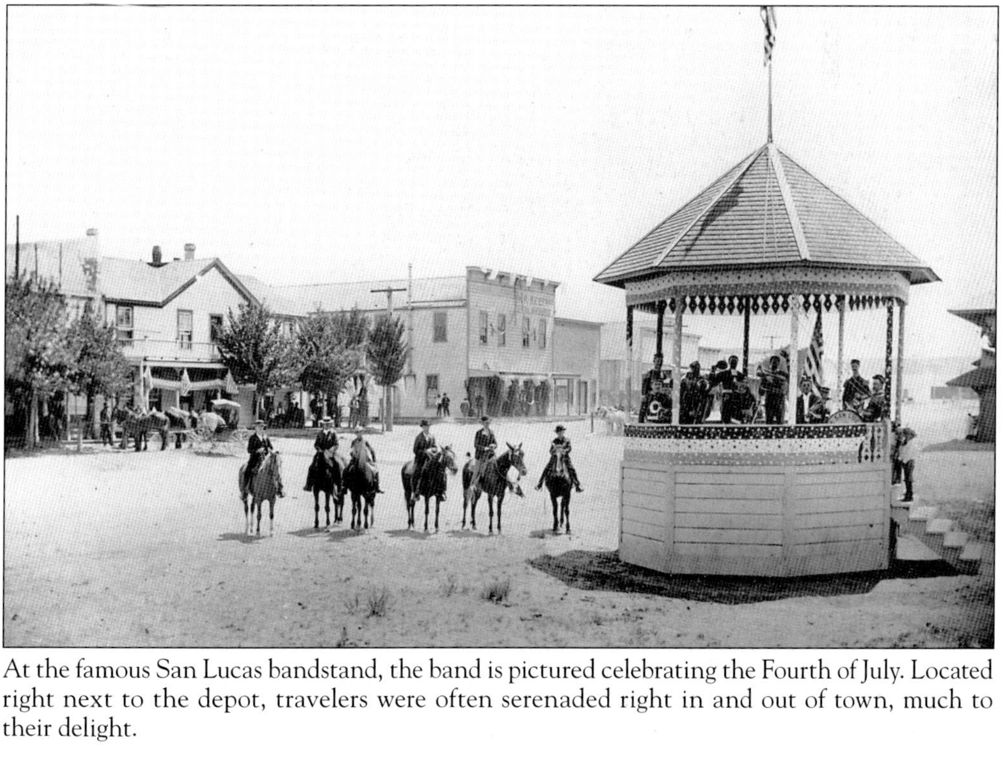

At the famous San Lucas bandstand, the band is pictured celebrating the Fourth of July. Located right next to the depot, travelers were often serenaded right in and out of town, much to their delight.

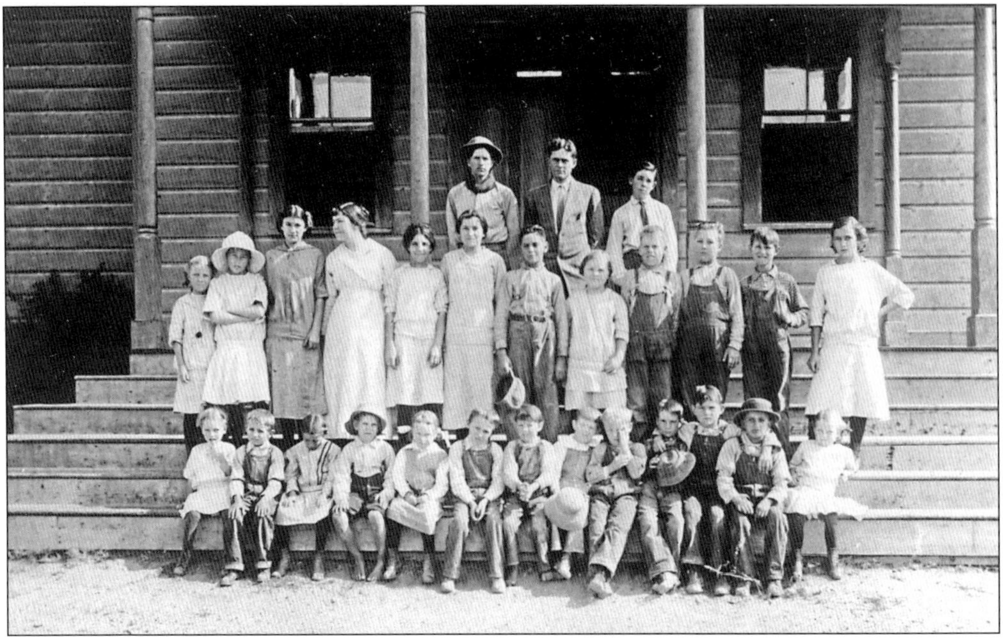

San Lucas students pose on the school house steps for a class portrait. Pictured, from left to right, are (first row) Esther Somerville, Ernest Gnesa, Mary Gnesa, John Gutherie, Egridio Gnesa, Paul Colgar, Clifton Beasley, Adolph Jessen, Dave Crette, Austin McKinsey, Aldo Gnesa, and Marion Jessen; (second row) Thelma Jensen, Viola Beasley, Charlotte Colgar, Marguerite Crette, Muriel Joppini, Edna Crette, Bruce Joppini, Carol Bunte, Bert Crette, Loran Bunte, Glenn McKinsey, and Violette Daniels. Teacher William Crook stands on the top step flanked by students Ted Koester and Louie Hill.

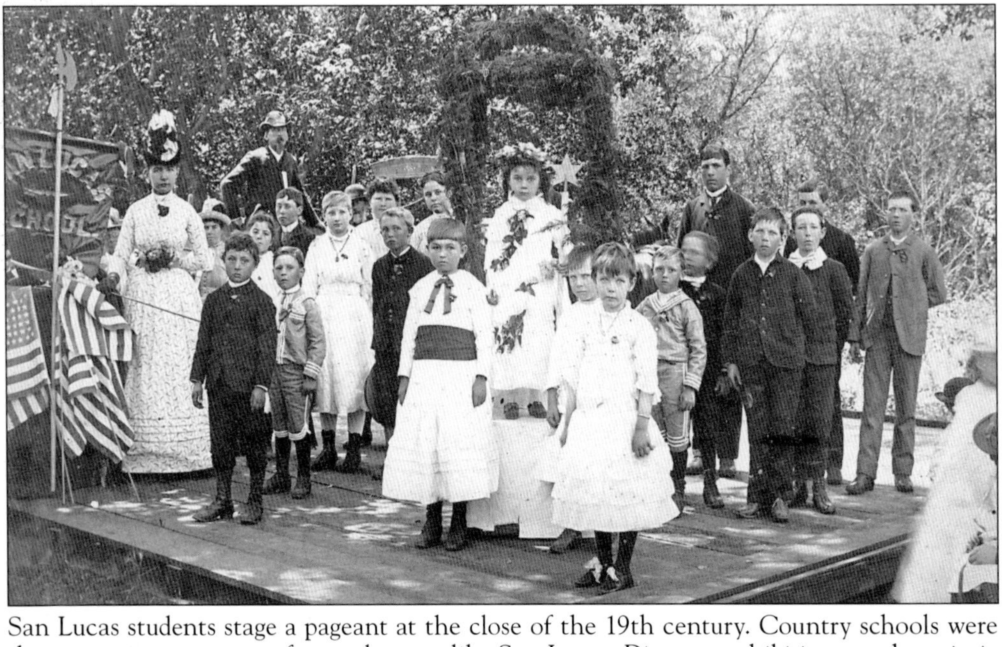

San Lucas students stage a pageant at the close of the 19th century. Country schools were the entertainment center for rural towns like San Lucas. Dinners, exhibitions, and patriotic entertainment were often held at the school.

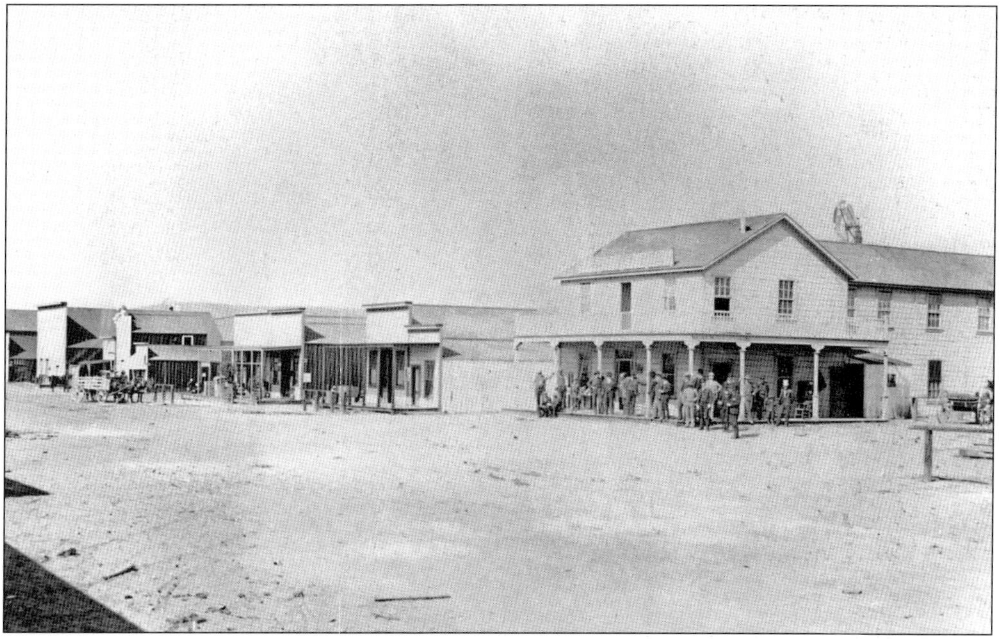

San Lucas was once the principal town of southern Monterey County. In this photograph, the Pleasant View Hotel stands in the foreground. Other businesses included 2 more hotels, 2 livery stables, 2 blacksmith shops, and 10 saloons.

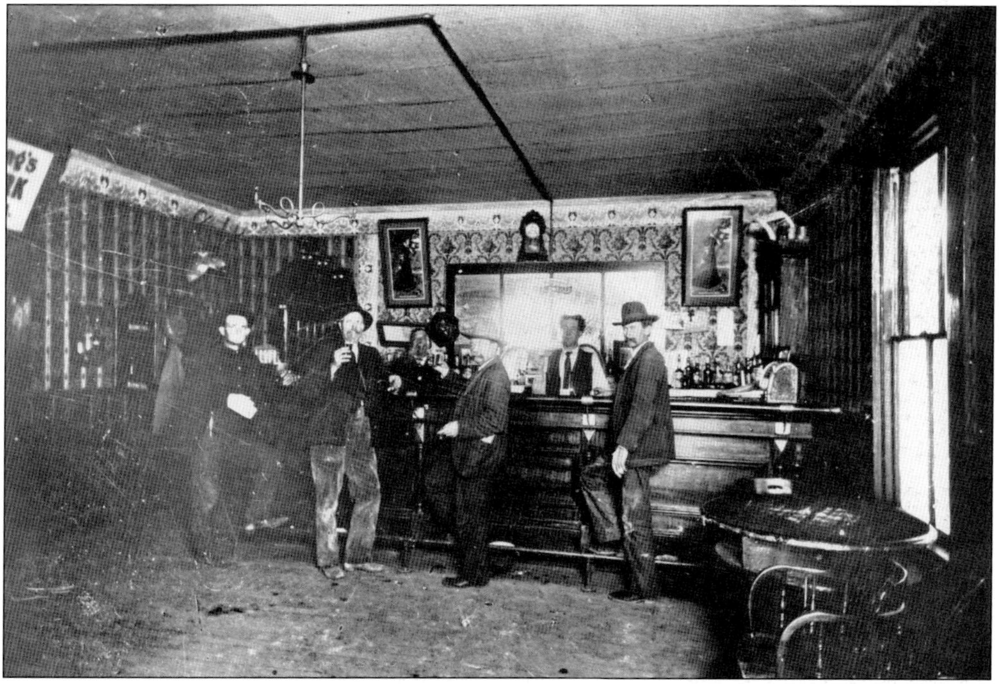

In 1899, the *San Lucas Herald* reported that "Frank E. Adams of the Pleasant View Hotel has had a new apparatus put in the bar room of the hotel, which will draw a nice cool glass of beer direct from the cellar. He invites all to call and see the machine work."

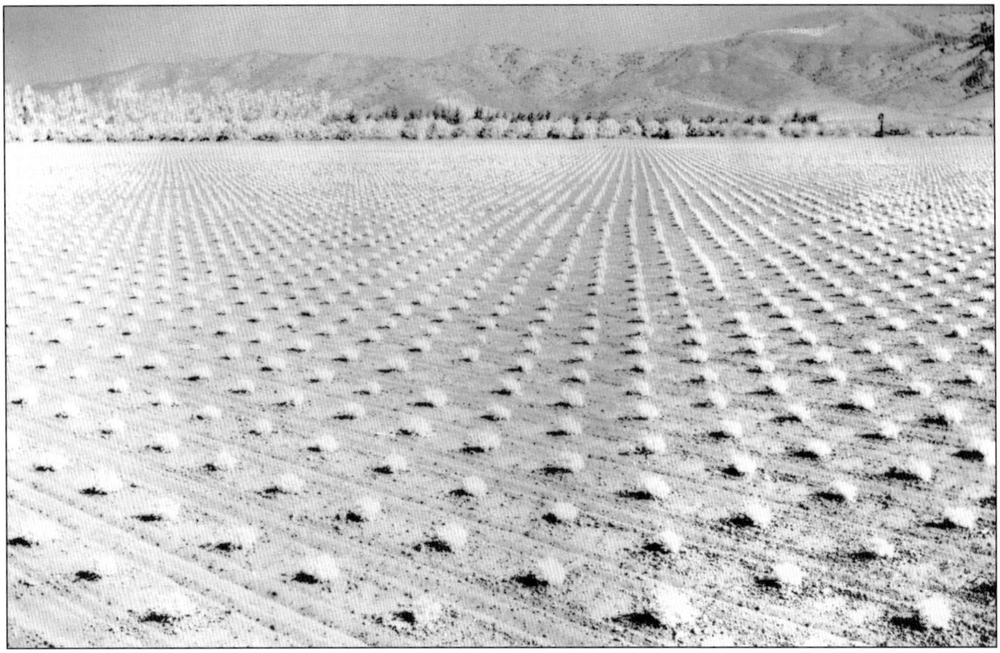

In 1925, the U.S. War Department planted 8,000 acres of guayule in the Salinas Valley as an experiment. In case of a national emergency, natural rubber could be processed from the plant. Resembling sagebrush, guayule grew three to four feet tall. Six years later, an extraction mill was built six miles south of Salinas at Spence Siding, producing an average of 700 pounds of rubber per acre.

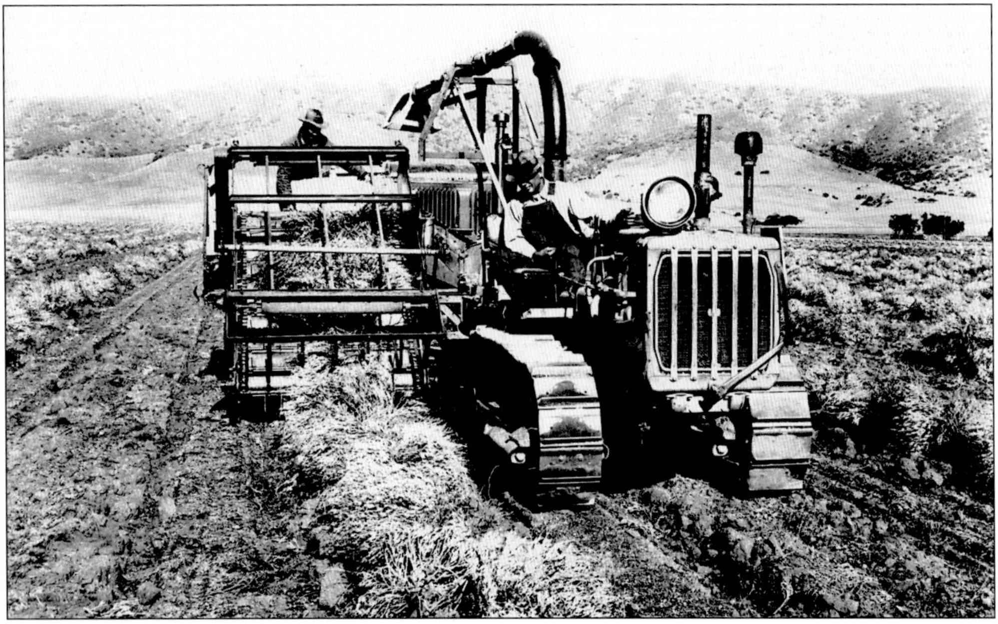

During World War II, the guayule market skyrocketed when the Department of Agriculture instituted the Emergency Rubber Project. Guayule acreage in the Salinas Valley expanded to 40,000 acres and was concentrated near San Ardo, King City, and San Lucas. After only 20 years, pressure from competitive interests closed down the project. In 1946, all plants in Salinas Valley fields, representing 21,000,000 pounds of rubber, were destroyed.

Eight

San Ardo

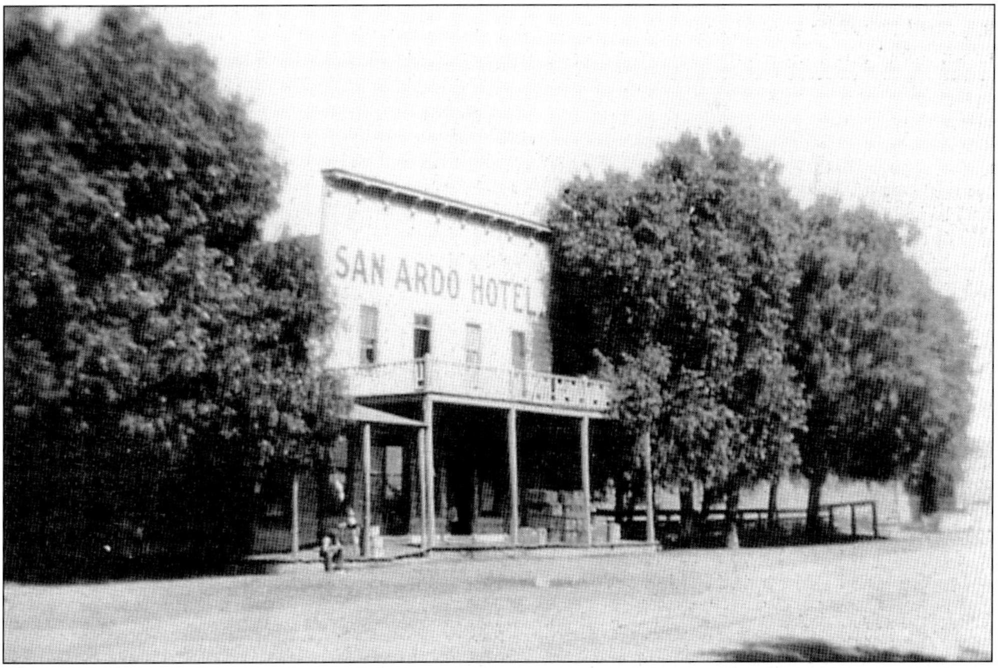

In 1886, the year San Ardo was founded, hotel proprietor Columbus Carlton advertised, "Hotel services at the new town of San Bernardo, Monterey County, are now ready and no pains will be spared to accommodate travelers and make them comfortable." Until the hotel was completed, Carlton rented rooms in his farmhouse. Three years later, the building burned and was rebuilt by new owners Timothy and Maria Lamb. (Courtesy of the Monterey County Library, San Ardo Branch.)

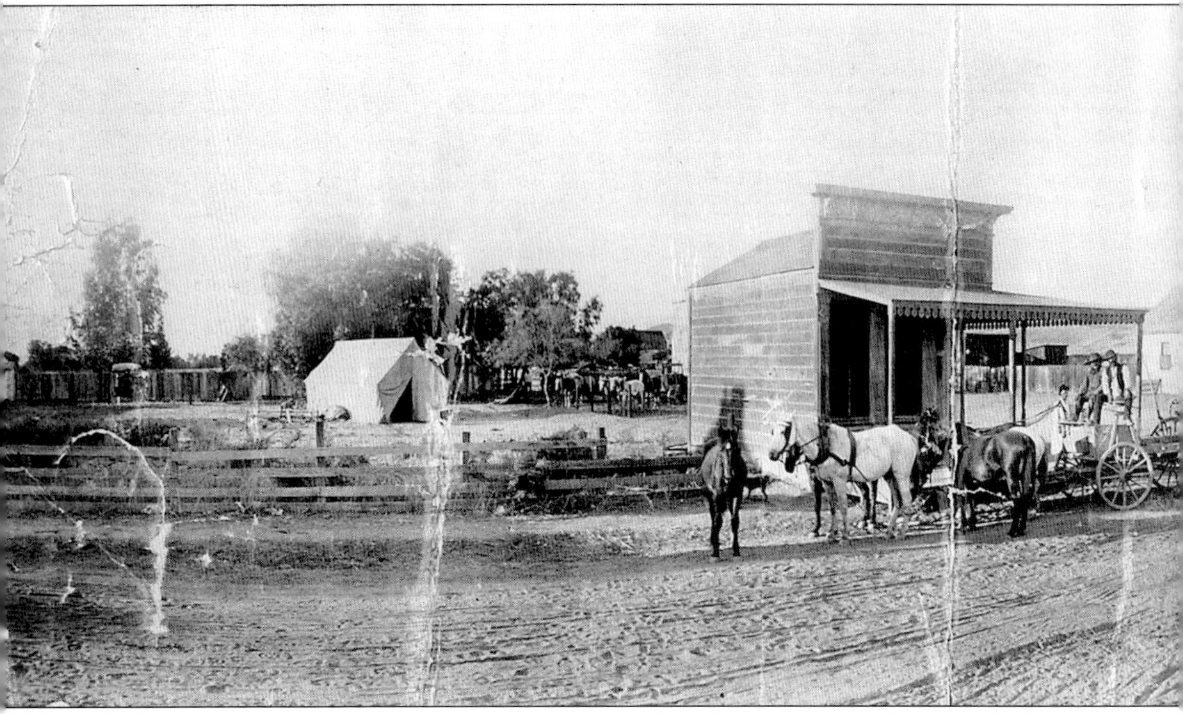

In 1871, two well-known butchers from San Francisco, Meyer Brandenstein and Edmond Godchaux, bought two-thirds of the Rancho San Bernardo. They established a town, San Bernardo, in the middle of the ranch and convinced the Southern Pacific Railroad to make it a stop on their line.

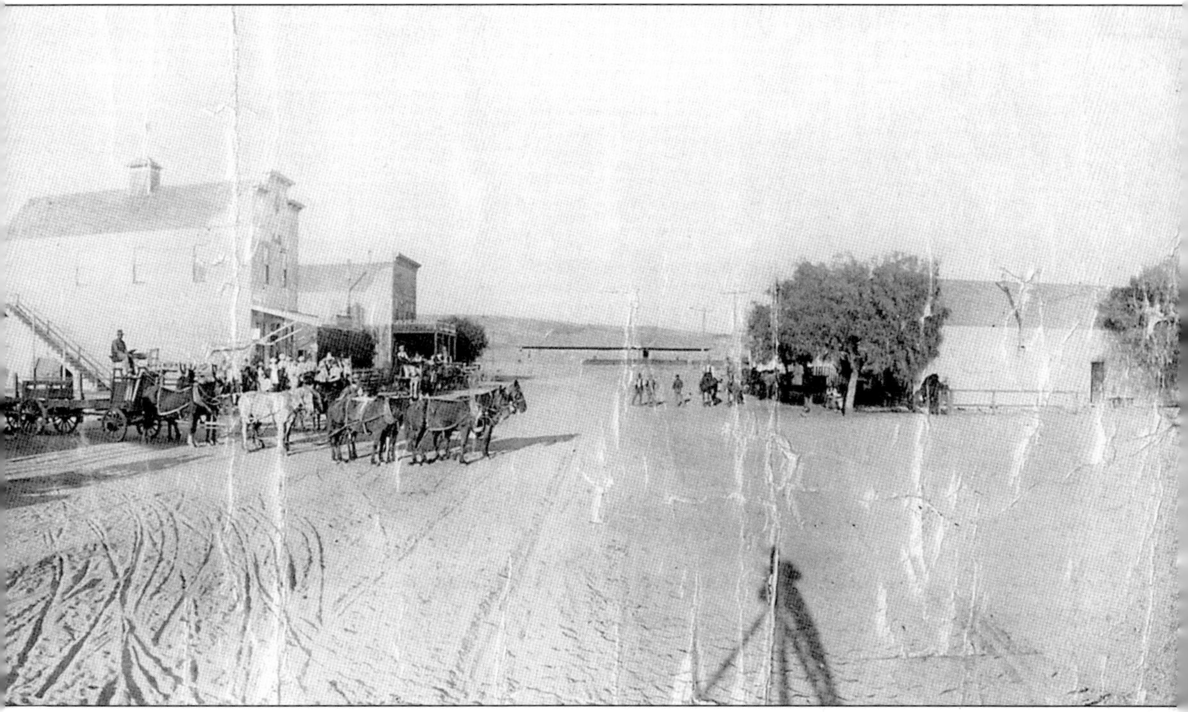

The town's name was later shortened to San Ardo, due to some confusion with the post office at San Bernadino. Pictured is the business section of town along Jolon Street in the early 1890s. (Courtesy of the Monterey County Library, San Ardo Branch.)

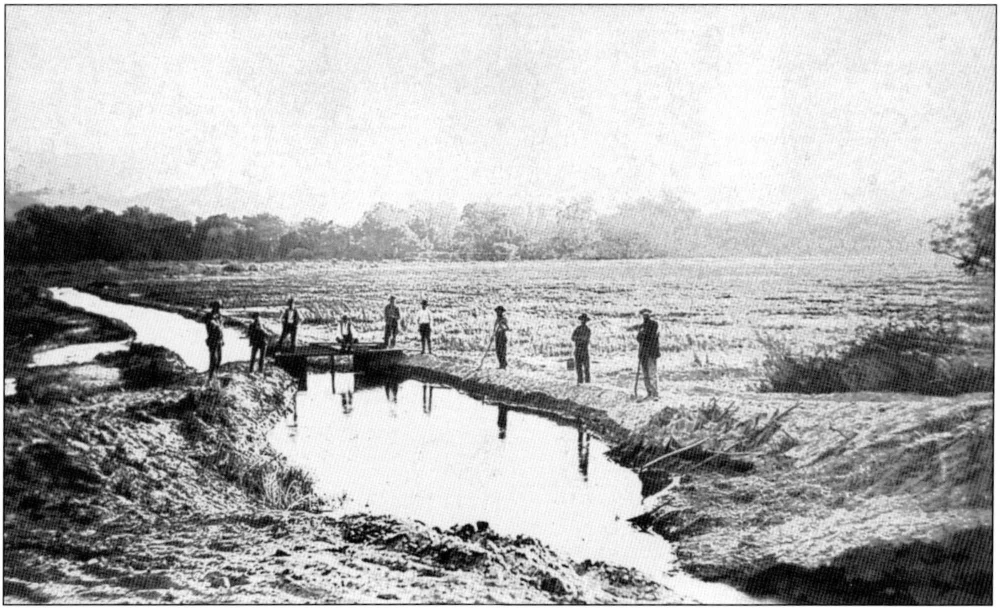

In 1882, Brandenstein and Godchaux filed a claim for Salinas River water. Two years later, they formed the San Bernardo and Salinas Valley Canal and Irrigation Company. A 50-foot canal was dug from the river to the ranch, carrying three feet of water. With diverging ditched and dams, they were able to irrigate up to 6,000 acres of alfalfa.

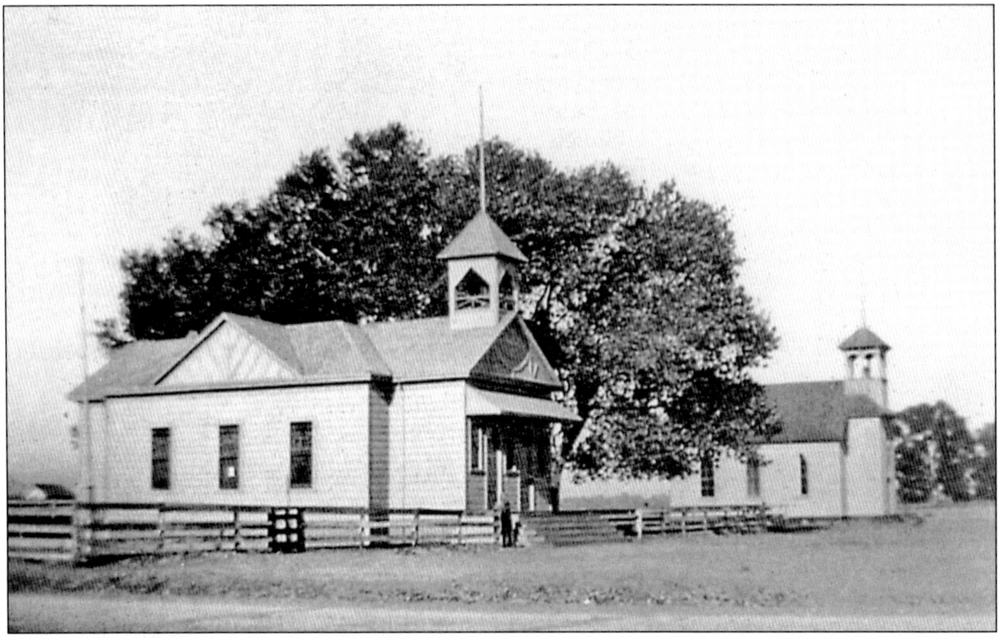

In 1900, the San Ardo School was built on College Street. In 1939, the school was sold and moved to the Hames Valley for use as a grange. The building burned in 1939. (Courtesy of the Monterey County Library, San Ardo Branch.)

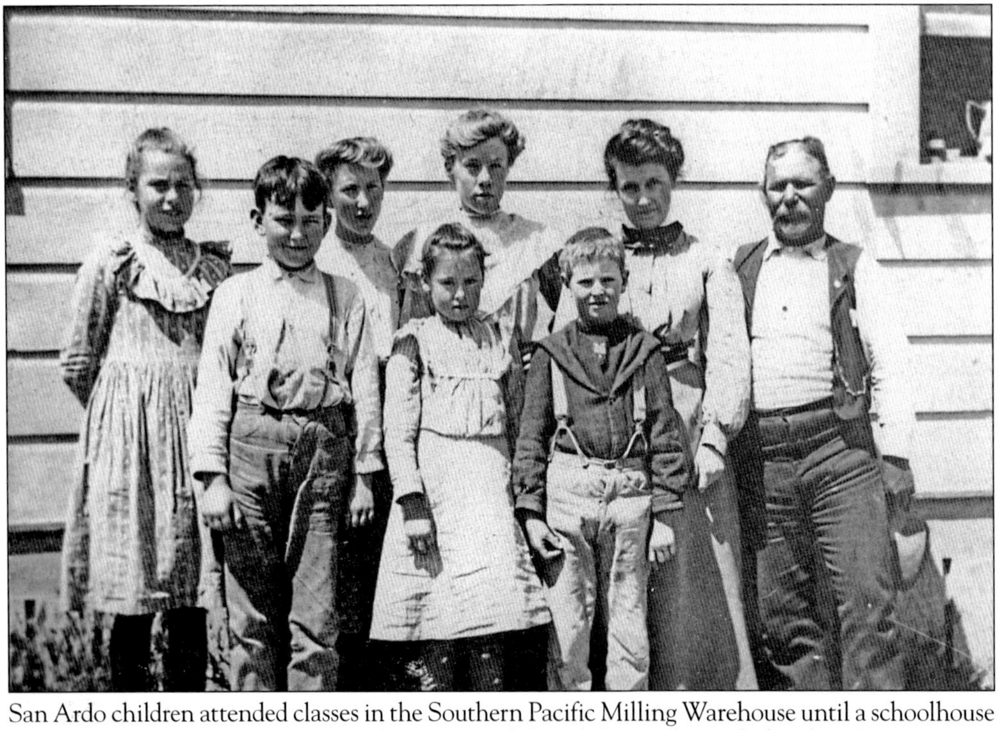

San Ardo children attended classes in the Southern Pacific Milling Warehouse until a schoolhouse was built near the Salinas River. Students pictured, from left to right, include Alice Crette, Varian Brown, Addie Brown, Nellie Crette, Emma Buschard, Bob St. Clair, Miss Rafter (teacher), and Perry Brown.

In 1886, Meyer Brandenstein donated a lot to build a Catholic church in San Ardo. Pioneer resident Kate McLaughlin said that the French started the construction and the Irish finished it. Called Our Lady of Ransom, the church was served by priests in San Miguel. They traveled by horseback to say mass once a month and stayed with local families. (Courtesy of the Monterey County Library, San Ardo Branch.)

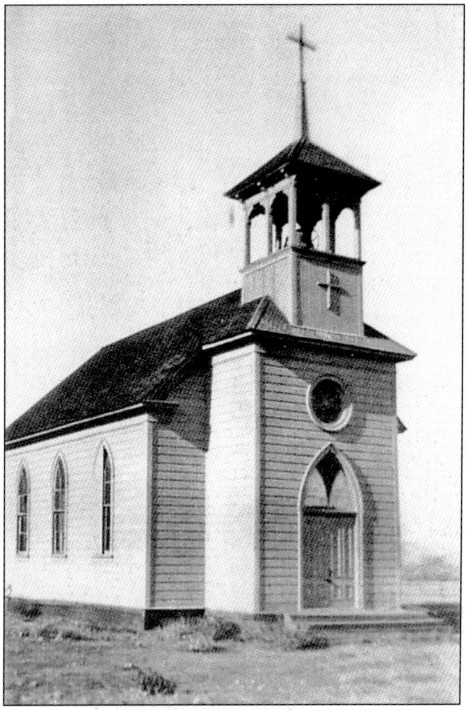

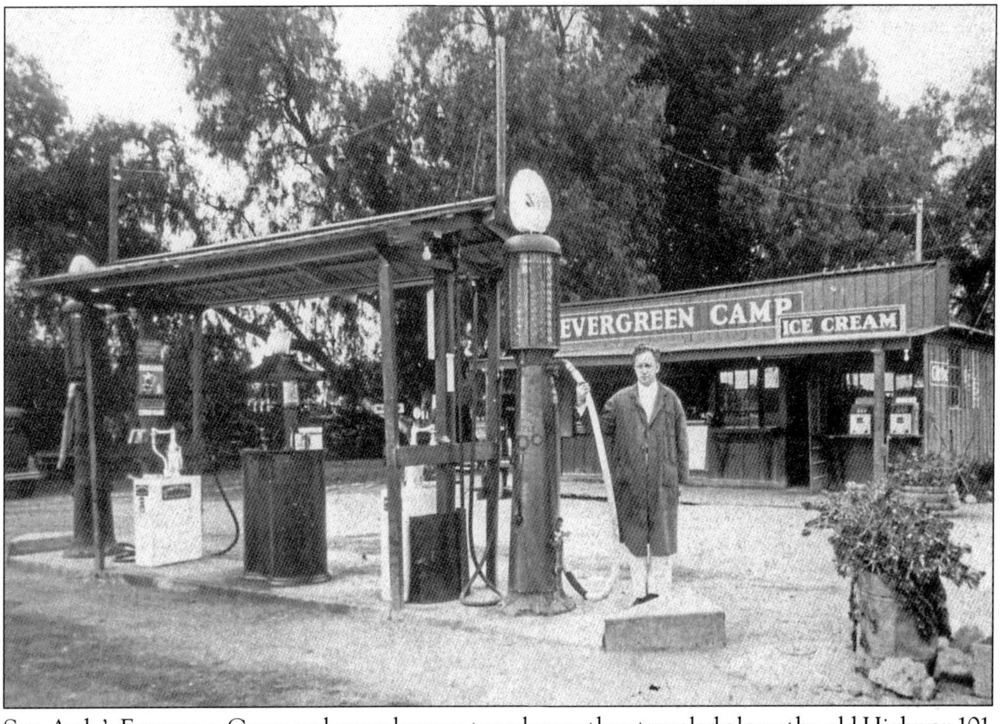

San Ardo's Evergreen Camp welcomed weary travelers as they traveled along the old Highway 101 route. Operator George Zin, pictured here, offered gas, groceries, and an opportunity to try your luck by playing slot machines (located to the right of the front door). (Courtesy of the Monterey County Library, San Ardo Branch.)

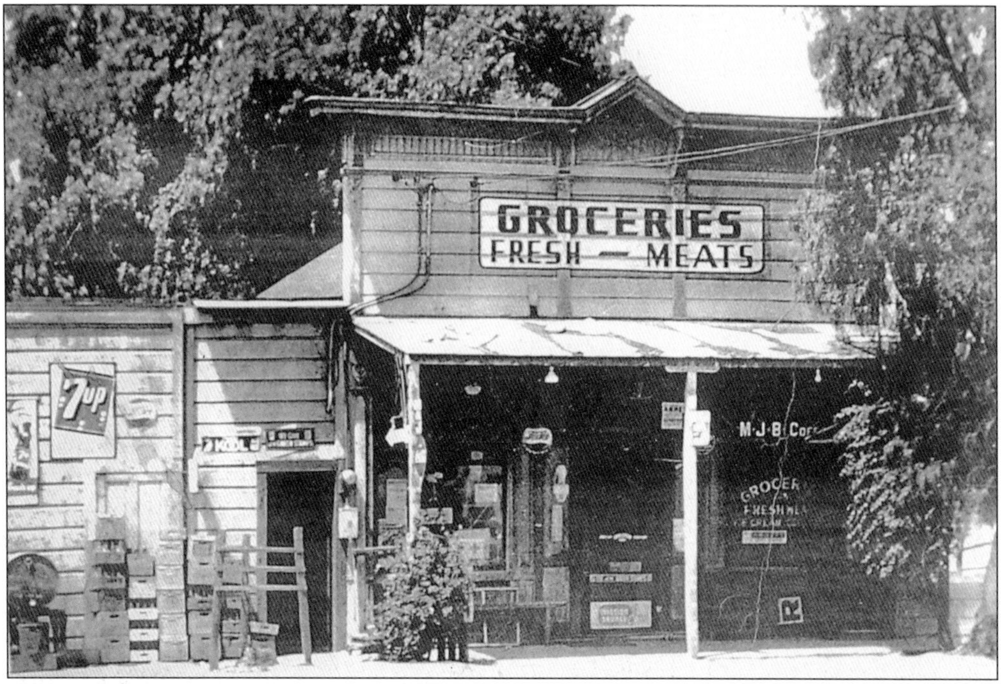

Jose Alvarado's grocery store in San Ardo also featured a beer counter and did a good business for many years during Prohibition. Jose kept bootleg whiskey behind a loose board at his house. Those in need of a drink pulled the bottle out, took a drink, and left some coins. This other business was run entirely on an honor system. (Courtesy of the Monterey County Library, San Ardo Branch.)

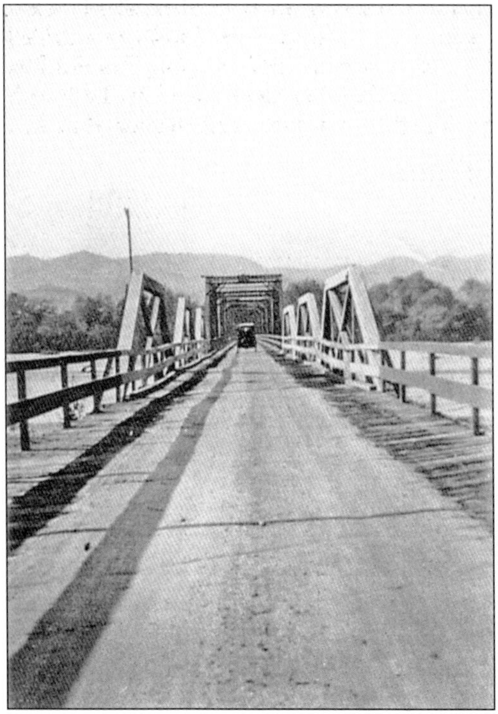

Until 1907, travelers had to ford the Salinas River to reach San Ardo. When a bridge was built, its opening was marked by a gala celebration complete with music provided by the town's 26-piece brass band. Seven years later, flood waters washed over the floor of the bridge, carrying away about 330 feet of the pile trestle approach. (Courtesy of the Monterey County Library, San Ardo Branch.)

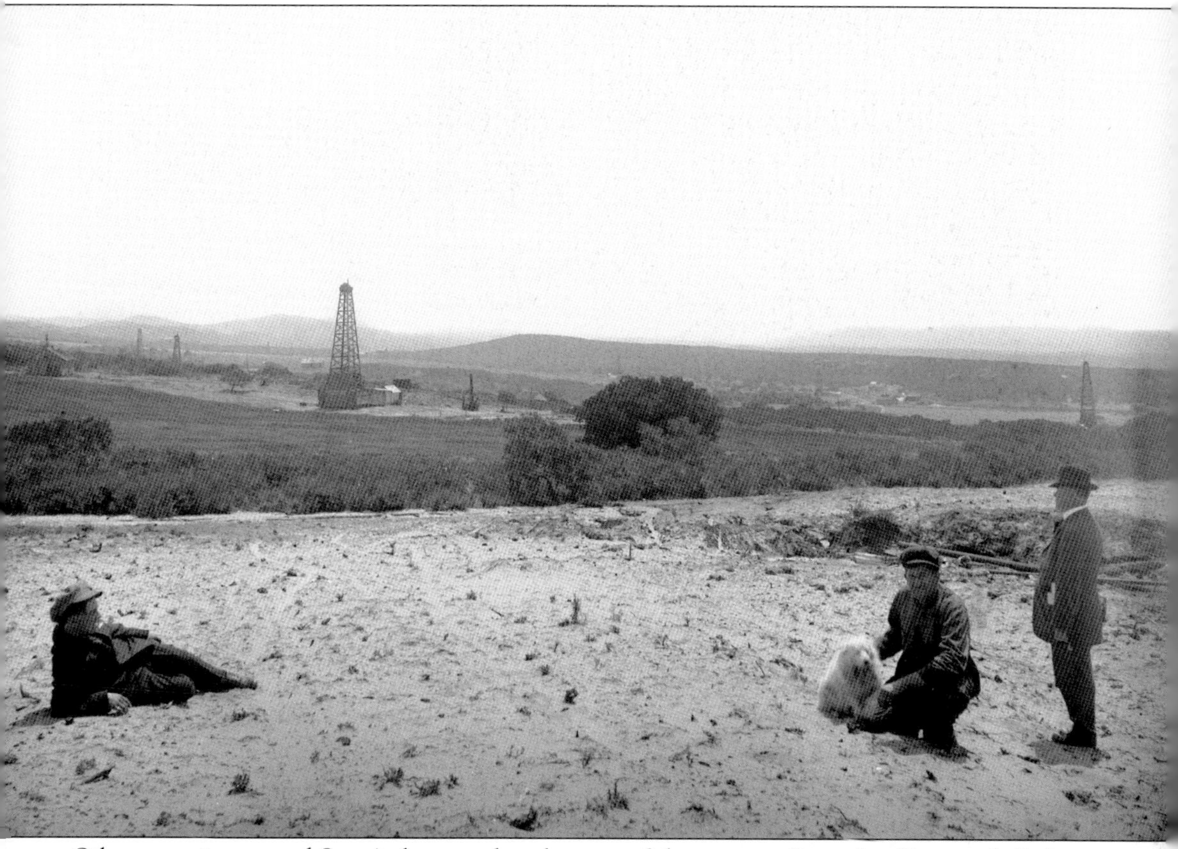

Oil prospecting around San Ardo started at the turn of the century. Several wells were drilled but none met with commercial success. However on November 7, 1947, the *King City Rustler's* headliner proclaimed, "Texas Company strikes Oil at San Ardo" on land owned by the Joseph Lombardi Family. Two more discoveries followed quickly on the Orradre and Rosenberg Ranches. (Courtesy of Pat Hathaway, California Views.)

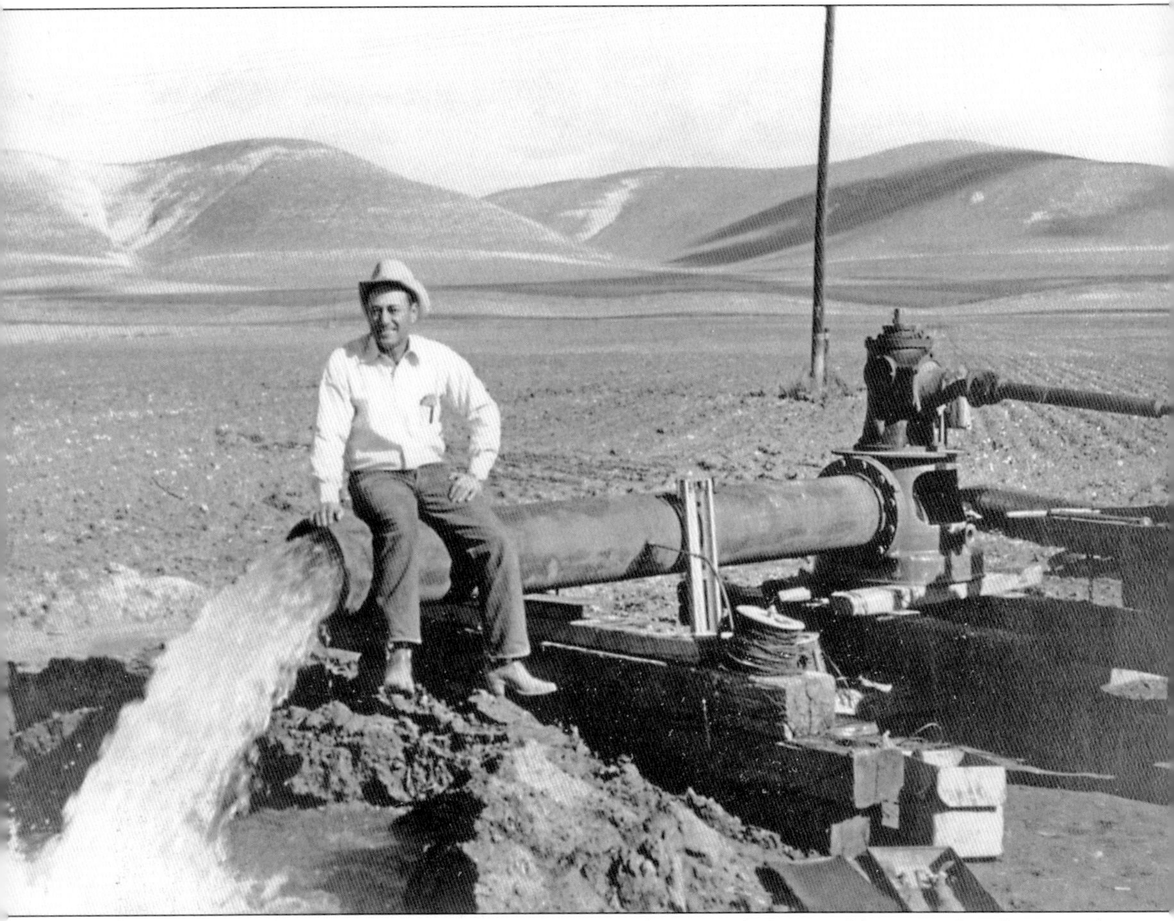

Kenneth Eade is pictured on his ranch, Three Tanks, in 1951. Located between San Lucas and San Ardo, his well pumped 1,500 gallons per minute.

Nine

BRADLEY

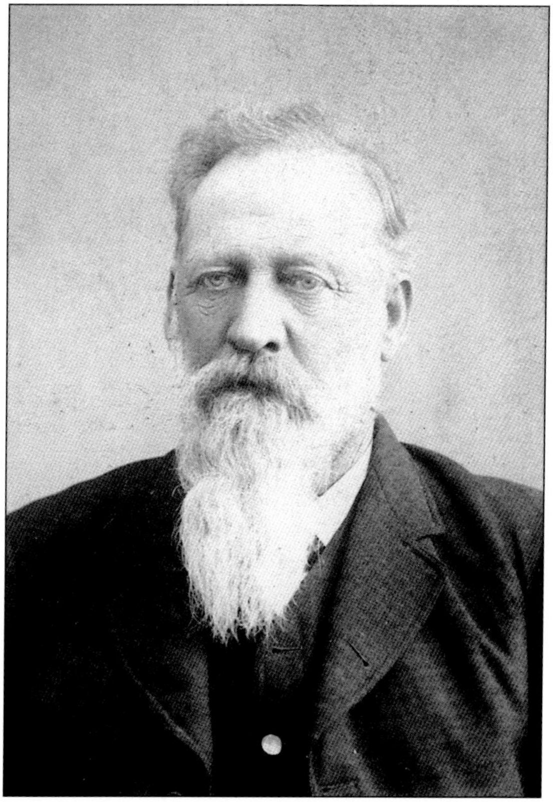

The town of Bradley, founded in 1886, was named for Bradley Varnum Sargent, on whose ranch the town was laid out. The ranch was known as La Pestilencia for the stench of several sulfur springs on the property. Sargent served as a Monterey County supervisor and, in 1886, was elected as joint senator of Monterey and San Benito Counties. (Courtesy of the Monterey County Historical Society.)

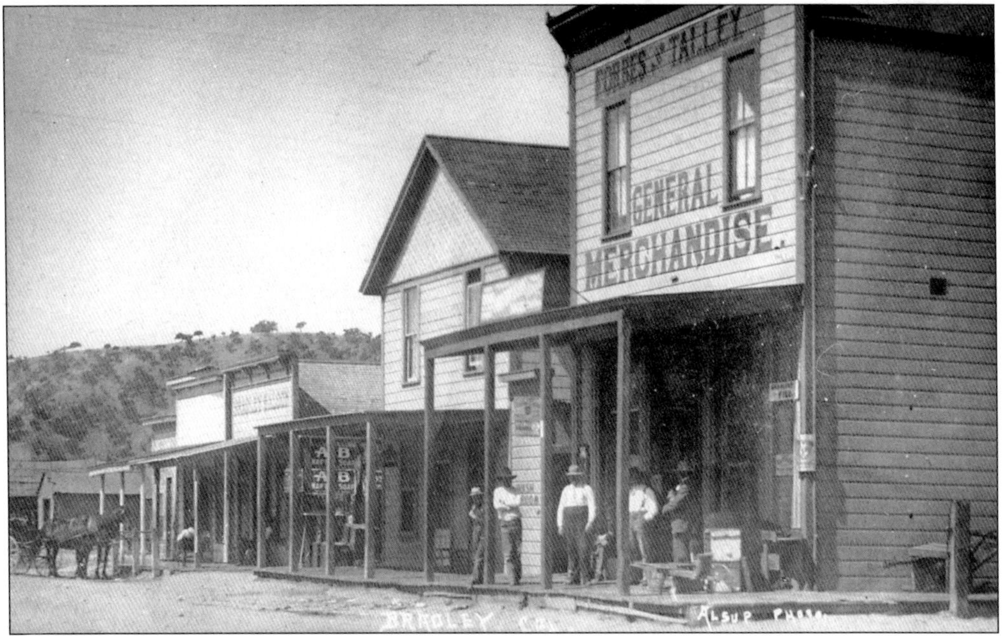

Henry Jacques Gimbal and his son Alexander Francis opened Bradley's first general store, called H. Gimbal and Son, pictured in the foreground. Leroy Gimbal, Henry's grandson, remembered that the store clerks would give him a bag full of candy or cookies for a penny. The town's first telephone was located in the store.

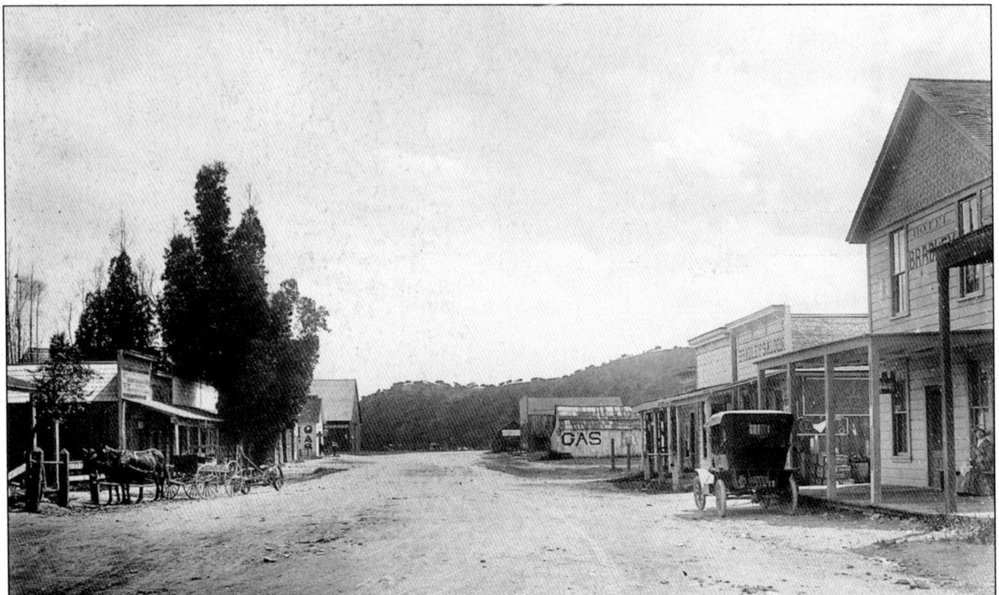

In 1915, Bradley's dusty main street was the embodiment of the Old West. That year, the *King City Rustler* wrote that Bradley "is a small village . . . comprising a hotel, store, meat market, blacksmith shop, garage, post office, livery stable, Southern Pacific railway station and Southern Pacific Milling Company's large grain warehouse." A branch of the county library was housed in the Hotel Bradley, seen in the foreground. (Courtesy of the Monterey County Library.)

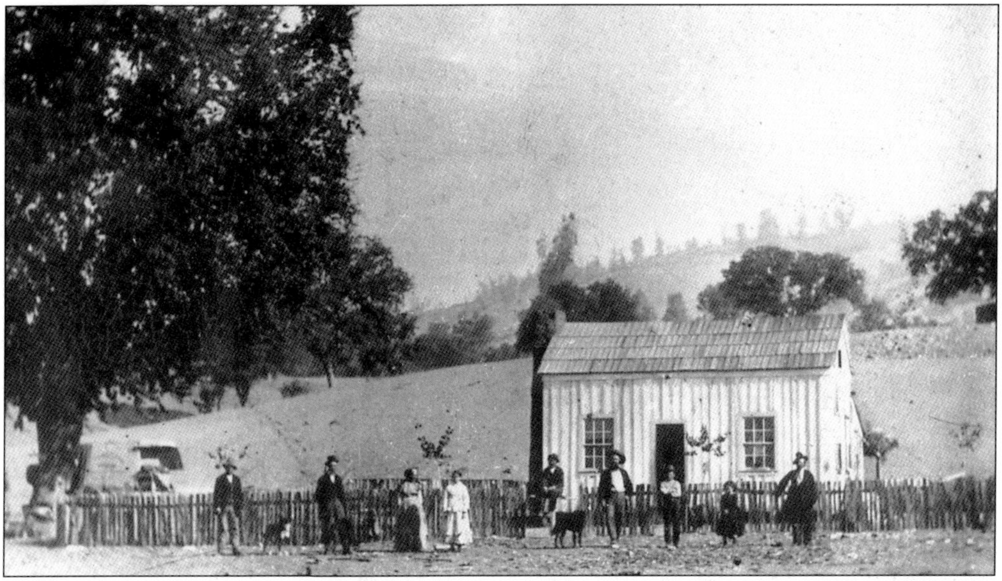

In the 1860s, Illinois natives Enoch and Eli Lee and their families settled outside of Bradley in the very southernmost part of Monterey County. They were considered squatters, as the section survey was not completed until the mid-1870s. Once they had a legal description of the property, they were able to file for a 160-acre homestead.

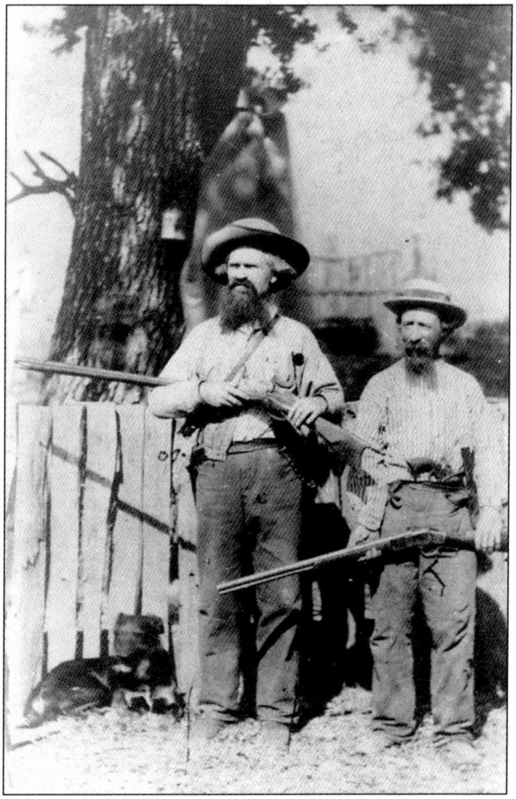

Homesteader Eli Lee (on the left) poses with neighbor Frank Brass on the Lee place near Bradley. While they appear friendly, the Lees were not especially fond of Brass, as Brass was a "Confederate man" and the Lee ancestors were "Union men."

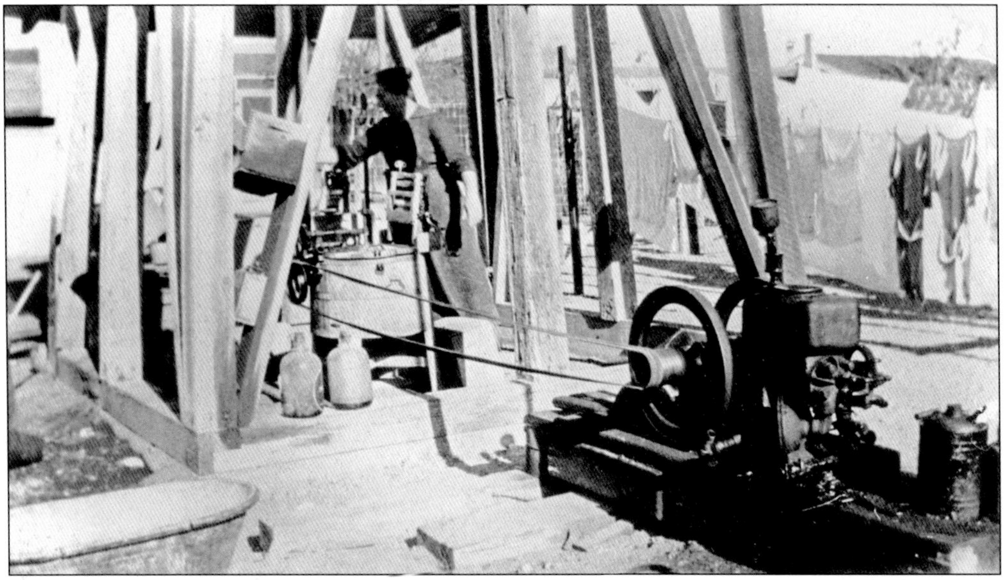

Wash day, or blue Monday, named for the bluing process used to whiten clothing, was a weekly task on farms throughout the Salinas Valley. Here a Bradley housewife sets up her washer, powered by a stationary engine under the windmill, on a sunny day in 1923. Monday was the traditional wash day, as most people changed clothes on Sunday.

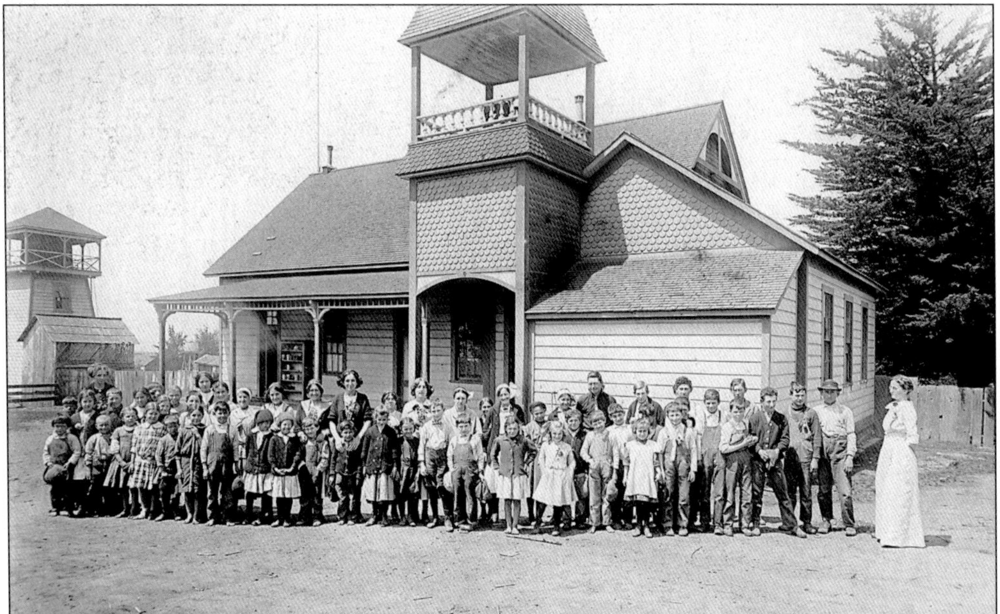

Children line up for their portrait in front of the picturesque Bradley school at the turn of the century. Resident Leroy Gimbal remembers that the school "was one room where the teacher taught all nine grades to about 25 kids. Included were children within horse-riding distance. I begged my mother to go also, but I was too young, so she agreed to teach me at home. When I finally got to go, it was an experience. The oldest farm boy had a stubby mustache as he never had time to finish school previously. I believe we learned quite a bit from listening to the older kids in these mixed grades as we heard them recite."

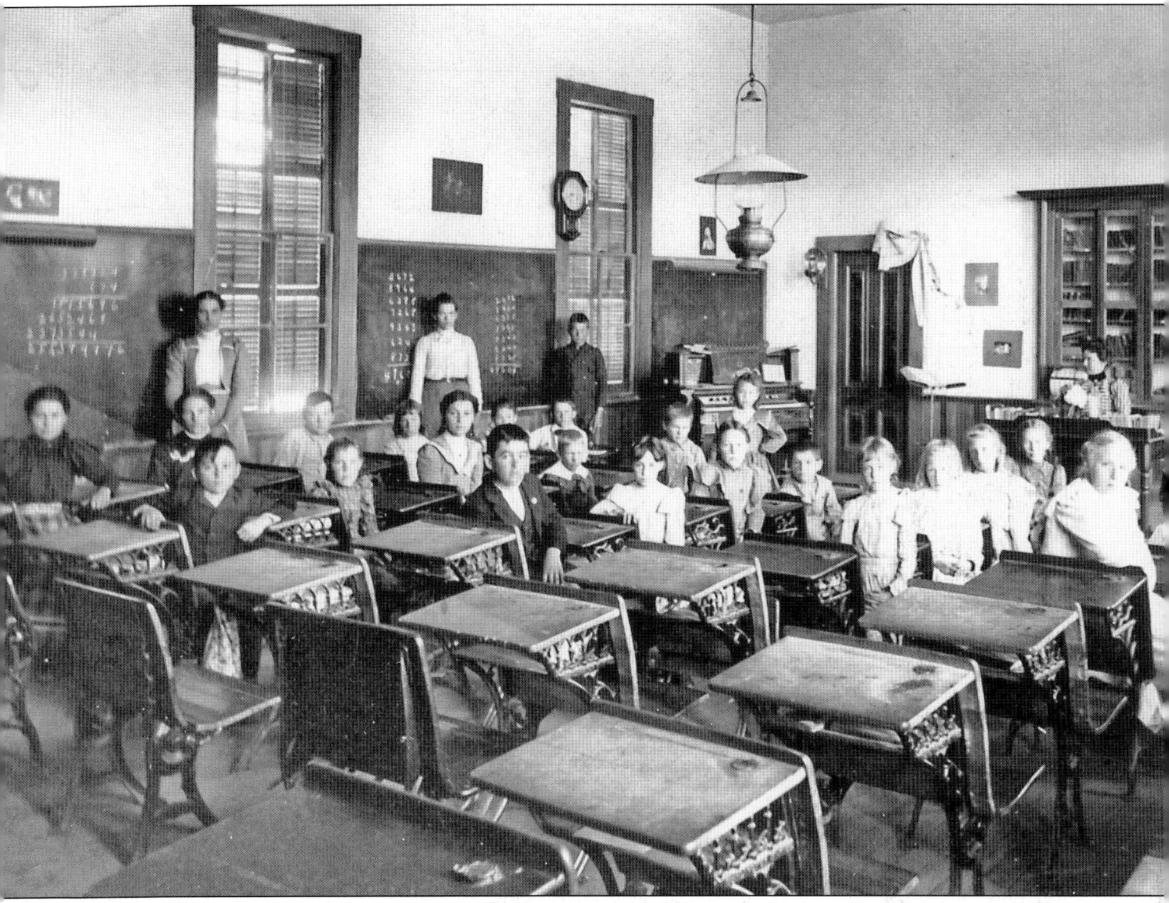

In 1906, teacher Mary Smith (seated at her desk) presided over her well-equipped, one-room school in Bradley. Solemn pupils turn toward the camera as their patient classmates wait by the blackboard to cipher their numbers.

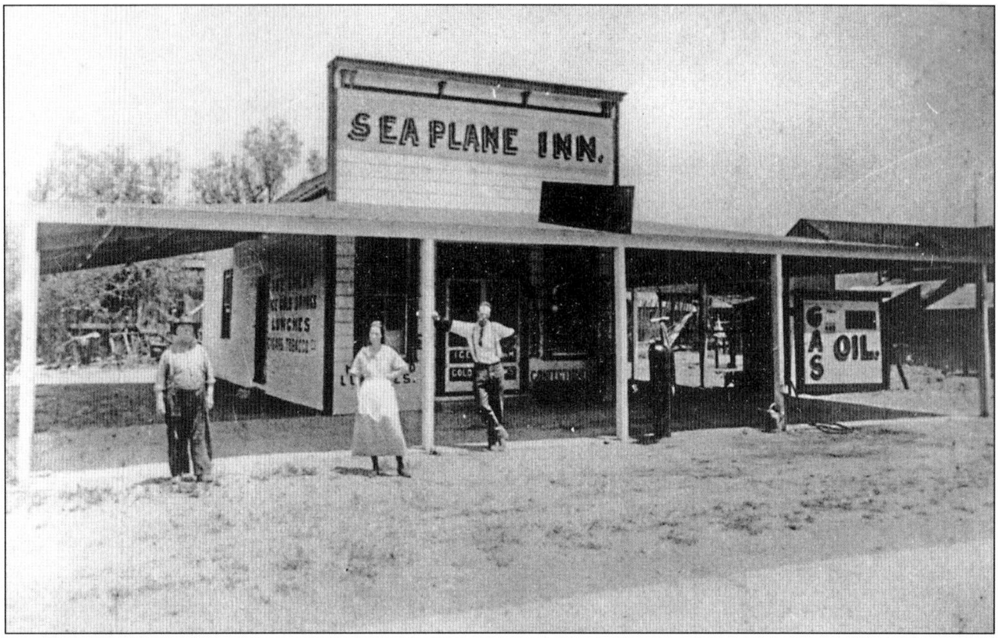

In 1916, Henry Veach bought out a small store in Bradley and moved it to the state highway. He opened Bradley's first gas station and established an automobile camp, the Sea Plane Inn, which was also known as "the zoo." The name derived from his large collection of wild animals, including bears, deer, monkeys, raccoons, foxes, coyotes, magpies, pheasants, parrots, and Chinese sacred birds. During Prohibition, Henry supposedly hid liquor in the bear's cage.

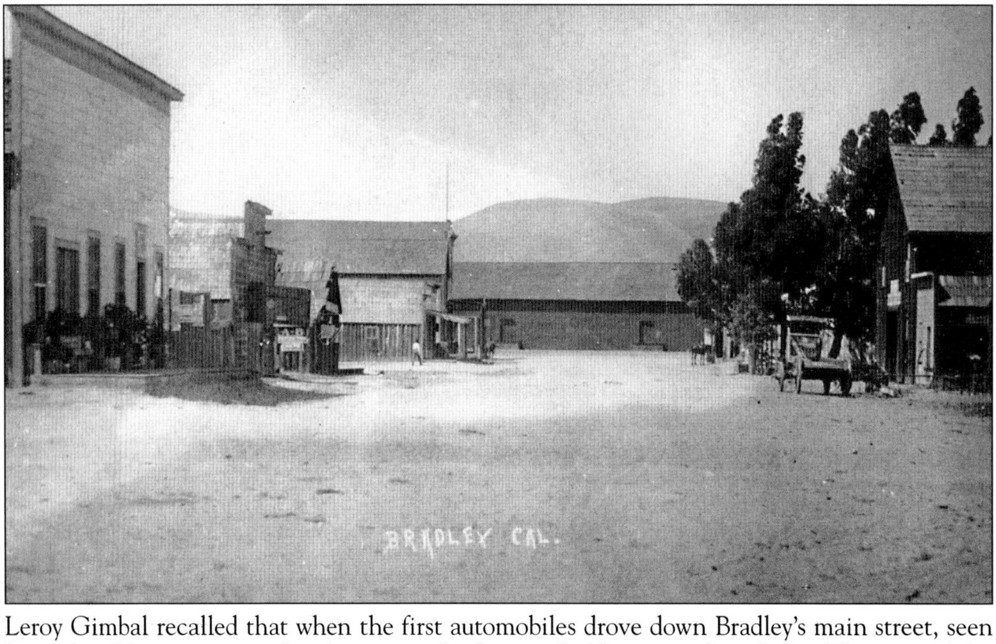

Leroy Gimbal recalled that when the first automobiles drove down Bradley's main street, seen here, that "they were considered very unsafe; they might blow up and catch fire. They scared the horses and caused runaways. The county government was going to completely ban them at first. The next step was to give horse-drawn vehicles the right-of-way. The auto had to stop, turn off the engine, and let the horse pass."